THE BUSINESS OF CRIME

THE
BUSINESS
OF CRIME

Italians and Syndicate Crime
in the United States

HUMBERT S. NELLI

New York

OXFORD UNIVERSITY PRESS

1976

Copyright © 1976 by Oxford University Press, Inc.

Library of Congress Catalogue Card Number: 75-32350

Printed in the United States of America

for Elizabeth

CONTENTS

PREFACE

This study is an outgrowth of my work on the Italian immigrant adjustment in Chicago. Research for that work included intensive examination of Italian involvement in crime during the decades between 1880 and 1930, and as a result I became interested in the question of whether the Chicago experience in crime was repeated in other cities throughout the country, or whether significant differences existed. To that end, between 1970 and 1973 I made a number of extended research trips to Boston, New York City, Philadelphia, Baltimore, New Orleans, Pittsburgh, Cleveland, Detroit, Chicago, Kansas City, Denver, Los Angeles, San Francisco, and Washington, D.C.

During the years since I began the research for this book, a deluge of literature on Italians and American crime has appeared. Most of these writings deal with the period since 1950 and, in addition to lacking historical perspective, show evidence of limited use of primary source material. So many writers have accepted and repeated myths and distortions of fact so many times that inaccuracies have become accepted as truths. Furthermore, most of the studies have concentrated on the experience in one city, New York, and have generalized from that situation about the entire country. Certainly New York has been of great importance in the emergence and growth of syndicate crime in the United States; at the same time, significant differences among cities did exist, and still exist.[1] On the basis of information obtained in

1. A notable exception is John Kobler, *Capone: The Life and World of Al Capone* (New York, 1971), which is marred, for scholarly purposes, by an absence of footnotes or

the fourteen cities in which I conducted research, I have completed
what I believe to be the first comprehensive history of Italians in
American crime during the period from the murder of Police Chief
David Hennessy in New Orleans in 1890 to the United States' entry
into World War II at the end of 1941.

In order to provide a basis for comparison with the situation in the
United States, the first chapter presents the political, social, economic,
and cultural conditions in Southern Italy and Sicily that fostered the
appearance and growth of secret criminal societies, particularly in the
later decades of the nineteenth century. The remainder of Part 1 examines in detail the murder of Chief Hennessy, the events leading up to
this crime, and its profound impact on the American consciousness.
Although Italian immigrants already had a reputation for violence and
illegal activity, the New Orleans Incident created nation-wide an
image of a criminal conspiracy with roots in the Old World.

Immigrant colony crime and the beginnings of Italian involvement
in syndicate activities in the decades prior to the enactment of the
Eighteenth Amendment are discussed in Part 2. During the decades
between the Hennessy killing and enactment of national prohibition,
no aspect of Italian immigrant activity received so much attention or
excited the interest of the American public as greatly as did crime. Although Black Hand extortion was probably the most sensational,
widely publicized, and (at least in the view of the general public) the
most "Italian" form of crime, it was only one aspect of Italian criminality in the United States. In the long run, it was neither the most significant nor the most lucrative.

Part 3 examines the role of prohibition and of the Depression of the
1930s in the emergence of the powerful, wealthy, and politically well-
connected Italian-American criminal entrepreneurs. Supporters of the
Eighteenth Amendment predicted that it would usher in a new era of

other forms of documentation. Two excellent recent studies are Francis A. J. Ianni, with
Elizabeth Reuss-Ianni, *A Family Business: Kinship and Social Control in Organized
Crime* (New York, 1972), an intensive examination of one of the New York "families";
and Joseph L. Albini's critique of the existing literature on Italian-American syndicate
crime, *The American Mafia: Genesis of a Legend* (New York, 1971).

"clean thinking and clean living." The results of prohibition differed widely from these lofty objectives. For young ethnics, prohibition provided the means by which they could enter the mainstream of American entrepreneurial crime; but repeal of the Eighteenth Amendment did not bring about a decline in their fortunes. After repeal—and, in fact, during the prohibition era—criminal entrepreneurs engaged in other types of illegal (but highly lucrative) activities, including gambling, narcotics, prostitution, and business and labor racketeering. In the process of developing their businesses, syndicate leaders created organizations loosely and imperfectly patterned on those in existence in the legitimate business world—organizations that effectively filled the needs for which they were created.

Although there was some transfer to this country of personnel from Southern Italian criminal societies, such men (at least until the Fascist campaign of the 1920s against the *mafia*) usually were low-ranking members whose area of operation lay in the Italian districts and colonies of American cities. Members of the criminal syndicates of the twenties and thirties, on the other hand, came predominantly from the American generation. These entrepreneurs were born in the United States or, more typically, immigrated as infants or children and grew to maturity in an urban environment that glorified success. These slum area youth knew that *success,* which meant money and the things it could buy, should be sought through any means, at any cost.

Much of the confusion concerning the Italian experience in American crime is related to unclear and imprecise terminology used by writers. This confusion has been true especially of two terms, *organized crime* and *mafia*. In fact, *organized crime* has appeared in so many different contexts, and to describe such a varied range of illegal activities (from relatively unstructured to highly centralized), that it has now no semblance of a precise meaning and is not utilized in this study. Instead, the text distinguishes between the various levels and types of crime involving Italians in the United States from the 1890s to World War II, as well as the differences between the situation in this country and the development of criminal societies in Italy's

South. Thus a distinction is made between *mafia,* the loose network of secret criminal groups that existed from at least as early as the 1860s (and which continue to exist) in western Sicily, and "Mafia," which refers to the centralized, structured organizations that developed in Italian neighborhoods of American cities during the pre-World War I decades of almost unrestricted immigration. Although these immigrant colony gangs claimed descent from Old World models, they exhibited significant differences.

During the twenties and thirties, the "Mafia" gangs were eliminated by, or absorbed into, criminal syndicates functioning mainly in the wider American urban environment. The syndicates were illicit business organizations established by the American generation of Italian criminals, typically in cooperation with members of other ethnic groups in order to further their endeavors in illegal (and widely patronized) economic activities such as bootlegging, gambling, loan-sharking, prostitution, narcotics, and business and labor racketeering.

Grants from the National Endowment for the Humanities (1972–74) and the Kentucky Research Foundation made it possible for me to collect material for this book in the fourteen research cities mentioned previously. The grants enabled me also to employ two efficient researchers, Joanne Bosche and William Broberg, and to make use of a computer to gain new perspectives on Black Hand extortion gang activities and on the origins of criminal syndicate leaders of the early 1930s. My NEH grant not only speeded the collection of source material, but also made it possible for me to devote a full academic year to writing.

A vast number of people in cities across the country provided information through interviews, or facilitated the gathering of manuscript and printed material. In addition to oral sources I found rich collections of information in federal and local law enforcement agencies, local crime commissions, private police agencies, federal and local archives, labor unions, and newspaper libraries.

I want to thank Robert Hess, Richard Lowitt, Sheldon Meyer, Mark Haller, and my father, Humbert O. Nelli, who read part or all of the manuscript and made valuable suggestions. I wish also to thank my wife, Elizabeth, for typing and editing early drafts and Mary Preece for typing the final manuscript.

H.S.N.

Lexington, Kentucky
July 1975

PART 1

FROM ITALY'S SOUTH TO AMERICA'S SOUTH

Italy's South and *La Mala Vita*

Over the centuries a succession of conquerors extracted as much wealth as they could from Southern Italy and Sicily and usually showed indifference toward the interests, needs, and welfare of their subjects. Such acts of pillage, rape, and robbery of the various regimes were all executed within the law and under the protection of duly constituted government. From anguished experience, Southerners knew that governments cared nothing for them and offered no protection for the poor and needy.

At the beginning of the present century, Palermo police chief Antonio Cutrera observed of the situation in Sicily that long domination by succeeding invaders had produced people who were suspicious, diffident, intolerant, and above all, enemies of government—any government—and of all law enforcement. Thus, disrespect for laws, hatred of authority, and contempt for all those who had dealings with authorities characterized Sicilians. This hostility toward the law, Cutrera concluded, led to hatred of all those in positions of power and of all efforts to enforce the laws. From necessity each man faced a hostile environment alone with whatever resources he could muster. As Italian journalist Luigi Barzini, Jr., asserts, "From very ancient days Sicilians have considered it below the dignity of a real man to appeal to official justice for the redress of wrongs. One defends one's honor." This self-styled dignity, however, is not limited to Sicilians or to Southern Italians, as Barzini recognizes. "This unwritten code is common to other Mediterranean countries like Spain, Corsica, and Sardinia, and not unknown in parts of the United States. It is an obvious derivation from feudal ideals of chivalry.'' [1]

Local peasant sayings reflected this contempt for the law as well as its corollary, a recourse to a personal, individualized code of behavior:

The gallows is for the poor man:
the law courts for the fool.

He who has money and friends can sneer at the law.

A fish begins to stink from its head
(i.e., corruption sets in at the top).

He who steals from the king (the State)
commits no crime.

The fat pig pays no taxes. [2]

Writing at the turn of the century, British historians Bolton King and Thomas Okey concluded that prevailing conditions in Southern Italy and Sicily were "the inevitable result of history," explaining that "the rule of Spaniards and Bourbons, the late survival of feudalism, only abolished in a half-hearted manner at the beginning of the [nineteenth] century, threw the country generations in arrears of civilization." [3]

Between the Congress of Vienna and the year 1860, when the Bourbons fled from Naples, weakness, corruption, and lawlessness characterized the government in the South. Bourbon officials permitted and even encouraged small-scale illegalities if assured that criminal leaders would not cause trouble for the regime. In effect, during the decades prior to the creation of the unified Italian Kingdom, the Bourbons virtually abdicated control. Banditry (which, as Eric Hobsbawm has observed, grows in time of social tension and upheaval), flourished in the 1860s and 1870s—the first two decades following unification of the country under the Piedmontese. A landowner described the situation for a commission of the Italian government: "Public security . . . leaves very much to be desired and many of us are forced to pay tribute to some famous bandit or to a criminal organization." [4]

Although launched with high hopes, the new Italian Kingdom provided only limited benefits to the long-oppressed peasants of the South. As Elizabeth Latimer observed in the 1890s, "the Sicilian and Neapolitan peasantry have been a disaffected population ever since the formation of the Kingdom of Italy." As for the southern part of the Kingdom, Deputy (later Senator) Giustino Fortunato likened the situation of the South at the turn of the century to that of Ireland in the United Kingdom. [5]

Throughout history the South Italian peasant was exploited, but after unification his lot worsened as the result of a rapidly increasing population without a corresponding increase in agricultural productivity. Although the yoke of the Bourbon monarchy had been thrown off, so far as the Southerner was concerned the foreign domination continued, now in the form of a more efficient and ruthless (and to many, more oppressive and exploitive) government in Rome. Northern Italians controlled this government. They looked down upon, and discriminated against, their southern compatriots, derisively referring to them as "Africans." The South, which had been fertile during the days of ancient Rome, was by the time of the Risorgimento an impoverished land, despised and victimized by the rest of the nation.

In the decades following unification, peasants fell deeper into *miseria*. Repressive taxation and usurious interest rates further undermined whatever initiative remained and discouraged efforts at self-improvement. In addition, a series of natural disasters shook the South in the late nineteenth and early twentieth centuries: earthquakes, droughts, volcanic eruptions, floods, and landslides wiped out whatever gains the peasants had been able to achieve. To many it must have appeared that both nature and God had turned against the Southern peasant. [6]

In this impersonal and hostile environment the peasant could count on only the nuclear family—the immediate members of his household. Each person was expected to mind his own business and that of the immediate family, which in the South comprised one and the same thing. Envy, jealousy, and suspicion typified his contacts with and attitudes toward the extended family—aunts and uncles, nieces and nephews, cousins of varying degrees of closeness. The man of the family turned to relatives only when he needed a favor; but because his own prestige increased in proportion to the loss of a relative's prestige, he acted prudently if he did not completely trust the words or advice of kinsmen. Although such relatives could occasionally be trusted, outsiders—non-family members—never deserved confidence, unless they had earned a position of friendship. Sicilians believed that "a proven friend is worth more than a relative."

Although in Southern Italian and Sicilian villages most residents were related, there was little closeness, cohesiveness, or feeling of unity among the villagers. A sense of community did not exist. Southerners had a fierce loyalty to their town but, as one authority has pointed out, this loyalty was not synonymous with "a strong sense of civic responsibility, or sacrifice for the common welfare, at least as this is understood in northern Europe and the Anglo-Saxon countries." [7]

Contemporaries emphasized the individualistic character of late nineteenth- and early twentieth-century Italian society. "Individualism runs rampant," observers King and Okey noted; "there is little mutual trust or cooperation," and "the masses have small sense of cohesiveness or hope or effort." Recent scholars have verified these findings about the situation of forty to eighty years ago, and maintain that these characteristics are still essentially functional. Jeremy Boissevain reports that the quality of character most highly regarded in the Sicilian village he investigated was that of "minding one's own business." He continues, "The supreme accolade of a man's character is *Christu fa i fatti sui!* ['He looks after his own interests!']." One was (and is) expected above all to look after "the moral and economic well-being of his family," and "not intervene in the affairs of others."[8] Sicilian proverbs transmitted these folkways through generations of peasants:

Of that which does not concern you
say neither good nor evil.

The man who talks little is wise.

Hear, see and be silent
if you wish to continue living in peace.[9]

Sicily was the land of the *latifundia,* the large landed estate. Throughout history, as Hobsbawm has pointed out, Sicilian peasants operated under the double yoke of a remote, foreign, centralized government and of a local regime based on the large estates usually owned by absentee landlords and run by overseers (*gabellotti*) who enriched themselves at peasant expense. Although absentee ownership did not originate under the Bourbons, it expanded greatly under that rule, and what with the increasing attractiveness of urban life during the nineteenth century, it increased even more after unification. The Italian census of 1901 reported that two-thirds of the landlords in Sicily, two-fifths of those in Calabria, and three-eighths of those in Basilicata were absentees.

Predictably, peasants viewed themselves as subsisting in surroundings that threatened individual and family security, and saw all officialdom and all gentry as malefactors seeking to impoverish and destroy them. Thus, helpless farmers and tenants sought a protector and benefactor, a man of standing to look out for peasant interests in time of need. Such a man became the patron of a large number of people, non-relatives as well as kin; he became a locally important person, a *capo mafioso.*[10]

Addressing the Italian Parliament in the 1870s, Diego Trajani, a prominent jurist and himself a Sicilian, described the situation under the Italian Kingdom in terms that applied also to preceding regimes:

> We have in Sicily the laws scoffed at, . . . corruption everywhere,
> favouritism the rule, justice the exception; crime enthroned where the
> guardian of public weal should be; criminals in the place of judges;
> judges become criminals, and a horde of persons interested in crime
> become arbiters of the liberty, honour and life of the people. By
> heaven! What is this but chaos; what but the worst of all evils? The
> anarchy of government before which a hundred brigands or a hundred
> malefactors more or less sink into insignificance.[11]

Under conditions such as these the *mafia* in Sicily and the *'ndranghita*
(*fibbia*) in Calabria functioned and flourished as an extralegal (and
"parallel") form of government. (In addition to other designations the
Calabrian groups were also called the "Honored Society," a term that
came to identify the *mafia* as well.) [12]

As *mafia* expert Giuseppe Montalbano cautions, one must distinguish between the *mafia* "as a medieval sentiment expressing the
Sicilian disdain of everything foreign"—that is, from outside the island—and *mafia* "as an association of evildoers joined by rules and
statutes either written or absorbed, for the purpose of criminal activities." Clearly the criminal *mafia* must have grown out of the tradition
of disdain and contempt for the law and thrived in this environment.
The general term denoting criminality in Southern Italy was *Mala
Vita*. As Gino C. Speranza, a native Italian, described it in an American magazine, "*Mala Vita* is the Italian phrase for that evil and para-
sitic class we call the 'criminal element' or the 'underworld.' " Although writers often classified the Sicilian *mafia*, Calabrian *fibbia*, and
the Neapolitan *Camorra* together under the term *Mala Vita*, there were
important differences, which related to their differing relations to the
rest of society in Calabria and Sicily on the one hand and in Naples on
the other, as well as to the internal structure of the different organizations.[13]

The early *mafia* was in large part a rural development concentrated
primarily in the western portion of the island in the provinces of
Palermo, Girgenti (Agrigento), Trapani, and Caltanissetta. Each *mafia*
group controlled criminal activities in its own town or district. In cities
each group specialized in its own type of criminal activity: one con-

1. *Garzoni di Mala Vita* (Lads of the Evil Life) lounging alongside a Southern Italian road. Photo taken about 1890. (*Illustrated American*)

trolled docks, another taxi drivers, a third the slaughterhouses; and, in theory, no group interfered in the territory or activity of another. On those occasions when they did cross boundaries, bloody feuds resulted, sometimes lasting for years and costing numerous lives.

Curiously, the *mafia* did not exist in the eastern provinces of Sicily. In a report prepared in 1876 for the Italian Parliament, Leopoldo Franchetti called eastern Sicily "the tranquil provinces," which contained areas "where it is possible to go around the countryside without fear of being killed or blackmailed," a situation that did not apply to the western provinces. This "promised land," as he termed it, lay in the provinces of Messina, Catania, and Syracuse.[14]

A number of factors contributed to this "tranquility." Eastern Sicily entered the factory age earlier, because of the decline of local handicrafts and increasing competition from northern industry. Moreover, the area's inhabitants had greater recourse to group action as a means of self-protection. Again, eastern Sicily offered richer soil, diversified agriculture, and estate owners who tended to live on their land and take a personal interest in their tenants and farms.

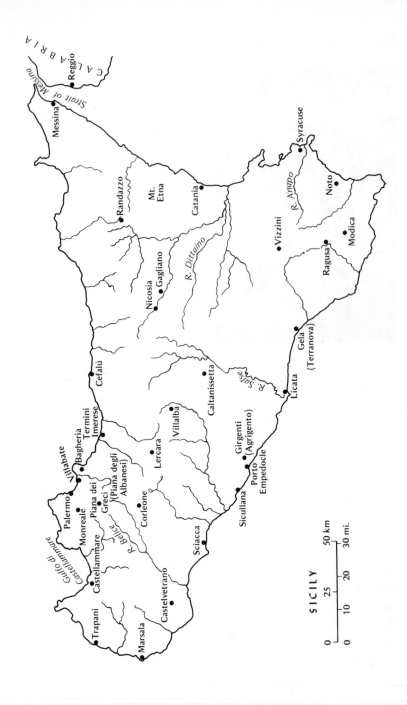

SICILY

TABLE 1
AVERAGE RATE OF MURDER, ROBBERY, AND EXTORTION IN SICILIAN PROVINCES, 1902–6

Province	*1902–6 ANNUAL AVERAGE PER 100,000 INHABITANTS* Murder	Robbery and Extortion
Caltanissetta	44.52	41.41
Catania	13.87	24.76
Girgenti	38.75	46.80
Messina	8.13	7.19
Palermo	29.06	33.65
Syracuse	8.20	10.30
Trapani	26.12	76.84

Source: Henner Hess, *Mafia and Mafiosi: The Structure of Power* (Lexington, Mass., 1973), p. 23. Based on *Inchiesta parlamentare sulle condizioni dei contadini delle province meridionali* (Inchiesta Lorenzoni), Vol. VII, Roma 1909, p. 853.

The *mafia* appears to have developed its greatest strength in the cattle-raising and fruit-growing areas around Palermo and in the sulphur-mining regions of Caltanissetta and Agrigento. Landowners in these locations hired armed *mafiosi* to protect their produce from cattle rustlers and fruit thieves, as well as to collect rents and intimidate workers; or, in the sulphur regions, to organize and control the mine workers. The overseers (*gabellotti*) employed the *mafia* not only to exploit the peasants but also to intimidate the owners in order to rent the *latifundi* on easy terms. There were *mafiosi* in every class, and they were involved in a full range of illegal activities, including crop burning, fraud, robbery, extortion, and murder. While they engaged also in non-criminal and non-violent activities, their legal operations and, in fact, the immense power they wielded, rested on the widespread knowledge that they could and would use violence and any type of crime necessary to gain their ends. Crime was the ultimate sanction on which they relied to increase their patronage and the fear on which they depended. They infiltrated local government, the big urban markets, the orange groves, and any area of life where crime could be made to pay.

Over time these "protectors" became powerful in their own right. For each job performed for landowners and *gabellotti,* the *mafiosi* gained "a proper share" of the proceeds. They accumulated cattle, land, and money. Instead of earning the enmity of lower-class Sicilians, successful *mafiosi* enjoyed special prestige in their own locality, stemming in large part from the fact that they made themselves "respected." This notion of respect, as Anton Blok has pointed out, was based on "the capacity and willingness to coerce with physical violence." In a land where the mass of people suffered daily humiliation with no redress, *mafiosi,* as *uomini rispetati* ("respected men"), suffered insult from no one and became objects of admiration and envy. They were, in brief, "the male ideal." Furthermore, although they did not usually flaunt their wealth, they enjoyed a higher standard of living than did their compatriots. In a static, closed society like that of western Sicily in the decades after unification, members of the laboring class had little hope of improving their condition of life unless they chose to emigrate. Thus, the *mafia* and other forms of criminal activity (such as brigandage) provided one of the few means available for ambitious young men to realize some degree of upward social and economic mobility. According to Blok,

> *Mafiosi* were recruited from the ranks of the peasantry to provide the large estate owners with armed staffs, to confront both the impact of the State and the restive peasants, especially in the inland areas of the island where the Bourbon State failed to monopolize the use of physical power. . . . Thus while on the one hand *mafiosi* heightened class tensions through their control over land, they checked open rebellions and sustained revolts in several ways: by force; by keeping a hold on outside influences; by opening avenues for upwardly mobile peasants; and by turning outlaws and bandits into allies.[15]

Local *mafia* leaders paid absentee feudal owners lump sums as rent for whole estates, and then sublet these (at large profits) to the peasantry. Gradually these *mafiosi* became men of wealth, and replaced the feudal owners as the new rural ruling class (in *mafia* areas, virtually all leaders seem to have been *mafiosi*). This transfer of power from the feudal landowners to *mafiosi,* their patrons, and their clients formed the basis for the parallel government. The *mafiosi* had a deleterious effect on the economic and social situation on the island because, as Montalbano has noted, they thrived on and perpetuated a system of feudal relations and economic arrangements, and thus hampered the development of a truly capitalistic system in Sicily.

Political considerations lay at the core of *mafia* control. *Mafiosi* made effective use of the elective system set up under the Italian Kingdom; elections became the means by which they established themselves as political powers in local communities. Not only did they control elections; through elected representatives they exerted considerable power in governmental affairs within Sicily and in the central government at Rome as well. Hence when a *mafia* leader or member was in trouble or required special consideration from police, courts or legislators, he called on the officials he had helped elect and demanded the repayment of the favor. The effect was an alliance between the *mafia* and corrupt elected officials, impotent or conniving policemen, and a bought judicial system. Conditions seemed to be a continuation of the Bourbon system. As King and Okey stated, "Where the *mafia* is strong, it is impossible for a candidate to win a Parliamentary or local election unless he promises it his protection." In their view, "Nothing is more sinister in Italian life than the alliance of *mafia* and Government to assist and shield high-placed swindlers." [16]

Permeating the entire system was the atmosphere of *Omertà,* which Franchetti, in his important study of Sicilian social and political conditions in 1876 (and later writings on the Sicilian *mafia* seem to agree), viewed as part of the heritage, part of the national way of life in Sicily. *Omertà* was a code of silence which, as Cutrera explained it in 1900, sealed Sicilian lips even in their own defense, and even when the accused were innocent of charged crimes. Cutrera quoted a native saying first uttered (so goes the legend) by a wounded man to his assailant, and soon to epitomize the spirit of *Omertà:*

> If I live, I'll kill you;
> If I die, I forgive you.[17]

The suspicion of being a "stool-pigeon," a *cascittuni,* constituted the blackest mark against a Sicilian's manhood, according to Cutrera. Each individual had the obligation of looking out for his own interests and of proving his manliness by not appealing to legally constituted authority for redress of personal grievances. A wronged person was expected to avenge himself, or find a patron who would see that the job was done. This attitude showed clearly in the adage "Blood washes blood," one of the sayings most commonly associated with the *mafia* and *Omertà*.

In this sense the *mafia* developed only after 1860, and its period of greatest glory came after 1890. The explanation of its power and in effect that of its existence as a state within a state, was its exploitation by central governmental authorities and by members of the upper class as a means of controlling the peasants. The modern *mafia,* the criminal organization with statutes and initiation rites, quickly developed a distinction between "old" and "young" *mafia* groups which is clearly reflected in the sect of the *Stoppaglieri* of Monreale, a hill town just outside Palermo.

By 1872 the local *mafia* was so strongly entrenched that the police decided upon a drastic step designed to break its power, or at least to weaken its influence. The police hoped to ally themselves with young hoodlums, to use the youth gangs to combat and destroy the "old" *mafia* with the "new." The alliance achieved some success at first, as the "old" *mafia* lost face and suffered some degree of disgrace. Then it counterattacked with propaganda, labeling the new rivals police flunkies and bestowing upon them the epithet *Stoppaglieri* (an old word meaning "cork" or "bottle stopper"). Although the exact purpose of the term was never clarified, possibly it was intended to designate the youth gangs as a police device, a cork, to bottle up the real *mafia;* it indicated that the new group served as allies of the hated police. The "old" and "new" *mafias* came into armed conflict, with losses on both sides. The expectation of the police of destroying the "old" *mafia* ended when the two *mafia* groups reached an understanding and merged to form a more effective and vastly more powerful group than had ever existed before. This merger occurred within a year or two of the initial formation of the *Stoppaglieri*.

The *Stoppaglieri*, with 150 members in the commune of Monreale, was divided into sections in each portion of the commune. A directive council headed the society, and governing was achieved through statutes. The organization made use of signs, passwords, and initiation ceremonies. To enhance its prestige and to provide an appearance of legitimacy, the group formed as a mutual benefit society, but in contrast to the goals of most mutual-aid organizations, members of the *Stoppaglieri* pledged themselves to help each other in robberies, revenge, fights, and secret-keeping. The governing statute listed four commitments:

1. To exchange help and aid to a member, and to wipe out offenses against any member with blood.

2. To assist and carry out the defense of members who fell into police hands; to cooperate in securing witnesses in his defense and to contribute toward paying defense costs.

3. To distribute among the members (according to executive decisions) the proceeds of ransoms, extortions, robberies, and other crimes perpetrated in the common cause; those most in need were to receive special consideration.

4. To keep the oath and to maintain secrecy on pain of death within 24 hours for violation of the statute's provisions.[18]

Associations of *mafia* criminal groups with statutes, initiation rites, passwords, and the like, began to appear sometime after 1863, according to Montalbano. The statutes and rites were similar to the type used by the *Stoppaglieri*. The *Fratellanza* (Brotherhood) of Agrigento was founded on the pattern of a "mutual aid" society. Members pledged themselves to cooperate in criminal activities, to protect each other from harm, and to assist each other in any and every form of crime engaged in, as well as to work for the release of members in prison and to prevent successful prosecution of members where possible. As reproduced by Colacino in 1885, the oath of allegiance of the *Fratellanza* (taken at quasi-religious initiation rites) was:

> I swear on my honor to be faithful to the *Fratellanza* as it is to me. As we burn this saint and these few drops of my blood for the *Fratellanza*, and as these ashes cannot reconstitute the saint, nor the drops of blood return to my veins, so will I not be able to leave the *Fratellanza*.[19]

With the passage of time, *mafia* groups abolished the rites and statutes and came to rely on tradition to hold allegiance and to maintain their standards of performance.

The *mafia*, which, as we have seen, developed during the decades after Italian unification, was not a highly formalized, centralized, or unified organization with a "Grand Council" or an elected "boss of bosses." It was, rather, a loose federation of small groups (seldom of more than ten or twelve members) located in each town and each quarter or every city in western Sicily. Each group functioned on the basis of an informal patron-client set of relations. In the words of Michele Pantaleone, the *mafia* "has had no hard-and-fast regulations establishing rules and disciplines, duties, responsibilities or ranks." Individual members established their own position in the hierarchy by means of the "respect" they could command. Another recent writer (Henner Hess) after examining the history of the *mafia* over the past hundred years, concluded that instead of a rigid organizational structure, there developed "a great number of separate *associazioni* or *cosche* [literally, leaves of an artichoke], each with a *capo* of its own. Relations between *cosche* are not uniform or regulated; there may be hostility or refusal to accept their existence, or co-operation." [20]

The *cosca*, maintains Hess, comprised "the closest clientage dependent on him, consisting chiefly of a number of men of violence who thus relieve the *mafioso* of the need to practice violence himself." This strong-arm group formed the element generally referred to as the low (*bassa*) *mafia*. Included in the high (*alta*) *mafia* were a number of persons who cooperated with the *cosca* "without themselves displaying any *mafioso* attitudes." These "protectors" were highly placed and socially prominent "holders of institutional power," including landlords, noblemen, clergy, politicians, judges, and law enforcement officials; these were the *capo*'s faction or *partito*. This vitally important network of relations was maintained by continuous reciprocal services.[21]

The situation in western Sicily was such that it was necessary, if not essential, for one to belong to a clientage, as Giuseppe Alongi observed in 1887. "Private and public life can be understood not only as a life led within the realm of the laws but invariably also as one lived within the *partito*." Ironically, "the honest person, even if he is rich but isolated, is exposed to the arrogance and chicanery of the first person who comes along, while the common crook finds help in the *partito*, and champions in the struggle against rival groups." The system that thus evolved was, in the words of Boissevain, one of *"mafiosi* with their exclusive, non-overlapping groups of colleagues and henchmen, who are also called *mafiosi*, and each of these with his network of patrons and clients." [22]

Membership in a *mafia* group was usually based on family relationships, either through blood or marriage. The mass of the population, composed of the illiterate and extremely poor, provided the victims exploited by both the government and the parallel and extra-legal governments of the *mafia* in Sicily, the *Camorra* in Naples, and the *fibbia* (Honored Society) in Calabria, as well as by local brigands.

The Calabrian *fibbia*, like the Sicilian *mafia*, operated as a parallel system of law in each village. It apparently originated as a form of mutual assistance against oppressive governments and overbearing aristocrats. Like the *Stoppaglieri* of Monreale, the *fibbia* had rituals, passwords, and governing regulations. It functioned with the support, or at least the acquiescence, of the local population. Leaders were men of dignity who commanded respect without demanding it and exerted a profound influence in the local economy and politics. To them the people brought their problems, such as difficulties with the law, and job and money needs, and the patrons solved them in return for favors and pledges of support and respect. In the process the patrons accumulated immense power and influence, and although they lived quietly, frugally, and inconspicuously, they also acquired great wealth. Functioning as the friend and champion of the oppressed, the *fibbia,* like the *mafia,* also allied itself with local landowners and politicians and exerted a generally decisive influence in elections in exchange for helping to control the local population.[23]

In contrast to the *mafia* and the *fibbia,* the *Camorra* operated entirely outside the "legitimate" sphere. It was a criminal guild or fraternity concentrated largely if not exclusively in the city of Naples. Unlike the more decentralized *mafia,* the *Camorra* was "rather tightly, centrally and hierarchically organized." Further, as Albert Falcionelli notes, *Omertà* in Naples was "a purely criminal manifestation," in contrast to its role in Sicily as part of the heritage.[24] Its principal operations were organized extortion, prostitution, theft, raids on gambling houses, usury, smuggling, and counterfeiting. As was discovered by Arthur Train, former Assistant District Attorney of New York County and an observer of the famous *Camorra* trial held at Viterbo in 1911–12, the Neapolitan organization "levied blackmail upon all gambling enterprises, brothels, drivers of public vehicles, boatmen, beggars, prostitutes, thieves, waiters, porters, marketmen, fruit-sellers, small tradesmen, lottery winners, and pawnbrokers, controlled all the smuggling and coined bogus money." Moreover, the Camorrists used religion for their own purposes by exacting tolls from the people, under the pretense that they were intended for religious purposes. As Alongi said, "That the Neapolitan *Camorra* is so mixed up with religion is due to the fact that the local criminal unites ferocity with religious superstition." *Camorra* members met at the Church of Mount Carmel in Naples to worship as well as to plan extortion and other criminal activities. In their own view they behaved as devout Catholics and good family men; they attended church regularly and contributed lavishly to parish needs.[25]

The *Camorra* had initiation ceremonies, passwords, governing regulations, and a hierarchy among its members. Ernesto Serao described "a *capo'ntrine*—a sectional head—and a *capo in testa,* or head-in-chief of the *Camorra,* a kind of president of the confederation of all the twelve sections into which Naples is divided and which are pre-

sided over by the *capi'ntrini.''* Thus the organization operated in each
of the city's twelve sections. For *Camorra* purposes each quarter was
in turn subdivided into *paranze,* or local gangs. Gang members elected
the chief of each *paranza,* and if he did not lead the group in a satisfactory manner—that is, if his leadership did not result in profitable
activities—he could be removed.[26]

Like the *mafia,* the *Camorra* existed on two levels and made effective use of politics. On one level there was the criminal organization
(otherwise known as the *Camorra bassa*) and on the other a number of
politicians and businessmen with widespread connections in the upper
classes of Neapolitan society, either directly or through some of the
more fashionable and influential members. There was, King and Okey
stated, ''an 'upper *Camorra'*—without the ritual of its lower counter-
part, but well understood—the 'kid-glove *Camorra'* of Deputies and
municipal councillors and journalists and professional men, who live
on jobs and malversation of public moneys.'' They, in cooperation
with the police, made possible the evildoing of the *Camorra bassa.* Of
central importance to the orderly functioning of the entire system was
control of the political process. ''From the advent of Garibaldi to the
present time [1912] the strictly criminal operations of the society have
been secondary in importance to its political significance.'' In consequence the government made sure that ''more honest citizens'' made
no serious efforts to curb or control ''their infamous trade in vice and
cowardice.'' [27]

The *Camorra* began in the prisons of Naples, but moved out of the
jails in the early decades of the nineteenth century to form a mutually
beneficial arrangement with the Bourbon government and the police.
In exchange for helping to keep working-class discontent under control, the *Camorra* received free rein to conduct its illegal activities in
Naples. During the revolution of 1860 the *Camorra* reached its height
of power and prestige when the Liberals handed over the maintenance
of public order to the criminal gang. Under the Italian Kingdom a
series of campaigns—the first in 1862—was undertaken to destroy the
Camorra. Because of its highly centralized organization, the *Camorra*
was vulnerable to vigorous and concerted governmental action; thus,

governmental efforts achieved largely successful results by the early part of the twentieth century.

Americans opposing Italian immigration complained of the arrival of large numbers of criminals escaping Italian justice, or looking for lucrative opportunities in the New World. Some criminals did migrate to the United States, but it is impossible to determine how many were members of the *mafia, Camorra,* or *fibbia.* Probably the number was not large and those who came were the lower-ranking, since the leaders generally were not vulnerable to police action—their arrangements with the police and the government protected them.

In the aftermath of the murder of New York police lieutenant Joseph Petrosino in Palermo in March 1909, "A Veteran Diplomat" in Italy observed that "it is to the United States and the Argentine Republic that the lower classes of the *mafia* have recourse in difficulties of this nature." On the other hand, "The *Pezzi Grossi,* the 'Big Potatoes' [Big Shots] of the *mafia,* when forced to leave for a time their country for their country's good, as a rule betake themselves to Cairo and to Alexandria." The "Big Potatoes" chose the location of their temporary exile with care. The Egyptian cities were close to home, and Egyptian officials, for a price, took a tolerant attitude toward the presence of prominent Italian criminals in their country, so long as the stay was of short duration.[28]

Moreover, leaders of the *Mala Vita* had an important stake in the system in Italy, which provided them with insulation from punishment from criminal acts. To be accused, arrested, and tried for a crime (and particularly a serious one) increased the prestige of a *mafioso*—provided he had the connections to ensure that he was acquitted or his case dismissed. Those of lower rank, who carried out orders and actually committed the misdeeds ordered by the hierarchy, might find it necessary to depart if they angered a powerful boss, or if witnesses could not be bought or intimidated. Brigands and petty criminals, and those committing violent acts of passion or vendetta, often emigrated in order to escape punishment. A criminal record in Italy placed a stigma on a man and brought him under close and continuing police scrutiny. Complete records were kept in the town of birth, and wher-

2. Emigrants departing Naples for the United States at the turn of the century. (*Charities and the Commons*)

ever a man went in Italy his movements were reported back to his birthplace, where his records were available for use by the police. If he got into further difficulty his previous record could be—and generally was—used against him. Unlike the Anglo-Saxon system of justice, whereby the accused is assumed to be innocent until proven guilty, Italian justice adhered to the Napoleonic code, in which the burden of proof of innocence rested with the accused. Evidence of character, previous reputation, circumstantial evidence, and hearsay could be used by the prosecution almost without restriction.

The majority of the Italians emigrating overseas were peasants seeking economic opportunity denied them or made difficult in the closed society in Italy; often these were men who lacked the intelligence, native ability, ruthlessness, or contacts to enter the priesthood, *mafia,* or any other institution that could provide means of upward mobility. As a result of the miserable conditions (unequaled elsewhere in Italy) under which most Southern Italian peasants lived and the limited opportunities for improving their status, emigration stood out as one of the few (and for some, the only) means of earning money and provid-

TABLE 2
ITALIAN IMMIGRATION TO THE UNITED STATES 1880–1930

Year	Number	Year	Number
1880	12,354	1908	128,503
1881	15,401	1909	183,218
1882	32,159	1910	215,537
1883	31,792	1911	182,882
1884	16,510	1912	157,134
1885	13,642	1913	265,542
1886	21,315	1914	283,738
1887	47,622	1915	49,688
1888	51,558	1916	33,665
1889	25,307	1917	34,596
1890	52,003	1918	5,250
1891	76,055	1919	1,884
1892	61,631	1920	95,145
1893	72,145	1921	222,260
1894	42,977	1922	40,319
1895	35,427	1923	46,674
1896	68,060	1924	56,246
1897	59,431	1925	6,203
1898	58,613	1926	8,253
1899	77,419	1927	17,297
1900	100,135	1928	17,728
1901	135,996	1929	18,008
1902	178,375	1930	22,327
1903	230,622		
1904	193,296		
1905	221,479		
1906	273,120		
1907	285,731		

Source: U.S. Department of Commerce, Bureau of the Census, *Historical Statistics of the United States, Colonial Times to 1957*, pp. 56–57.

ing for family needs. Prior to the 1880s, emigration flowed first in sizable numbers from the Northern and economically more advanced areas of Italy. But Southern adherence to tradition and resistance to movement from the place of origin began to break down after unification. Over the decades after unification the gap between North and South grew wider, and the government in Rome chose to pamper the North and penalize the South. The government's treatment of the South as a colony or conquered territory finally made its impact, and after the 1880s immigrants from the South flooded into the New World to comprise some 90 per cent of the Italian newcomers.

This shift in source coincided with a shift in destination. Throughout most of the nineteenth century, Italian movement overseas was directed toward Latin America, especially Argentina and Brazil. Because of economic and political troubles in these countries in the latter years of the century and expanding economic opportunities for unskilled labor in American industry, the mainstream of Italian emigration was diverted toward the Northern Hemisphere. In the decades before World War I Southern Italians spread across the United States, settling in Colorado, California, Alabama, and Texas, although they tended to concentrate in the urbanized industrial states of the East and Midwest such as New York, Rhode Island, and Illinois. One of the most popular destinations in the early years of Southern Italian immigration was Louisiana, and particularly its metropolis, New Orleans. As we shall see in the next two chapters, the city's attractiveness for these immigrants faded rapidly after 1891, when a lynch mob killed eleven Italians alleged to be *mafiosi* connected with the death of a police chief.[29]

2

Italian Immigrants and Criminals in New Orleans

From its beginnings in 1718 New Orleans was notorious for crime, violence, and official corruption, and increasingly attracted unscrupulous elements intending to profit from the opportunities there. Southern Italians, who began to pour into the city during the late nineteenth century, did not bring with them unusual criminal capability; the easygoing traditions and lush pickings in political and extra-legal areas simply drew criminals and opportunists, and they comprised a small but influential element within the immigrant group. New arrivals included those who intended to comply with the laws of their new homeland, and would realize economic betterment for themselves and their families within the existing legal system. Among new arrivals were also those who intended to circumvent the laws or break them outright in their quest for money, power, and prestige.[1]

New Orleans and the State of Louisiana had attracted Sicilians and other Southern Italians even before the great immigrant wave from the Kingdom. Italian immigrants had trickled into the Bayou State during pre-Civil War years, and in 1850 some 915 of them resided there—the largest number to be found in any state of the Union: by contrast, 835 lived in New York, 288 in California, and 196 in Massachusetts. On the eve of the Civil War, 1,134 Italians resided in Louisiana. The Italian population of New Orleans in 1850 and 1860 was not recorded, but probably three-quarters of the immigrants to the state could eventually be found in the city. The number of Italians in New Orleans increased during the decades after the Civil War, from 1,571 in 1870 to 1,995 in 1880, and to at least 3,622 by 1890. The 1890 federal census grossly undercounted the foreign-born in American cities; on the other hand, contemporaries in New Orleans firmly believed that the city contained between 20,000 and 25,000 foreign-born Italians and their children—a figure that was clearly excessive. The actual number was probably between 10,000 and 15,000. Unlike New York, Chicago, and other northern cities, New Orleans contained no sizable established enclave of Northern Italians. Even before 1880, its Italian community was largely Southern, particularly Sicilians, in composition.[2]

New Orleans held out a wide range of attractions for these newcomers, from expanding economic opportunities and familiar Roman Catholic traditions to comparable climate and superior living conditions. An editorial writer in the New Orleans *Picayune* described one of these attractions:

> Italians from the coast and islands of the Mediterranean have turned their attention to New Orleans and our gulf region, and they have found here so much that encourages them that we must look for a constantly increasing immigration. Here they have an interior sea, another Mediterranean, reaching to the tropics, and furnishing every possible facility for their maritime operations in fish and fruits. Here they find the orange, the fig and the pomegranate growing in the greatest perfection, besides the sugar cane, cotton and rice, the culture of which is well suited to their people from the rural districts.[3]

In contrast to that of northern American cities, the weather in New Orleans exhibited considerable similarity to that of Southern Italy. Although housing conditions in the central city were far from ideal, tenement living provided more space and more bearable shelter than in many other American cities. Because of the almost year-round warm weather, crowded quarters did not weigh too heavily on the newcomers, since they could be outdoors much of the time. Periodic floods and cyclical epidemics of yellow fever, cholera, typhoid, and malaria plagued the city, but diseases and natural disasters were not unknown to former residents of Southern Italy and Sicily. As D. Mack Smith has noted, "most southerners lived in squalor, afflicted by drought, malaria and earthquakes." Furthermore, New Orleans lacked the heavy population concentration endured by immigrants in the industrial centers of the East and Middle West. With 242,039 inhabitants in 1890, New Orleans ranked as the twelfth largest city in the United States, and extended over 23,739 acres, with 43,000 dwellings housing 48,582 families. The average population per dwelling was 5.63 persons, and there were 10.20 people to an acre. In contrast, Cleveland, an industrial center and the tenth largest city in the country, with a total population of 261,353, occupied 15,923 acres and contained 43,835 dwellings and 53,052 families, with an average of 5.96 persons to a dwelling and 16.41 persons to an acre.[4]

By the 1890s, Sicilian immigrants congregated along St. Philip, Ursulines, Chartres, Dumaine, Decatur, Royal, Barracks, and other streets in the French Quarter in the vicinity of the waterfront and the French Market, in sufficient numbers for the neighborhood to be called "Little Palermo" by older residents. "Little Palermo" was not, however, a permanent, static community, but rather an area of settlement for new arrivals to the city and for transients who would soon move on to find employment on sugar, cotton, and rice plantations outside the city. Thus, in November 1905 the Louisiana Immigration Association estimated that ten thousand Italians would pass through New Orleans en route to the state's planatations during the summer months.[5]

Immigrants who remained in New Orleans, like their urban counterparts elsewhere, were not confined to any one part of the city. When Italians, like other European immigrants, began to move up the socioeconomic ladder, they found it possible to leave their ethnic enclaves if they wished to do so: obviously the type of discrimination that prevented free residential mobility among blacks did not operate among white newcomers.[6] City directories and tax ledgers reveal that by 1890 Italians (although still heavily represented in core area neighborhoods) lived in every section of the city, and some had accumulated considerable wealth. Thus, Antonio Monteleone, who in

1890 was a shoe manufacturer with $37,000 in taxable property, was one of the Italian colony's success stories. A native of the town Contessa Entellina in the province of Palermo, Monteleone arrived in New Orleans in 1870, an impoverished immigrant boy. He began working as apprentice to a shoemaker, later opened his own store, and then started the first shoe factory in the city. In the early 1890s he built the Commercial Hotel on Royal and Customhouse (now Iberville) streets; later he expanded and renamed the building. The Monteleone Hotel still stands, one of the famous hostelries in the French Quarter. Monteleone became a director of two banks (the Whitney-Central Bank of New Orleans and the Bank of Hammond, Louisiana, where he owned extensive property) and owner of a brewery.

Antonio Lanata of 159 Esplanade, who dealt in real estate, was one of the wealthiest Italians in the city, with $184,600 in real and personal property. Shipping-line owner, fruit importer, and merchant Salvatore Oteri, 205 Royal, was worth $108,000; the Solari family—John B., Angelo M., and Joseph, eminently successful in the grocery and liquor businesses—lived on fashionable St. Charles Avenue and possessed nearly $200,000 in taxable property. Clearly the Italian community in New Orleans contained men of financial substance who dealt in a variety of economic activities.[7]

As noted above, New Orleans offered many economic opportunities, particularly in view of its importance as a seaport. Although by the 1880s the Irish and the blacks monopolized waterfront jobs, large numbers of Sicilians found employment as fishermen, stevedores, and longshoremen. Others became importers, exporters, and retail merchants; still others, fruit and vegetable peddlers and dealers. Italian "enterprise and capital" played a key role in the development of the fruit trade with Latin America and other sources overseas, as the *Picayune* editorialized, "from a mere peddling business conducted in a few sailing schooners, to the dignity and proportions of a great commercial interest employing a score and more of steamships and hundreds of thousands of dollars of capital."[8]

In 1881, by which date Italians had firmly established themselves as stable, hardworking, ambitious residents of New Orleans, Southern Italian criminality made its first impact upon the city, when a prominent Sicilian bandit was arrested there.

Western Sicily in the 1860s and 1870s was overrun with brigands, and Giuseppe Esposito was one of the most daring, successful, and vicious of them. Born into a good family, he "early in life exhibited an unruly and wild disposition." By the early 1860s, although barely out of his teens, he emerged as the leader of a gang of about 160 robbers and extortionists who grew wealthy by terrorizing the rural areas in the vicinity of his native Palermo. A broad-shouldered, powerfully built man, Esposito was above average in intelligence, although when he wished to dissemble he appeared to be a simple peasant. Apparently the only telltale mark on his body was a small scar between his eyebrows, and this proved to be an important factor in identifying him during his trial in New York City.[9]

A bold and daring leader, for almost fifteen years Esposito enjoyed a reputation for being one of the most successful brigands on the island. Through the judicious outlay of bribery money, he achieved virtual immunity from the periodic government expeditions through the mountains of western Sicily. Esposito specialized in kidnapping prominent businessmen and holding them for ransom. His most widely publicized exploit was the capture in November 1876 of an English curate, John Forester Rose, who was sightseeing in the Sicilian countryside. Rose was held for a five-thousand-pound ransom, and when his wife refused to submit to the blackmail, Esposito sent her one of the curate's ears. A week later the wife received another letter demanding the money; included with the letter was her husband's other ear, and a threat that the next letter would contain his nose. (Mrs. Rose sent the money, and her husband was released.)

The world-wide publicity growing out of this affair shamed the Italian government into dispatching a force of *carabinieri* with orders to capture the brigands. Esposito eluded the authorities for more than three months, although governmental pressure gradually caused the gang's membership to decline. The troops finally caught up with what remained of the outlaws. In the ensuing fight nine bandits died and fourteen were captured, among them the chieftain. Esposito and five of his men escaped from prison after bribing the guards, and the chief returned to his mountain hideout and his criminal activities. By 1879, however, Esposito found the situation in Sicily intolerable and decided to leave the island. After a short stay in New York, he traveled to New Orleans, where he took the name Vincenzo Rabello (or Rebello). Early in 1880 he married Salle Radazzo, a widow with two small boys, and the couple had a child in February 1881. They lived in a small house on Customhouse, between Burgundy and Rampart streets, in the Italian colony.

In Sicily, banditry was not a *mafia* operation: brigands like Giuseppe Esposito worked outside both the law and the extra-legal system of the *mafia*. Nevertheless, they could not function for any length of time without the knowledge and acquiescence of local *mafia* leaders, who received a percentage of the profits in exchange for permitting the banditry, and expected brigands to do an occasional favor, such as kidnapping or killing a rival. Thus Esposito did not have the status equivalent to that of a *mafia* leader; he was merely an outlaw. After his arrival in New Orleans, he apparently set up a system similar to that which had functioned effectively for him in his homeland. At that time (1881), no *mafia* of the type found in western Sicily existed in the Crescent City.[10]

On July 12, 1881, Esposito was arrested by police detectives Mike and Dave Hennessy and two police officers sent from New York to take the Sicilian to that city for extradition proceedings. On his arrival in New Orleans, Esposito had purchased a small fishing boat, called a lugger; upon his capture, he claimed that he had lived in New Orleans for years, working as a fisherman (although apparently he did not know how to sail the boat).

Esposito's downfall was not the result of intrepid police work, since, except for a small number of Italian residents, no one knew that the Sicilian brigand lived in New Orleans. Unfortunately for Esposito, he had a disagreement with another Sicilian immigrant, Tony Labousse (or Labuzzo), who had supervised construction of his lugger. When Labousse, by then a successful Italian merchant, delivered the boat, he lost the ensuing argument over his remuneration, and got his revenge by revealing Esposito's identity and whereabouts to the authorities (he might also have been influenced in his decision to betray his friend by the $5,000 reward that the Italian government had placed on Esposito's head). Labousse never received any compensation for his part in the capture, for on July 15, just three days after Esposito's arrest, he was shot and killed at the corner of Exchange Alley and Bienville Street. His assailant, Gaetano Arditto (Garditto), was seriously wounded in the exchange of shots, but survived to stand trial for murder, and was found guilty.

Labousse's death resulted from a vendetta growing out of his involvement in Esposito's capture. Arditto, a lemon peddler, had met Esposito shortly after the bandit's arrival in New Orleans. The two men became warm friends, and Esposito even advanced money to Arditto "to engage in the business of stevedore on the Levee," as the *Picayune* reported on November 9, 1881. As Esposito's closest friend, Arditto saw it as his responsibility to avenge the betrayal. Esposito, Arditto, and perhaps also Labousse, apparently belonged to a gang that specialized in kidnapping wealthy Italians in New Orleans (and elsewhere in Louisiana) for ransom. Tony Matranga, who later played a central role in the *Mafia* Incident (see Chapter 3), was allegedly a member of the group. Joe Provenzano, who appeared prominently in the events leading up to the Incident, testified in Esposito's favor at his extradition trial in New York City.

A final indignity capped Esposito's American experiences. Not only was he returned to a prison cell in Sicily, but also he was cheated by the friends to whom he had entrusted the care of his wife and family. Another friend, Giuseppe Grande, took Esposito's lugger and registered it as his own, leaving Esposito's wife and children destitute. Contrary to Sicilian tradition, Esposito turned to the law courts. In November 1881 he sued some of the wealthiest Italian fruit merchants in New Orleans, including Angelo Cusimano, "for the sum of ten thousand dollars and other sums of money exceeding in amount the sum of five thousand dollars additional," but was unsuccessful in his attempt to have the New Orleans District Court protect his wife's interests. And then in 1889 Esposito's wife sent his son Joseph to an orphanage. According to the New Orleans *States* (April 25, 1889), she applied to the mayor to have the boy and another child placed in an orphan asylum, "as she could not support them." The article concluded, "It was done." Apparently the traditions of *Omertà,* of settling one's own problems, of friends who looked after interests of a jailed leader, were weaker in the New World than in Sicily.

Some writers have traced a connection between young Officer Dave Hennessy's arrest of Esposito in 1881 and the murder of Police Chief David Hennessy ten years later, allegedly at the hands of Italian assassins. This theory confirms the legend that retribution follows any thwarting of *mafia* wishes, regardless of the passage of time or the precautions taken by the victim. Yet Esposito's friends quickly deserted him or turned on him, took his money and boat, and ignored the needs of his family—a flouting of Sicilian tradition that weakens the theory of revenge against Hennessy after a ten-year lapse. Another widely accepted theory, propounded by local historian John S. Kendall, held that Esposito "created" the *mafia* in New Orleans during the 1880s. The bandit's lack of influence among his compatriots tends to nullify this hypothesis.[11]

3. New Orleans Police Chief David Hennessy. (*Illustrated American*)

After Chief Hennessy's murder in October 1890, the New Orleans police department released a list of "assassinations, murders, and affrays committed by Sicilians and Italians" in the city during the period between August 1866 and the spring of 1891. The list purported to give an accurate picture of Italian criminality and violence, as well as a description of the operations of organized Italian gangs, in New Orleans. Officials and the public accepted the information provided, and writers since then have based their conclusions on its contents; no one at the time or since bothered to check the accuracy of the information. Comparisons with other sources of information indicate that the list was completely unreliable.[12]

In 1891 the view predominated that a *mafia*-style organization existed among Sicilians in New Orleans. Superintendent of Police D. G. Gaster had prepared the list for Mayor Joseph A. Shakspeare, who himself firmly believed that the *mafia* planned to take control of the city and intended to kill him as it had killed Hennessy.[13]

Official coroner reports and the files of city newspapers during the 1880s reveal that murders in that decade involving Italians were due, with few exceptions, to vendettas or "personal difficulty." Organized criminal activity and brutality existed among Italians in one form or another, as events in 1890 indicated; and yet a great amount of misinformation was deliberately disseminated by officials and unquestioningly accepted by the general public. Inaccuracies become strikingly evident when the Gaster list is compared with the coroner reports. Gaster's report contained errors in almost every case outlined, and each error served to blacken the reputation of New Orleans Italians.[14]

● Thus, the police department report stated, for example, that Pedro Escaro and Joseph Bilboa were killed on the steamship *Humaçoa* by a man named Silverio on December 24, 1883. The victims' names were, according to the coroner's report, Pedro Echave and José Maria Bilboa; their place of birth did not appear on either report, but they were probably of Spanish background; and the ship was the *Humaçao*.

Unreliable police reports at time (handwritten margin note)

• Then, the Gaster list recorded a murder on the night of June 14, 1885, involving a victim named Juan Martini. The stabbing, reported Gaster, had the appearance of being a *mafia* killing. In contrast, the coroner's report stated that the victim's name was John Martin, that he was born in Germany, and that he had died of a gunshot wound.

• On January 18, 1887, Dominica Tribiga shot and killed Jean Tamora, according to Gaster's list; the impression given was that victim and killer were Italians. The coroner's report indicated that both Dominique Trebigue and Jean Marie Trebigue (the actual names) were natives of France.

• According to the Gaster report, on the night of June 30, 1889, Manuel Mangeloa was shot and killed by "unknown Sicilians" while he slept. According to the coroner, the name of the victim was Marcel Mangelon, he was French, and the nationality of the killer or killers remained unknown.

While nearly all the reported murders involving Italians during the 1880s resulted from vendettas or personal problems, as the coroner's files indicate, some probably occurred through the attempts of organized gangs to extend their own power and influence. According to New Orleans authorities and writers on crime in that city (who often neglected to substantiate their assertions), imported Sicilian *mafiosi* committed these murders. Thus, partly on the basis of the Gaster compilation, John Kendall (in a 1939 article) asserted that the *mafia* had murdered three men in 1889. According to the coroner's report, on January 19, 1889, the corpse of a white male, 35 to 40 years of age, with a large cut at the base of his neck, was found "in the marsh, on the left side of the shell road, between the toll gate and the West End." The coroner's office identified neither the victim nor his assassin(s). The New Orleans *Picayune* article on the same day the body was discovered did not name the corpse, but the reporter who wrote "Murder Mystery. A Dead Man Found in the Swamp," purporting to

writes + miss reports helped form idea of mafia in peoples heads (handwritten margin note) reflect "the views" of police officers, conjectured that the *mafia* had committed the murder.

The Gaster list identified the corpse as Vincencio Ultonino. According to Kendall, the victim was a Sicilian named Vicenzo Ottumvo. Then, to entertain his readers, Kendall provided a colorful dramatization of the cut at the base of the neck, which the coroner had identified as being possibly the result of a knife wound. Kendall stated that the victim had been participating in a card game when someone "crept up behind him and with a razor, at one stroke, very nearly severed his head from his body. . . . The body was tumbled into a wagon, hauled to the Canal, and thrown into its muddy waters." Kendall had no doubts: the killing was "distinctly a *mafia* murder." [15]

These inaccuracies and embellishments, repeated in subsequent articles and books, became accepted as truth. The officially unidentified body found in the New Orleans marsh in 1889 involved, in crime reporter Nicholas Gage's book, *The Mafia Is Not an Equal Opportunity Employer,* "the first recorded Mafia killing in the United States," and occurred "when a man named Vincenzo Ottumvo was murdered in New Orleans during a card game. A gang war followed that ultimately led to two grand jury investigations." [16]

The "gang war" alluded to by Gage was a real and deadly struggle between the Matranga and Provenzano clans, but no evidence suggested that it grew out of the January murder. Two murders with political connections occurred, however, and yet neither was mentioned by Kendall or Gage. The first took place during a street fight between rival groups of Italians on December 12, 1886, when Vincent Raffo was shot and killed. Then on January 5, 1888, Antonio Bonora died of a shot to the abdomen. Rocco Geraci (or Gerachi) was arrested and charged with the first murder, and was accused of perpetrating the second; he was convicted of neither. The *Times-Democrat,* summarizing events in the Provenzano-Matranga feud up to October 21, 1890, stated that at the time of the murder trial in 1886, "it was charged by the defense that Rocco Geraci had murdered a shoemaker named Vincent Raffo in 1886," and he was arrested, charged in criminal court, and placed under $5,000 bond. So flimsy was the evidence given against him," however, that the district attorney suggested dismissal of that case. Geraci was a prominent Italian politician of the Sixth Ward and a member of the Matranga faction. (Five years later he would be one of eleven Italians murdered by an angry crowd at the Parish Prison.) Both the 1886 and the 1888 murders might have been steps in the escalating power struggle that culminated in the Hennessy assassination of 1890 and the lynchings in 1891.[17]

Kendall cited another murder, one that took place on February 24, 1889, when, according to the coroner's report, Giuseppe Mattaino's throat was cut, his face burned beyond recognition, two-thirds of his skull cut out, and his legs, hands, and feet burned. Even though the Gaster compilation affirmed that Mattaino's wife and her lover had perpetrated the slaying, Kendall maintained that it "may have been" a *mafia* job.

According to the coroner's report, a third murder victim, Pietro Vit-trani, was a laborer from Jefferson Parish who had been in the city "a few hours" when, on March 9, 1889, he suffered "a compound fracture inflicted by a blunt instrument to the skull and brain" by person or persons unknown. In the Gaster version, the victim died "from the effects of gunshot wounds inflicted by three Sicilians, whom Vit-trani did not know." Kendall changed the victim's name to Camilo Victoria and the date of the murder to June. As in the Ottumvo (Ul-tonino) case, the killing took place at a card game "with three other Italians, when an unknown person made his way quietly into the alley alongside the building, and through an open door shot him in the head, killing him instantly." Apparently Kendall confused this case with the shooting of Camillo Vitrano during a card game on June 17, 1890; the killer or killers shot from an alleyway. This murder took place at the height of the struggle between the Provenzano and Matranga organizations for control of the Italian section of the New Orleans docks, and could very well have been a gang killing. It is also possible, as the New Orleans paper, *The Mascot,* observed in the story headlined "Another Vendetta Victim" (June 21, 1890), that the murder was part of a family feud or vendetta that had prompted the slaying of Ca-millo's brother Paulo in a similar manner (a gunshot wound in the

[handwritten margin notes: "Stiming" / "Kendall says Mafia job even when there is evidence against it"]

4. Contemporary cartoonist's rendition of the shotgun slaying of Camillo Vitrano on June 17, 1890. (New Orleans *Mascot*)

head) some six years earlier. The Gaster report, incidentally, stated that Paulo was stabbed to death.[18]

In the late 1880s, a number of Sicilians and other Southern Italians in New Orleans, some of them with criminal records in the homeland, took part in illegal and semi-legal activities. Such men were for the most part former brigands who, like Esposito, had emigrated when the situation at home became uncomfortable. Some, possibly, were accused or convicted of crimes of passion, and there may well have been a sprinkling of former *mafiosi*. As Sicilians and Southern Italians, these men were familiar with the traditions and characteristics of the *mafia,* whether or not they had ever had dealings with that society. In crime, as in so many other areas of life, immigrants tried to re-create what they remembered from the homeland; typically, however, they produced something differing in many respects from the original. In part this difference resulted from the fact that most of those who attempted to set up criminal gangs in the United States were usually not former *mafiosi*, but common criminals; those who had been *mafiosi* did not belong to the high-ranking leadership that was protected from punishment, but were, rather, low-level members (*picciotti*) who simply carried out orders.

It seems clear that the so-called *mafia* gangs in New Orleans during the late 1880s and the 1890s shared some of the characteristics of the Sicilian organization, like involvement in politics and desire to control activities in a particular line of work (in this instance, unloading ships engaged in the South American fruit trade). These gangs, however, lacked two basic characteristics of the Sicilian model: strict adherence to the code of silence, and support from the local Italian population. Furthermore, political involvement and business monopolies were not limited to Sicilians or to criminals. Hence, while crime existed and flourished among Southern Italians in New Orleans during these years, it could not accurately be ascribed to *mafiosi*.

The Matrangas and the Provenzanos led the rival factions in Italian New Orleans. Ward politics and the waterfront comprised the areas in which the struggle occurred most violently. For some ten years prior to 1888 the Provenzano brothers dominated the business of unloading ships engaged in the lucrative fruit trade with Latin America. From 1878 to 1886, in the words of Joseph P. Macheca (a leading Italian fruit importer in New Orleans), the Provenzanos "had the exclusive business of discharging fruit vessels." This monopoly ended in 1886 when a new stevedore firm, that of Matranga and Locascio, appeared on the docks. For the next two years that firm offered stiff competition to the established Provenzanos, and in June 1888 (as described in a *Times-Democrat* article of October 21, 1890) "the fruit merchants concluded to change their stevedores and employed the Matranga brothers because of certain disagreements with the Provenzanos." These "disagreements," according to Frank P. Demaio, a Pinkerton agent sent to New Orleans to investigate the Hennessy murder, resulted from a growing dissatisfaction with the Provenzano group's performance on the part of the shippers. The shippers then organized an association, discharged the Provenzanos, and gave all their business to the Matranga-Locascio firm. The new employers retained most of the laborers who had worked under the Provenzanos. Vincent Caruso, for example, one of the men later accused of Hennessy's murder and himself a lynch mob victim in 1891, had worked for twelve years for the Provenzanos before joining Matranga.[19]

It is impossible to determine the exact reasons impelling the fruit importers to give control of their stevedore work to the Matrangas. Possibly, as some writers have claimed, the Matrangas forced the shipowners to reach a decision in their favor.[20] Yet in the trial growing out of an ambush of the Matranga faction, two leading Italian fruit importers (Joseph P. Macheca and Salvatore Oteri) claimed that the shippers underwent no pressure to decide in favor of the Matrangas. The complete stenographic transcripts of this trial (as well as of the Hennessy murder trial) no longer exist, and it is necessary to depend on the summaries of proceedings taken in court each day by newspaper reporters and published in the daily press. While these summaries present the high points in testimony given, and the key questions asked by prosecution and defense attorneys as well as answers given, they are nonetheless incomplete.

From the evidence available, the shippers apparently based their decision on business factors. The Irish and black workers who controlled the docks were in the process of unionizing during this period, and the Matrangas may have been brought in to head a company-type union (it was this union that many New Orleanians meant when they alluded to the *mafia*). One may ask whether the Matrangas were engaged because they were in fact underworld leaders. When they brought charges against the Provenzanos in a court of law, they certainly did not behave as orthodox *mafiosi* were known to act. They did not observe a code of silence and they did not seek their own justice— as a parallel government is supposed to do—when they turned to the law and gave extensive evidence in court. It would seem that if they had headed an all-powerful *mafia* the Matrangas would have been able to settle accounts themselves with little difficulty.

Thus Charles Matranga testified in court that the Provenzanos had made threats to Macheca, Oteri, and other merchants in an effort to recoup the stevedoring business. He also stated that on several occasions Joseph Provenzano had approached him and "asked to let him go back into the business." When Matranga refused to permit Provenzano to join his firm, Provenzano vowed that "there would be bloodshed all along the wharf." While this is clearly biased testimony, the significant fact is that Matranga and a large number of leading Italian businessmen did aid the police and the court instead of maintaining silence and attempting to settle accounts extra-legally. Indeed, the business community tried to end the feud between the two factions, which continued throughout 1888 and 1889. Early in 1890 Macheca brought the Provenzanos and Matrangas together and, serving as mediator, encouraged them to air their grievances. The two parties (in Macheca's words) "came to an agreement and gave their word to the chief of police [Hennessy] that there would be no further trouble." The truce lasted approximately five months. According to an October 21, 1890, article in the *Times-Democrat,* "a few days before the shooting it was testified that a final demand was made by the Provenzanos for the work which was denied them, and they threatened trouble." [21]

In any event, on May 5, 1890, members of the Matranga workforce spent the day unloading bananas from the *Foxhall.* Shortly before midnight five of them—Anthony Matranga, Anthony Locascio, Vincent Caruso, Rocco Geraci, and Salvatore Sunseri—climbed into a fruit wagon driven by Bastion Cardona and started for their homes, a row of cottages known as "Greek Row" on Dorgenois, near Ursulines Street. While the men sang and laughed the wagon rolled down Claiborne Street; when it reached Esplanade, a volley of some twenty-five shots was fired from ambush, severely wounding Caruso, Sunseri, and Matranga. The men survived, although Matranga's left leg had to be amputated. The assailants escaped. According to a May 9, 1890, story in the *Times-Democrat,* "Many of the fruit and produce merchants have interested themselves in the case, and in behalf of the attacked party, with whom they are in sympathy, have contributed money and will exercise their influence in bringing the criminals to justice."

5. Members of the Provenzano faction arrested in connection with the May 5, 1890, shooting: (1) Gasparo Lombardo, (2) Nick Giulio, (3) Tony Pellagrini, (4) Tony Gianforcarro, and (5) Joseph Provenzano. (New Orleans *Democrat*)

These words and actions were contrary to Sicilian *mafia* tradition.

Taking command of the case, Hennessy arrested Peter and Joseph Provenzano, Tony Pellagrini, Tony Gianforcarro, Nick Giulio, and Gasparo Lombardo, and charged them with "shooting with intent to kill." They were brought to trial on July 15, 1890; leaders of the Italian community and members of the Matranga group testified against them, and on July 19 the jury found the accused guilty of shooting and wounding, with intent to kill members of the Matranga group. The verdict of "guilty without capital punishment" provided for a mandatory punishment of hard labor for life in the State Penitentiary. The *Times-Democrat* applauded the result, predicting that it would end the vendetta that had "existed in the Italian colony of New Orleans for years" (July 20). "When they found [that] the better classes of their own countrymen would come to their assistance," the article continued, "the victims of the ambuscade renounced the Mafia and appealed to the law." The Provenzanos had assumed "that the trial, like those of the past, would be farcical. That Sicilians would never settle their differences in the courts." An editorial in the same issue applauded "the new departure in the bearing of testimony" by New Orleans Sicilians. As a result of the "guilty" verdict, "confidence in the protective power of the law will replace timidity in the Italian breast and henceforth his evidence in court will harmonize with facts rather than be dictated by his fears."

The only sour note in the trial proceedings, as the editorial writer noted, was the testimony of police officers who swore under oath that they had seen members of the Provenzano group at the time the ambush took place, and thus provided the accused with alibis. As one newspaperman observed (in October 1890, looking back on the case), "A peculiar feature of the case was the large number of policemen who were witnesses for the defense." The *Times-Democrat* and other local newspapers called for an investigation to determine whether the officers had perjured themselves. On July 22 the police department formally requested the Criminal District Court to conduct such a inquiry. The grand jury reported, on July 31, that "they found the charge of dereliction of duty totally unfounded." Although the grand jury investigation was reported by the press to have been "exhaustive," it is impossible to verify the accuracy of this statement since the proceedings (which no longer exist) were not published at the time.

Despite the grand jury decision, no effort was made to indict any of the Italians, and there was no suspicion that the trial jury (which, after hearing all the evidence, found the Provenzanos guilty) had been tampered with, or that the evidence presented by the Matrangas or the Italian community was perjured. The grand jury, facing a choice between believing Sicilians who claimed that the Provenzanos were guilty, and officers of the law who maintained that the Provenzanos were innocent victims of Matranga wrath, elected to disbelieve the Italians and thereby protect the image of honesty and integrity that David Hennessy had been trying to create from the time he became police chief in 1888. (Prior to that time the police department had been noted for corruption, inefficiency, and incompetence.)

On August 1 attorneys for the Provenzanos won a new trial for their clients. The Matranga-Provenzano struggle thereupon entered a new phase. After numerous delays the trial started on January 13, 1891, and ten days later the jury returned a verdict of "not guilty." In this retrial new witnesses, among them leading machine politicians (members of the so-called "Customhouse Gang") and police officers (including all ranks up to captain), testified to the presence of the defendants in other parts of the city at the time the crime was committed. The prosecution was unable to refute the new testimony, in part because of the grand jury's finding that policemen who had served as witnesses in the first trial had not perjured themselves. This finding automatically made the police appear to be reliable witnesses. Furthermore, testimony of the Matrangas and Italian community leaders who supported legal action against the Provenzanos had become suspect. Most New Orleans residents refused to put any value on Matranga testimony following the murder of popular police chief David Hennessy, who had been listed as a witness for the Provenzanos in their second trial.[22]

The irony in the situation lies in the fact that the "better element" in the Italian colony had turned away from Old World traditions of settling disputes by personal and direct action and of keeping silent about wrongdoing. After the May shooting of the Matrangas, Italians had gone to the police. They furnished information, suggested channels of obtaining evidence, provided money to aid the prosecution in its preparation of the case for trial, and thus they proved, as one newspaperman claimed, "that they were themselves in dead earnest to break up the villainous methods of secret crime which their more reckless compatriots have introduced and sought to establish in this city." Unfortunately for the reputation of the Italian leaders, the police supported the Provenzanos and provided alibis for them.

An important fact, which Italian residents of the city undoubtedly recognized, was the court's acceptance of police testimony over that provided by Italian-American businessmen. New Orleans Italians probably asked themselves what gains had come from their cooperation with the legal system. A reasonable conclusion might be that, as in Sicily, it was better to keep quiet and settle problems by oneself. Yet, significantly, in the following months the Matrangas continued to report to Mayor Shakspeare threats that they alleged the Provenzanos had made. Repeatedly they asked the mayor to take legal action against their enemies. It is, of course, possible that the Matrangas and their supporters were *mafiosi;* but this accusation and evidence for it came from the Provenzanos, a highly biased source. (In fact, Manuel Politz, one of the accused in Hennessy's murder, also claimed that the Matrangas were *mafiosi;* but when Politz proved to be mentally deranged, the district attorney totally discredited his confession.) The Provenzanos countered Matranga claims against them by stating that their enemies were members of a local *mafia* group identified variously as the "Stilletos" and the "Stoppagliere Society," and that these *mafiosi* committed blackmail and murder among members of the Italian colony. After the police chief's death the Provenzanos also suggested that the Matrangas with their allies were responsible for that murder. They might have been right about the Matrangas' membership in the *mafia,* but none of the evidence, provided by the Provenzanos, linked the Matrangas directly with a criminal gang of extortionists.[23]

The Matrangas for their part claimed that their rivals were *mafiosi* and intended to destroy them. A May 16, 1891, article in the *Picayune* revealed that during the preceding months members of both the Matranga and the Provenzano factions had appealed to the mayor for protection, claiming that the opposing faction was part of the *mafia* and was "out to get them." Clearly this was no way for self-respecting Sicilians to behave, especially if they really were members in good standing of the *mafia.*

In more than one respect things were not what they appeared. The Provenzanos were not the injured and innocent parties they claimed to be in the trials of 1890 and 1891. The *Picayune,* which did not report the shooting incident that had occurred on May 5, was selective in its treatment of the Provenzano-Matranga struggle. The Provenzanos, who were pushed off the docks when the Matrangas gained a monopoly of the unloading of ships, did not meekly accept their fate. In addition to the May 1890 shooting, which led to the Hennessy murder and the *Mafia* Incident, the Provenzanos made a strong push to regain control of the business they had lost in 1888. On May 15, 1891, just two months after the lynching of members of the Matranga faction at the Parish Prison (see Chapter 3), Mayor Shakspeare directly warned Joe and Peter Provenzano and their followers that, as he put it, "This community has grown sick and tired of the intimidation and lawlessness you have carried on." If the intimidation did not stop, the mayor vowed, he would use "every means at my command to wipe from the face of the earth every member of your gang who tries to raise his hand against a person of this community." [24]

The cause of the mayor's indignation and the occasion for the show of force was the waterfront situation in the wake of the murder of fruit importer and steamship company owner Joseph Macheca at the hands of the lynch mob, and the dispersal of the Italian waterfront gangs who (under the direction of Charles Matranga) had controlled the unloading of ships from Latin America. Black longshoremen were attempting to fill the vacuum and to take over this work, which previously had been an Italian monopoly. Immediately after the lynchings at the Parish Prison, black longshoremen working under stevedore Henry Peters were given a contract to unload fruit ships owned by the Macheca firm. Then the Provenzanos apparently tried to force the blacks (who, along with Irish longshoremen, already controlled the rest of the waterfront) out of the jobs held by the Provenzanos prior to 1888. The situation became so intolerable that, on behalf of his longshoremen crew, stevedore Peters asked the mayor for "advice and protection." The short-fused Shakspeare immediately called the Provenzanos to city hall, related his conversation with Peters, and delivered his ultimatum: "This thing must stop, now and for all time." To Joe Provenzano the mayor stated, "I know well enough that you have long been at the head of a disturbing element here that has been a menace to the peace of this community." As Shakspeare admitted, he realized that Joe Provenzano had "sought to foment trouble here time and again," and that Charles Matranga had complained that "he cannot pass a Provenzano on the street without the latter spitting at him"—clearly not the way ordinary Italians treated a man who was supposed to be the head of a feared *mafia* gang. This and other actions must stop, or he would force the Provenzanos out of the city. Thus by May the Provenzanos could no longer maintain the pose of injured innocence adopted in the wake of Chief Hennessy's murder. (One wonders, too, about a police official who was a personal friend of such vicious and violent men.)

Some writers have presented the Provenzano-Matranga feud as a battle between *mafia* and *Camorra* groups in America. In a work first published in 1952, reporter Ed Reid assumed that the Matrangas were *mafiosi,* and conjectured that the Provenzanos "may have been connected with the *Camorra.*" Citing Reid as his source, Eric Hobsbawm asserted that in America the *mafia* "originally refused to deal with any but Sicilian immigrants, and fought notable battles against the rival (Neapolitan) *Camorristi,* e.g., the famous Matranga-Provenzano feuds in New Orleans in the 1880s, and similar battles in New York in the 1910s."[25] Less than a month after Hennessy's murder, a writer in *Illustrated American* concluded that "every circumstance in his death was that of a Camorrist 'removal,' " and that the Matrangas (rather than the Provenzanos) were "a gang of Camorrists who were terrorizing the small fruit-dealers in New Orleans."

Thus, depending upon the preference of the writer, the Matrangas and/or the Provenzanos became Sicilian *mafiosi* or Neapolitan *Camorristi,* although both the Provenzanos and the Matrangas originated in the province of Palermo in Sicily, as did most (but not all) of their followers. As testimony in the Provenzano-Matranga case brought out, none of the men came from Naples. Of the six Provenzano men tried for attempted murder, four were born in Sicily (Peter and Joseph

Provenzano, Gasparo Lombardo, and Tony Gianfarcarro); Tony Pella-grini was born in New Orleans; and Nick Giulio, born in Pensacola, Florida, lived in New Orleans from the age of nine months. So too, of the men killed by the lynch mob at the Parish Prison in 1891, Caruso, Bagnetto, Traina, Marchesi, Monasterio, Politz, and Geraci were natives of Palermo; Scaffidi was born in Messina, Comitz in Aquila (near Rome), and Macheca in New Orleans. Moreover, many members of the feuding factions had apparently been acquainted with each other for years, both in the United States and in Sicily. Thus Tony Matranga, who was born in Piana degli Albanesi and brought by his parents to New Orleans at the age of one, stated that he had known his would-be assassin Gianfarcarro "from boyhood." Rocco Geraci, a member of the Matranga group, testified that he had "known Joseph and Peter Provenzano since their birth together in Sicily," and that he and the Provenzanos had emigrated to New Orleans together seventeen years before.[26]

A *Times-Democrat* editorial of January 24, 1891, reflected the con-fusion of New Orleans citizens. A brutal ambush had taken place in May of the preceding year, men had been seriously wounded, and it was highly unlikely that the victims, the Matrangas, had staged the af-fair. The logical suspects were their rivals, the Provenzanos, but over-whelming numbers of prominent witnesses testified in their behalf at the retrial; furthermore, after Chief Hennessy's slaying, all Italians were held in low repute. The editorial writer commented on the inabil-ity of the police to find the guilty parties in the Matranga shooting, and of the courts to punish the accused. If the criminal justice system in New Orleans had broken down, speculated the writer, the sole alterna-tive lay in direct action by the people. "Have we come to that?" he queried. Just two months later a lynch mob provided the answer to his question.

3

What connection with Mafia how did they get this idea?

Hennessy's Murder
and the *Mafia*

David Hennessy, the popular and widely admired young police chief of New Orleans, was shot and mortally wounded at about 11:30 P.M. on October 15, 1890, within a few feet of his home at 274 Girod Street. It was a dark, dreary, rainy night. A low-hanging electric lamp provided some illumination at the intersection of Girod and Basin streets, about ten feet from where the shooting took place, but "at the time of the shooting this [light] was nearly out," according to the New Orleans *Picayune*.

Chief Hennessy, with several wounds in his body, was taken to Charity Hospital, where he lived for nearly ten hours. Witnesses at the murder trial identified the men who had fired at him, but the victim himself, who was closer to his assailants than were any of the witnesses, offered no such information during those last hours. As the *Times-Democrat* reported, "When he was asked if he knew who shot him he shook his head from side to side in a negative way. [Police Sergeant] Walsh asked, 'Don't you know?' and a like answer was returned." Neither did he indicate, as later accounts claimed, that he had collected evidence proving that certain individuals were members of a *mafia* gang and intended to kill him because he knew who they were. Just after he was shot, however, and again in the hospital, Hennessy was heard to say, "The dagos shot me." Apparently what prompted this conclusion was his involvement in the Matranga-Provenzano case; had he known the names of his assassins, or their

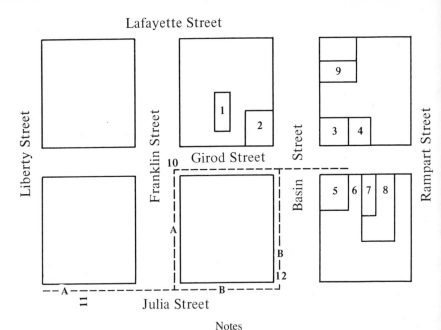

Notes

1. Chief Hennessy's residence.

2. Grocery.

3. Second-hand store in front of which the chief paused to draw his pistol and return his assailant's fire, falling upon the steps of the building as he fired his second shot.

4. Cottage in front of which the chief was passing when the first volley was fired.

5. Two-story frame dwelling.

6. Alley in front of which the second murderous volley was fired.

7. One-story frame building, the front room occupied by Monasterio as a cobbler's shop, and the rear room by a black family named Beverly.

8. Two-story frame dwelling.

9. Residence of Mrs. Gillis to which the chief walked after he was shot.

    A. Course taken by three of the fugitives.

    B. Course taken by two of the fugitives.

10. Point at which one of the men slipped and fell in turning the corner, and where the double-barreled gun was recovered in the gutter.

11. Point at which two shortened guns were found by the police in the gutter. (Based on New Orleans *Picayune,* October 17, 1890)

[handwritten margin notes: loading the name of Italians + Mafia exaggeration]

motives, he would surely have revealed them. The *States* and the *Picayune* relayed only the statement "The dagos shot me," and not his reaction to Sergeant Walsh's questioning. The jury in the murder trial never heard about the negative headshake or the question in the hospital.[1]

Hennessy's death shocked the citizens of New Orleans. His popularity and youth, a series of earlier tragedies in his family (such as the deaths of his father and cousin in line of duty), and the bereavement of an aged mother whom he had supported, combined to create city-wide sympathy and outrage and an overwhelming demand that the guilty parties be identified and brought to justice. Three factors directed attention toward Italians and specifically toward the Matranga element. One was Hennessy's statement that the "dagos" had shot him. The second was the widespread knowledge that Hennessy intended to testify in behalf of the Provenzanos. The third was the fact that the shots that hit the chief were fired from a shed that had for years been oc-

6. Girod Street shed used by killers of Police Chief Hennessy.
(*Illustrated American*)

cupied by Italians and ordinarily used as a fruit stand. As a *Picayune* report observed, these Italians were usually "new arrivals, who would leave the place after stopping for a month or two." At the time of the murder Pietro Monasterio had occupied the building for approximately two months and operated it as a shoe shop. On October 19 Joseph P. Macheca, a friend of the Matrangas, was identified as the person who had rented the Girod Street shanty for Monasterio's use.

Following the shooting, Mayor Shakspeare called the entire police force to duty, assuming the killers to be Italians, directed their energies toward that sector. "Scour the whole neighborhood," he ordered. "Arrest every Italian you come across, if necessary." The police followed these orders to the letter and arrested more than a hundred Italians. The jail was filled, one *Times-Democrat* reporter divulged, "with Sicilians, whose low, receding foreheads, repulsive countenances and slovenly attire, proclaimed their brutal natures." Similarly, Shakspeare fanned popular prejudice with an impassioned speech before the City Council on October 18:

> The circumstances of the cowardly deed, the arrests made, and the evidence collected by the police department, show beyond doubt that he was the victim of Sicilian vengeance, wreaked upon him as the chief representative of law and order in this community, because he was seeking by the power of our American law to break up the fierce vendettas that have so often stained our streets with blood. Heretofore these scoundrels have confined their murderings among themselves. None of them have even been convicted because of the secrecy with which the crimes have been committed and the impossibility of getting evidence from the people of their own race to convict. Bold, indeed, was the stroke, aimed at their first American victim. A shining mark have they selected on which to write with the assassin's hand their contempt for the civilization of the new world.
>
> We owe it to ourselves and to everything that we hold sacred in this life to see to it that this blow is the last. We must teach these people a lesson they will not forget for all time. What the means are to reach this end, I leave to the wisdom of the Council to devise.[2]

The mayor misrepresented the facts in positing the impossibility of obtaining evidence from Sicilians, since in the first Provenzano trial

Sicilians did appear as witnesses in open court. Nevertheless, his attitude reflected that of a large segment of the New Orleans citizenry, who took for granted, first, that the killers were Italians; second, that the *mafia* operated in large numbers; third, that the shooting was a declaration of war by the *mafia*.

In the issue of October 18, 1890, the New Orleans *Item* called the *mafia* a state within the state, with laws that are "surer of execution than the decrees of the State." Is there any reason, the reader was asked, to wonder why in a confrontation between the *mafia* and the American legal system Italians prefer "to risk the outcome of criminal prosecution in our courts than accuse or even testify against a member of the terrible order?" Accordingly, "unless the assassins of Chief Hennessy are captured, tried and punished, the victory is theirs," as the *Times-Democrat* editorialized on October 17, 1890, "and they will hold a constant threat over the community that whoever interferes with them will be killed. New Orleans must surrender to the *mafia* and vendetta," the paper warned, "unless it gets rid of these criminals, who have so openly defied its authorities." The writer concluded that "they must be crushed and annihilated unless we wish to banish law and order and establish murder in its stead."

On November 9 the grand jury began its investigation of the shooting. Indictments for murder and for lying in wait with intent to murder were returned against nineteen Italians: Pietro Natali, Antonio Scaffidi, Charles Traina, Antonio Bagnetto, Manuel Politz (or Polizzi), Antonio Marchesi, Pietro Monasterio, Bastion Incardona, Loretto Comitz, and Salvador Sinceri as principals, and James Caruso, Rocco Geraci, Asperi Marchesi, Joseph P. Macheca, Charles Matranga, Charles Patorno, Frank Romero, John Caruso, and Charles Pietza as accessories before the fact. All the accessories, with the exception of Pietza and Marchesi, were members of the Matranga faction. After a series of delays, some caused by the Provenzano retrial, the Hennessy trial came to court on February 16, 1891, exactly four months after the murder. For no adequately explained reason only nine of the accused were placed on trial: Scaffidi, Monasterio, Matranga, Asperi Marchesi, Macheca, Bagnetto, Politz, Incardona, and Antonio Marchesi.

The taking of testimony began on February 28, after twelve days for jury selection. The prosecution contended that Macheca rented the shanty at Girod for the purpose of preparing for the assassination of the police chief; that Asperi Marchesi served as lookout to advise of Hennessy's approach so that Monasterio, Scaffidi, Politz, Bagnetto, and Antonio Marchesi, armed with sawed-off shotguns and pistols, could fire when the chief drew opposite the shed; that the murder occurred to prevent Hennessy from delivering his damaging testimony against Matranga and his associates when the Provenzano case came up for retrial.

More than sixty witnesses were called. On October 17, 1890, according to the *Times-Democrat,* Mr. M. L. Peeler, of 273 Girod, identified Scaffidi as one of killers, by means of an oilcloth coat that police officers had found in Scaffidi's home. Detective Kerwin called Peeler "the most material witness" the police had, although admittedly Peeler had been unable to see Scaffidi's face during the assassination. The following day the newspaper carried an article stating that Peeler's story had been inaccurate.

Several of the suspects were arrested. Apparently the case against them was based on the charge that they behaved suspiciously. Thus, Antonio Incardona, an occupant of the wagon allegedly fired upon by the Provenzanos, had opened a fruit stall in the Poydras Market shortly after that May incident. According to the October 21 issue of the *Times-Democrat,* he was jailed because he was "a new Dago around the market" and "for this reason was suspected of complicity in the assassination." The evidence was so weak that District Attorney Luzenburg finally abandoned the case against him. Scaffidi, for his part, came under suspicion because he was not where he was supposed to be—at his job in Poydras Market—at the time of the killing; furthermore, he owned an oilcloth coat and fitted the general description given by Peeler. According to defense witnesses, however, Scaffidi had been at home at the time, tending his wife, who was having a miscarriage. The prosecution did not disprove this contention; the memoirs of Pinkerton agent Frank Dimaio supported it. As Dimaio remembered the incident some forty years later, another of the accused,

Frank Romero, stated that Scaffidi's wife "was delivered of a baby that night." [3]

One problem for the prosecution lay in the inconsistent testimony of its witnesses. Zachary Foster, who witnessed the shooting, stated that he saw the faces of four of the killers—three clearly and one indistinctly—and identified Scaffidi, Marchesi, Monasterio, and Politz. On cross-examination, however, "all he saw was in a short space of time, on a rainy day," according to the *Picayune* (March 1, 1891). "The four men he saw had on hats; he had never seen them before; but still he is willing to swear those men are like the four he saw that night. They look pretty much like them. He would not like to go any further than that."

Weather conditions created an additional problem. Although rain was falling at the time and the light at the corner of Girod and Basin was reportedly "nearly out," James T. Poole and other witnesses recalled that the scene "was as bright as day" and that they had no trouble seeing the killers. Such testimony raises the question of why Hennessy was unable to see his assailants clearly enough to identify them. If Monasterio was one of the gunmen, the victim would surely have recognized him, for the shoemaker had resided in the neighborhood for two months and had done work for Hennessy's mother. Since Chief Hennessy was constantly on the alert, he would doubtless have learned what Monasterio looked like, and possibly would have checked up on him. He probably knew some or all of the accused gunmen by sight and by name.

If one could credit an editorial in the *Times-Democrat* for October 19, 1890, Chief Hennessy "had collected important evidence in regard to Sicilian brigands in this city, and it was to prevent his giving his evidence that he was assassinated." The writer confided that Hennessy's papers contained "some valuable documents shedding light on this very matter, and giving some clue to the men who had every reason to fear him." Yet at no time during the trial did the "evidence" Hennessy was supposed to have collected on Italian criminals in New Orleans enter into the proceedings. If any such evidence existed among his papers, it was never found; and, significantly, no claims ever arose that any of Hennessy's belongings were distributed, stolen, or destroyed.

The erratic behavior of Politz comprised one of the more bizarre aspects of the trial. On March 2, speaking excitedly in Italian and gesticulating wildly as he struggled with the guards, Politz demanded to speak privately to the judge. At a conference in Judge Baker's chambers attended by Politz and lawyers for the defense and prosecution, the prisoner made a confession. For the remainder of the trial Politz's behavior varied between calm and violent, and at one point he tried to jump out a courtroom window. However seriously the local press and some subsequent writers took Politz's statements, his confession impressed neither the judge nor the prosecution lawyers. Although, as historian John E. Coxe notes, "some sort of confession was made," the district attorney "did not see fit to accept the confession and proceeded with the prosecution"—that is, Politz's statement could not be given credence in a court of law. Kendall described Politz as "a highly excitable person," whereas he was actually unbalanced, and the stress of the trial and rough treatment in prison proved to be too much for him. After Politz's lynching, a *Times-Democrat* reporter claimed that the mob's victim had confessed to him the details of the Hennessy murder, stating—as might be expected—that he alone among the accused was innocent, and describing the personnel and inner workings of the *mafia* in New Orleans. Yet, as Harris Myron Dulitz points out, "although many have accepted this confession, the sheriff, under whose constant surveillance the accused had remained, stated he heard nothing mentioned of the *mafia* in Politz's interview with the reporter." Although Kendall admitted that the confession could not be "taken very seriously," he still concluded that "it proved that the murder was the result of a conspiracy," the accused being mere tools in the hands of unidentified *mafia* higher-ups.[4]

Except for Politz, the accused controlled their emotions and entrusted their defense to a group of the ablest, best-known, and most successful lawyers in the city, among them A. D. Henriques, Thomas J. Semmes, Lionel Adams, and Arthur Gastinel. Also engaged was a prominent and reportedly unscrupulous private detective, Dominick C.

7. Joseph P. Macheca (*above, left*), John Matranga (*above, right*), and Manuel Politz (*left*), three defendants in the Hennessy murder trial. (New Orleans *Picayune*)

O'Malley, a long-time enemy and rival of the deceased Hennessy, who purportedly aspired to be chief of police and exhibited considerable resentment when Hennessy was named to that position. The press and public of New Orleans did not understand how Italian immigrants could afford such highly priced legal talent, and concluded that the *mafia* must have provided the money. The *Times-Democrat* for March 17, 1891, reported that from $50,000 to $75,000 had been raised by the *mafia* in New Orleans and other cities. Other papers claimed that money was pouring in from *mafia* organizations throughout the country. Had those interested checked, they would have found that subscriptions were raised by Italian-language newspapers in New York, Chicago, and other cities containing Italian colonies throughout the country. Moreover, the Italian community in New Orleans was financially well off, and the local Italian-American newspapers collected contributions for a defense fund.

Some of the defense lawyers, as well as O'Malley, had represented the Matrangas in the Provenzano trials and had helped the State present its case against the Provenzanos. In the Hennessy case the Provenzanos retaliated. Their lawyers helped the prosecution prepare and present its case against Matranga, Macheca, and the others accused of the shooting. The two murder cases were inexorably intertwined, not only in the public's eye but in the legal process itself.

In presenting the defense's case, Henriques and his associates called more than eighty witnesses who were able to provide alibis for all of the accused. The defense also sought to destroy the prosecution's case by pointing out gaps and inconsistencies in the evidence presented, and heaped ridicule on the reliability of prosecution witnesses. In Henriques's closing statement, according to the *Picayune* for March 12, 1891, he predicted that "when the jury saw so many glaring inconsistencies and contradictions, they would say it was a prosecution founded on theory and pushed forward upon that theory with all the vigilance and perseverance the police could muster." To the jury he pointed out that it was up to the prosecution to prove a case against the accused, and that "the jury could hardly be satisfied beyond a reasonable doubt by such contradictory evidence."

The case went to the jury at 6:15 on the evening of March 12; the jury returned a verdict the following day at 2:15 P.M. Jurors found In-cardona, Matranga, Bagnetto, Antonio Marchesi, Asperi Marchesi, and Macheca not guilty, and were unable to agree on a verdict concerning Politz, Scaffidi, and Monasterio. The verdict was greeted with anger and outrage in the court, and the jurors were hurried away through a back exit because of fears for their safety. Reporters followed the jurors out to learn how this totally unexpected verdict could have been reached. Jury foreman Seligman stated simply that "the state made out a poor case." Another juror said, "I'm sorry I couldn't please the whole community, but I had to do what I thought was right." [5]

After the trial a grand jury was empaneled to investigate jury-tampering rumors that circulated widely during the course of the trial. In the report returned in May 1891, the grand jury stated that it found no evidence that any member of the jury was offered or had accepted bribes, although it learned that O'Malley and his associates had offered money to several talismen to reach a favorable verdict if they were selected to serve on the jury. Thus it appears, at least on the surface, that the jury reached its verdict on the basis of evidence presented in court.

The public reaction was summarized by a *Picayune* editorial of March 14, 1891:

> The verdict in the Hennessy case was a thunderburst of surprise to the masses of the people of this city. It astonished every person who is accustomed to look to the courts for the vindication of justice.

All the newspapers greeted the verdict with fury and frustration, and most subsequent writers on the subject have sympathized with this reaction. Writing in 1936, popularizer Herbert Asbury stated that the evidence was as conclusive "today as it was when presented on the witness stand." In a recent study of New Orleans in the period from 1880 to 1896, Joy Jackson asserted that "the case against all but two was strong." None of the writers, including John E. Coxe (who pro-

duced the most detailed and scholarly account of the case), examined
the evidence carefully. After a detailed discussion of the indictment
proceedings and the mechanics of the trial, Coxe disposed of the days
of prosecution testimony against the five accused in this way:

> As the result of strong direct testimony, introduced by the state, An-
> tonio Scaffidi, Antonio Marchesi, Manuel Politz, Antonio Bagnetto,
> and Pietro Monasterio were identified as the parties who did the shoot-
> ing and who were seen fleeing from the place of ambush.

What that testimony consisted of, who presented it, and how it was
challenged by the defense, Coxe did not reveal. And, like other
writers on the subject (with the notable exception of Dulitz), Coxe neglected to point out that the state presented a weak case. High emotions and image-invoking prose of the principals and the press depicted
this case as symbolizing the issue of decent society versus the *mafia;*
but there is no reason why such myth-making should be perpetuated
without careful examination by subsequent writers on the subject. Instead of reviewing all the evidence impartially and asking probing
questions, later writers have tended to accept the theories of the time;
they have sifted through the material on the case, using that which
supported the accepted theories and dismissing or discounting what did
not. As Kendall has correctly concluded, "After all the police activity,
the court trial, the popular uprising, and the lynching, we never did
get to know exactly who killed Hennessey [*sic*]." [6]

   In the New York *Herald* for March 18, 1891, Pasquale Corte, Italian
consul in New Orleans, revealed that on November 5, 1890, Anthony
de Martini, a member of the New Orleans Italian community, and ex-
alderman Antonio Patorno had brought him a letter that De Martini
had received from a friend, John E. Duffy, who was in prison in
Baton Rouge. Part of its contents referred to Hennessy's murder.
Based on information he obtained from "a reliable friend who writes
[him]," Duffy claimed that five Americans had murdered the police
chief. According to him,

> These are Americans, and their names are as follows: D. C. O'Malley,
> as principal; "Tom" McChrystol, who lives in the Third Ward; Louis

Lay, who lives in the Third Ward also, and who was implicated in the "Chris" Clausen case for the killing of John Dimond at the Spanish Fort. E. P. Wallace, who, I think, lives in the Second Ward, is also one of the parties, and Thomas G. Washburne, of the Second Ward. The last named may be an alias.

In his letter Duffy explained that he had forwarded the information because he knew that the Italians accused were innocent, and hoped that his information might "be the means of helping your Dago friends." Upon receiving the letter, Consul Corte forwarded it to District Attorney Luzenberg. The prosecution possessed the letter during the preparation of its case but, as Corte noted in the *Herald,* ignored its existence, neither producing it in court nor indicating the possibility that the Matranga group might not be guilty. The reason for this official silence remains unclear, inasmuch as the District Attorney never responded to Corte's statement.

The manner in which the Hennessy slaying was carried out could indicate either a lack of professionalism or a deliberate frame-up on the part of professionals to implicate the Matrangas. On October 18, 1890, the New Orleans *Mascot* observed that "the locality where the assassination took place was evidently well chosen for the purpose, and from the traces of the shooting it is evident that the gang of assassins was well prepared." On the other hand, professionals would surely not have rented a shed less than a block from the intended victim's house, where their presence stood out. Then, on the night selected for the murder, experienced killers would not have loitered in front of the shed, in full sight of passers-by and residents while waiting for their victim (as one witness claimed that they did). And after the shooting, professional assassins would not have fled in panic, dropping weapons where they would be found rather than carrying them away and disposing of them. (Although the weapons, sawed-off shotguns, were of a type both police and public identified with Sicilian criminals, the police never traced the weapons to the accused.) In all, while events on the murder night contained all the ingredients for a frame-up, the murder could indeed have been executed in the bungling manner described by the police. None of the five accused appeared to be overly intelligent. Southern Italian criminals were often unsophis-

ticated and unforesighted enough to make the same type of unprofes-
sional blunders that occurred on the murder night—although more care
might have been expected of Macheca and Matranga.

During the days after the shooting, when the evidence was being
collected and suspects were being arrested, police work was marked
by feverish activity but neither by thoroughness nor by intelligence;
yet at the time the burning emotions of the crowd, irresponsibly
fanned by city leaders (including the mayor) and the press, masked
ineffective detective work. Apparently the police did not consider
alternate theories, assuming from the beginning that members of the
Matranga faction had murdered Hennessy. As soon as word of the
shooting reached headquarters, the police were dispatched to locate
Matranga and learn where he and his associates (including Macheca)
had been at the time. That the Matrangas' movements for that evening
could be accounted for by a number of non-Italian witnesses became
"proof"—not of their innocence but of their guilt. As the police
reasoned, the Matranga group, expecting to be questioned about the
murder of Hennessy, had prepared alibis to cover their whereabouts at
the time of the killing; the possibility that non-Italians, or Italians
other than the Matrangas, could have committed the crime was never
considered.

In general, although in 1890 the police department under Hennessy
had improved considerably in efficiency, it still contained (according
to the local press) many incompetent officers, and corruption plagued
the force. A grand jury in March 1890 found gambling taking place
throughout the city with the knowledge and complicity of the police
force, despite city laws prohibiting it. On March 8, 1890, the *Mascot*
suggested that "if the gambling houses must keep open, . . . they
pay directly to a fund of the city and refrain from contributing to the
individual purses of members of the police force." Such a practice,
the paper pointed out, "brings disrespect upon the force and can only
tend to horribly demoralize it." Whether because of widespread corruption or other reasons, in the public's opinion few police officers
exhibited devotion to duty and discipline. On September 30, 1890, the
Picayune reported that several officers had been called before the

police commissioner for slackness and dereliction of duty. Less than a month later, this same police force faced the Hennessy murder case, which meant identifying and locating the guilty parties, and providing solid evidence for the prosecution.

It is altogether possible that Italians other than the Matranga group had committed the crime. According to Consul Corte, about a hundred criminals had escaped from Italian justice by emigrating to New Orleans, and many of them were naturalized American citizens; they were also, as Corte claimed, deeply involved in local and state politics, where they were "caressed and protected by politicians." Hennessy had reportedly sent to Italy for information on the records of these criminals, and rumor or actual news of this step threatened every Italian with a criminal record and every political protector. Any one of them was capable of disposing of Hennessy, and the more enterprising among them would have made use of the Matranga-Provenzano case to divert suspicion from themselves. Considering the situation in New Orleans at the time, a machine-politician-police cover-up was entirely conceivable.[7]

For their own political reasons, reformers in the Shakspeare party, even if unaware of a cover-up, would have welcomed the opportunity of dealing severely with the Matranga group. The city's Italian population had increased, and was still increasing, rapidly. As immigrants became naturalized they swelled the ranks of the Irish-led political machine, which had been defeated by Shakspeare and his reform ticket in 1888. The reformers, feeling none too secure in their newly won political power, feared that the Irish bosses would use the swelling numbers of Italian votes to return power to themselves. Macheca, for example, not only ranked as a wealthy merchant but also figured conspicuously as a Democratic Party politician and an enemy of the Young Men's Democratic Association, the Shakspeare-led reform organization. Fear of the Italian machine votes coincided with public concern over the large numbers of Italians coming into the city— Southern Italians at that, generally considered to be an inferior group. The obviously increasing economic success of Italians stirred hatred, envy, and fear among the other citizens, and these emotions were aggravated by widespread belief in the prevalence of secret murder societies among the newcomers from Italy.

The Committee of Fifty, an extra-legal body appointed by the mayor to help bring Hennessy's assassins to justice, met after the news of the jury's acquittal and decided to hold a public meeting on the following day, "to remedy the failure of justice in the Hennessy case." Citizens were advised to "come prepared for action." [8] Accordingly, on March 14, a crowd variously estimated at 5,000 and 20,000 gathered at the Henry Clay statue on Canal Street. Reformers whipped the mass of people into a vigilante mob. William S. Parkerson, Shakspeare's campaign manager in 1888, James D. Houston, a prominent political leader, John C. Wickliffe, an editor on the New Orleans *New Delta,* and Walter Denegre, a corporation lawyer and prominent reform leader, delivered inflammatory speeches exhorting the mob to storm the Parish Prison and avenge Hennessy's death and the alleged miscarriage of justice.

With Parkerson in command, the crowd marched on the prison with the avowed purpose of dispatching the Italians who, although acquitted of the murder, were still to be held in prison until the charge of "lying in wait with intent to kill" could be *nolle prossed.* When word of the mob's approach reached the prison, the guards opened the cells and told the Italians to hide as best they could; the mob met with no resistance from the prison staff. [9]

Parkerson, Wickliffe, and other prominent citizens, armed for the occasion, entered and searched for the prisoners, and systematically shot or clubbed to death those they located—eleven at final count: Antonio Bagnetto, Antonio Marchesi, Joseph Macheca, Antonio Scaffidi, Manuel Politz, Pietro Monasterio, James Caruso, Loretto Comitz, Frank Romero, Charles Traina, and Rocco Geraci. On completion of this "vindication of justice," Parkerson emerged from the prison to the cheers of the crowd, and like a conquering hero rode off on the shoulders of admiring followers. [10]

In a letter to *Frank Leslie's Illustrated Newspaper,* Wickliffe explained his actions and those of the lynch mob.

8. Yard of Parish Prison, where six Italian prisoners were hanged on March 14, 1891. (*Illustrated American*)

> The afternoon of the acquittal [Friday], at the lugger landing, the American flag was torn down, trodden under foot and spat upon, and the Italian flag was run up with the stars and stripes beneath it, union down. Sicilians all over the city made the boast, "The *mafia* is on top now, and it will run the town to suit itself."

Wickliffe did not know—or did not reveal—that in addition to celebrating the acquittal of the accused Italians, the community was honoring, on the same day, the birthday of the King of Italy. Rather than being the action of a triumphant *mafia,* the tearing down of the American flag at the waterfront appears to have been the escapade of some drunken Italian sailors on a birthday spree. It is unlikely that Wickliffe or his friends understood the words of the Sicilians during their celebration (probably many spoke in dialect as well as broken English), so that his claim that the Italians boasted of *mafia* dominance in New Orleans may well have been rash judgment.[11]

Wickliffe and others involved justified their action by claiming the

right of the people to reverse the "unjust verdict of a corrupt jury."
Furthermore, he wrote, "only the eleven whose guilt was clear were
executed." He did not describe the method by which he and the mob
determined that guilt. Nor did he mention that four of the victims had
never been implicated in the Hennessy murder; they happened to be
Italian and in prison, and the self-styled avengers killed any Italians
they found in jail that night. Matranga, widely believed to be the
mafia leader in New Orleans and one of the men the vigilantes were
most eager to eliminate, eluded the searchers and so escaped death.
After the mob had dispersed, he was released from prison and returned
home. If indeed he had ever headed a *mafia* group, he lost this prominent position. Nothing occurring in the remaining fifty-two years of
his life connnected him with criminal activities. With his second wife,
Elizabeth Hazel Dullenty, he led a quiet life as a stevedore for the
Standard Fruit Company, later the United Fruit Company, until his re-
tirement after fifty years of service in 1918 (he had started to work at
the age of 11). He died in 1943 at the age of 86.[12]

Parkerson justified the mass lynching with the argument that "while
the *mafia* confined itself to killing its own members we did not resort
to violence," but that the killing of a prominent American was intolerable. "After the execution of the prisoners," Wickliffe went on, "the
Cotton Exchange, the Stock Exchange, the Sugar Exchange, the Mechanics', Lumbermens' and Dealers' Exchange, and the Board of
Trade held meetings, and each unanimously passed resolutions endors-
ing the act." He then queried, "Do the acts of these commercial bodies count for nothing with the world?" [13]

These efforts at self-justification seemed necessary because while
the killings met with general approbation in Louisiana, people in other
parts of the country reacted with dismay and disgust—although not
unanimously. According to Alexander Karlin, who examined opinions
expressed by 105 newspapers in various parts of the country, opinion
was divided, 42 newspapers approving of the lynchings, 58 opposing,
and 5 expressing no opinion. The South and West Coast generally supported the mob action; opinion in the East and Middle West opposed
the philosophy and actions of the killers. Whereas the New Orleans

Picayune argued that "the work done was a marvel of moderation when we consider the terrible nature of the forces at work," the Detroit *Tribune* observed that "the citizens of New Orleans who defend and applaud the massacre of Saturday stand practically alone. The rest of the country, judging from all the evidence at hand, deplores and condemns the acts of the mob." [14]

Foreign opinion strongly condemned what was viewed as the latest proof of American barbarism. At least three of the murdered men were Italian citizens, and the Italian government formally protested the slaying of its nationals in New Orleans, demanding punishment of the mob and financial compensation for the victims' families. [15] For a short time in 1891, war between Italy and the United States appeared to be imminent. President Harrison eased the situation when, in his annual Message to Congress (December 9, 1891), he called the event "a most deplorable and discreditable incident, an offense against law and humanity." Tempers cooled and relations between the two countries improved after Harrison offered an indemnity payment. [16]

If the reformers had hoped to destroy one basis of boss power in the city—the Italian immigrant vote—their efforts achieved little success. When Shakspeare ran for re-election as mayor in 1892, he was defeated by the Democratic machine candidate John Fitzpatrick by more than 3,000 votes (20,547 to 17,289). The Italian vote went overwhelmingly against the incumbent for at least three reasons: his violently anti-Italian statements before and during the Hennessy trial; the fact that many of his close political friends had taken positions of leadership within the lynch mob; and the fact that he had made no noticeable effort to prevent the mass meeting that preceded the lynching, and, by his absence from public view that morning, gave his tacit approval, if not his support, to the killings. In the ensuing years Italian voters continued to be a bulwark of the machine. [17]

The grand jury charged with investigating the killings of March 14 reported that "the power of the *mafia* is broken," but exhibited considerable confusion with regard to its definition of *mafia,* which, according to this body, consisted of "socialists, nationalists, or whatever it may be . . . [whose] members create and disseminate seditious opinions with a manifest tendency toward overt acts, whose commission partakes of the rankest treason.'' [18] To those who shared this concept, the *mafia*'s objective was to establish its own power and authority over that of the city's duly elected officials by murdering the chief of police and intimidating the mayor with threats on his life. Such a view assumed the existence of a highly centralized and structured organization, but certainly did not betray accurate observation of the situation in New Orleans in 1891 with regard to Italians and crime. Still, by the time of the murder trial, New Orleans residents were hysterical, and their feelings were encouraged by Mayor Shakspeare, who (whether for personal or for political reasons) desired to bring the Italian community to heel. The local newspapers fostered the belief that acquittal of the accused Italians represented part of a *coup d'état* that necessitated swift, unequivocal repudiation on the part of honest and law-abiding citizens.

Crime indeed existed within the Italian community, but on a primitive level—that is, by way of kidnapping and extortion of economically successful Italians by small gangs of criminals, most of whom, like Esposito, had operated as brigands in Southern Italy. It appears that both the Matrangas and the Provenzanos were among the objects of blackmail attempts. In any case, up to 1891 crime involving Italians in New Orleans seems to have been limited to the Italian community. If the Matrangas were responsible for Hennessy's murder, the killing was merely part of a vendetta involving two feuding factions and did not represent an effort to establish *mafia* control over the city.

Despite the vigilante action in March 1891, Italian criminals continued to extort and to murder other Italians. The New Orleans press reported on December 9, 1892, that the "dreaded *mafia*" had struck again, and in subsequent years robberies, vendettas, extortion attempts, and murders in the Italian colony were publicized in New Orleans newspapers. So long as Italians victimized other Italians, however, their behavior met with expressions of concern but no action on the part of the "better people" of New Orleans. [19]

PART 2

THE IMMIGRANT ERA

4

The Black Hand

In the wake of the Hennessy murder and the lynchings in New Orleans, murders involving Italians in that city and elsewhere in the United States were generally attributed (by police and reporters) to the *mafia*. Thus, nine days after the New Orleans lynchings a New York *Tribune* editorial claimed that *mafia* organizations existed "not only in New Orleans, but generally in large cities throughout the country." If Americans saw the hand of the dreaded Sicilian organization in almost every act of immigrant violence, Italian-language newspapers and colony leaders denied its existence either in the homeland or in the United States, and usually branded reports of such criminality as unfounded, inaccurate, and distorted.[1]

It is nevertheless clear that by 1891 criminal bands were at work in any American cities that contained sizable Southern Italian immigrant populations. As early as 1878 a gang composed of expatriate Sicilian bandits carried on a flourishing extortion business among successful residents in Southern Italian communities in San Francisco and surrounding towns. To ensure maximum publicity and to capitalize on the prestige of the Sicilian society, the San Francisco brigands called themselves "La Maffia." The San Francisco *Examiner* described the gang as "a neat little tea party of Sicilian brigands" who were "attempting to bulldoze such of their countrymen who would stand their blackmailing tricks." The "villainous gang" had for its objective "the extortion of money from their countrymen by a system of blackmail, which includes attacks on character and threats to kill.'' This gang disintegrated when the corpse of a Sicilian immigrant named Catalani was found near Sausolito. When evidence pointed to Rosario Meli, Iganzio Trapani, Salvatore Messino, and Giuseppe Bianchi, they were arrested and eventually convicted—not of murder, which authorities were unable to prove—of robbing Catalani prior to his death.[2]

Giuseppe Esposito, who shortly after he arrived in New Orleans in 1880 apparently organized a "band of seventy-five cut-throats" specializing in kidnapping, was not the first to practice extortion in Italian New Orleans. After Esposito's arrest in July 1881, prominent Southern Italian residents confided to American newsmen that for years prior to his arrival affluent residents of the community had been forced to submit to extortion. These activities were not organized, and were not the deeds of "idle men who spend their ill-gotten gold in riotous living," but rather those of "thrifty, industrious people who work hard but grumble at fate because some of their countrymen are more wealthy than they." Usually the extortionists were common laborers who needed money for one reason or another. They were not, however, ordinary members of the laboring class: because of a criminal record in Italy or a reputation for violence and viciousness, they elicited fear and acquiescence from compatriots. Extortion was apparently conducted on a personal basis at this time in New Orleans. Thus Gaetano Arditto, who was convicted of the murder of Tony Labousse in late 1881, sent a note to a prominent Italian citizen demanding $4,000 on pain of death. Arditto signed his name and (as the New Orleans *Times* reported the event) "the victim well knowing the character of the man was forced to submit to the demand." [3]

Blackmail activities continued through the 1880s. During the course of the decade, however, they became more impersonal and the extortionists more circumspect. Vincent Provenzano received an unsigned note dated September 24, 1886, advising him to deposit $1,000 at a designated location while wearing a white handkerchief in his hat for identification purposes, and to comply with the demand within three days. Other Italians, including the Matranga brothers, indicated that for years they had submitted to extortion demands from unknown blackmailers.[4]

Immigration from Southern Italy increased rapidly during the 1890s and after the turn of the century, and 90 per cent of the newcomers settled in cities, particularly those of the East and Middle West. As more and more Southern Italians flocked into urban America, they provided an increasingly tempting source of money, readily intimidated as they were because of the evil reputation of secret societies in the homeland.

In 1908, amid a flurry of Black Hand (*Mano Nera*) activity, American and Italian-American writers sought to determine the origin of the term "Black Hand." Alessandro Mastro-Valerio, publisher and editor of Chicago's *La Tribuna Italiana Transatlantica,* claimed that Carlo Barsotti, editor of *Il Progresso Italo-Americano* (New York), had coined the term in order to avoid using the word *"mafia,"* and in the hope that the offenses thus identified would be viewed as responses to American conditions. For his part, Gaetano D'Amato, former President of the United Italian Societies of New York and friend of Police Lieutenant Joseph Petrosino of that city's Italian detective squad, held that the name had first been used in Spain in the 1880s by a society of thieves and murderers who styled themselves protectors and guardians of the downtrodden against persons of wealth. The term was first used in the United States "about ten years ago," according to D'Amato, and "probably by some Italian desperado who had heard of the exploits of the Spanish society, and considered the combination of words to be high-sounding and terror-inspiring." After a few successful ventures, "the newspapers finally applied it to all crimes committed by Italian banditti in the United States." [5]

American journalist Lindsay Denison believed also that the name was of Spanish origin, but that it was first used during the Inquisition by "a secret society which fought the government and the church." When it ceased to exist in Spain, "the secret societies of Southern Italy were its heirs." Then during the 1870s and 1880s, continued Denison, "a false report was raised in Spain" that it had been revived. The story, he said, "lingered in the brain of a [New York] *Herald* reporter, and one fine day he attempted to rejuvenate waning interest in a puzzling Italian murder case by speculating as to the coming to life of the Black Hand among Latin immigrants in America. The other newspapers seized on the idea eagerly, and kept it going." [6]

All the writers seemed certain that the term *Mano Nera* first appeared in the United States around 1898. They were mistaken. Its initial appearance in relation to Italian-American crime was in September 1903, in the aftermath of the gruesome "Barrel Murder Case" in New York.

Extortion and blackmail gangs had apparently begun to operate on a large scale in the Italian colonies in Manhattan and Brooklyn in 1901. During the subsequent two years, when groups operated under such names as "La Società Camorrista," "La Mala Vita," and "Mafia," police estimated that they "reaped a harvest from hundreds of wealthy Italians." In September 1902, Charles Bacigalupo, so-called "Mayor of Mulberry Bend" (the Lower Manhattan Italian district), told a New York *Herald* reporter that the extortionists were "bad people to deal with, and are, I believe, working in all cities in this country where there are Italian colonies." In New York, Bacigalupo continued, "a great many doctors, bankers and others have received blackmailing letters in the last few months, and, from what I hear, most of the recipients sent the money asked." Bacigalupo himself had never paid a cent in tribute or even received a blackmail letter—"but if I did receive one I hardly think I would ignore it." [7]

On rare occasions during this early period police were successful in capturing blackmailers. In January 1902 Detective Petrosino managed to persuade Stephen Carmenciti, a prosperous wholsesale tailor living on East 103rd Street in the East Harlem Italian neighborhood, to agree to a rendezvous to pay $150 to an extortion society calling itself "Holy House." Two Holy House members were arrested—Joseph Mascarello of East 107th Street and Carmine Mursuneso of East 106th Street—but the men were found innocent when the merchant refused to testify, fearing for the safety of his family.[8]

There was grave concern among residents of the Italian colony over this situation and the dozens if not hundreds of crimes that never came to official attention during 1901, 1902, and 1903. The event that focused the American public's attention on the blackmail activities taking place in the city's Italian neighborhoods was the Barrel Murder, which, ironically, had no connection with extortion. On April 14, 1903, the corpse of a man with seventeen stab wounds and the head nearly severed from the body was found stuffed in a barrel in a vacant lot at East 11th Street and Avenue D on Manhattan's Lower East Side. There was no identification on the corpse, and the case appeared to be unsolvable. Detective Petrosino remembered having seen the victim, but for a time could not recall when or where. Finally he "placed" the dead man at the trial of a counterfeiter, Giuseppe De Priemo, at the Federal Court in New York a year or so earlier. Since at the time of the Barrel Murder De Priemo was at Sing Sing, the detective traveled up the river to interview him there. As soon as De Priemo saw a photograph of the dead man, he cried, "That's my brother-in-law, Benedetto Madonia," and added that the victim had recently visited him in the company of a man named Tomasso Petto, who was known as "Petto the Ox." [9]

The few existing scraps of evidence pointed to Petto, either as the murderer or as one who knew a great deal about the events surrounding Madonia's death. A pair of gloves found in the barrel bore the label of a Buffalo store—and Petto had recently lived in that city. Furthermore, according to De Priemo, his brother-in-law always carried a watch with certain distinctive markings "on the neck." A watch chain, but no watch, was found on the body. Pawn shops were checked, and Madonia's watch was found in one of them. Petto was identified as the man who had pawned the watch (for a dollar), and when he was arrested the pawn ticket was found in his possession. Petto did not deny pawning the watch but did deny that he had obtained it from Madonia: an Italian named "John," whom he had known for three years but whose last name he did not know, had given it to him. Not wanting or needing it, Petto said, he had simply pawned it.

Madonia was apparently an agent for a counterfeiting ring. His job

Concerning the murderer

was to distribute bogus bills to dealers throughout the country. As Secret Service agents conjectured, either he could not account for counterfeit bills that were to have been put into circulation, or he had held out proceeds from the sales in the course of his travels; then when fellow gang members learned of his double dealing, they murdered him. The manner in which Madonia was killed and the decision to leave his corpse where it could be found quickly (the body was still warm when it was discovered) indicated that the murder was intended to be a warning.

Leaders of the gang were Ignazio Saietta ("Lupo the Wolf") and his brother-in-law, Giuseppe Morello, who were to play a part in New York's crime until the mid-1930s. Another member was Madonia's brother-in-law. Petto was a known member of the gang; his work usually consisted of strong-arm assignments. Physically powerful but unintelligent, he apparently could not resist the temptation to steal the only valuable (and traceable) possession on the body—the watch. It seems certain that he participated in the murder, but probably not as the sole knife wielder. The state's case against Petto was insufficiently strong to convict him, particularly after Madonia's wife, son, and brother-in-law refused to help. Petto the Ox went free.

Although the Barrel Murder was an internal gang matter, probably not even connected with the blackmail wave then sweeping the city's Italian district, it became a major factor not only in riveting Italian-Americans' concern on these activities but especially in focusing the attention of America at large on immigrant community crime. Thus, in the midst of the Madonia investigation an article appeared in the *Herald* headlined "Scores of New York Business Men Pay Blackmail to *Mafia*," and recounting that prominent Italian bankers, merchants, and physicians had "corroborated the accounts of blackmailing schemes perpetrated by the same class of men who are charged with the murder of Benedetto Madonia." As these men were generally successful in collecting thousands of dollars from their victims, apparently with little risk of punishment (according to the story), the Barrel Murder and its resultant publicity doubtless encouraged still more crooks to turn to this line of business. In the following months

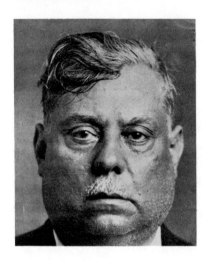

9. 1936 photograph of Ignazio Saietta ("Lupo the Wolf"), who came to public attention following "Barrel Murder" of Benedetto Madonia. (United Press International)

crimes of extortion increased in New York's "Little Italies." Finally, on September 13, 1903, a fear-inspiring name was given to this form of criminal activity, when "Black Hand" (*Mano Nera*) appeared for the first time in the American press—in a *Herald* article captioned " 'Black Hand' Band in Extortion Plot," an account of how one Nicola Cappiello, a wealthy Brooklyn contractor and dock builder, had been the target of blackmail efforts for more than a month.

On August 3, 1903, Cappiello received the following note embellished with three black crosses surmounted by a skull and crossbones (in translation):

> Nicola Cappiello
> If you don't meet us at Seventy-second Street and Thirteenth Avenue, Brooklyn, to-morrow afternoon, your house will be dynamited and you and your family killed. The same fate awaits you in the event of your betraying our purposes to the police.
>
> *Mano Nera*

black mail note,

Cappiello decided to ignore the demand. Two days later he received another letter.

You did not meet us as ordered in our first letter. If you still refuse to accede to our terms, but wish to preserve the lives of your family, you can do so by sacrificing your own life. Walk in Sixteenth Street, near Seventh Avenue, between the hours of four and five tonight [August 5].

Beware of *Mano Nera*

Because of his stubbornness and unwillingness to listen to reason, the Black Hand next demanded $10,000. A few days later, three of his oldest friends and a fourth man whom he did not know called on him and offered to intercede in his behalf with the blackmail band, promising that if he could provide $1,000 they would do their best to persuade the blackmailers to spare his life. Cappiello delivered the money on August 26, but within days the four men were back for an additional $3,000. Convinced now that the gang intended systematically to drain him of his fortune (estimated to be in excess of $100,000), Cappiello reported the threats to the Brooklyn police. As a result, the original four Black Handers—Mariano Esposito, Fortunato Castellano, Annunziato Lingria, and Biaggio Giordano (three of them the contractor's "best friends" who had proffered their intercession), along with a fifth man, Antonio Giordano, who had not been with the helpful quartet—were arrested, brought to trial, and found guilty.

Although this first case ended more favorably for the victim than did hundreds of others that were to follow, the pattern was set at the very beginning of Black Hand history. The extortion campaign usually began with the delivery of a note demanding payment and threatening dire consequences if the victim ignored it. If the recipient did not comply at once, additional notes were sent, to be followed by the appearance of a delegation, usually including trusted friends, who offered to deal with the blackmailers. The "friends" returned with a demand for a sum of money often beyond the victim's ability to pay. A series of bargaining sessions followed, and a compromise figure was reached; the victim usually paid this negotiated sum. Sooner or later, however, the extortionists demanded still more money, and the process continued until the victim was drained of his resources (or gave a believable appearance of being penniless), turned to the authorities, was killed, or left the city. All this while, the Black Handers worked diligently to create a pervasive atmosphere of terror among the potential victims. This feeling of impending evil was reflected by Mrs. Cappiello, who lamented to a *Herald* reporter that "For more than a month we have been living in constant expectation of death. We know not whom to trust." [10]

With the Cappiello case the *Herald* began applying the term "Black Hand" to all Italian-colony blackmail cases. This policy was soon followed by the other city papers. The *Times,* which did not report its original use by the Cappiello criminals, first mentioned *Mano Nera* on January 17, 1904, noting that the term had been in use "for some time." Newspapers in other cities soon recognized the possibilities in such an attention-getting name. It had a sinister quality. When applied to Italian criminals in the United States it caught the public's fancy in a sensational manner and gained wide currency. The extent of its use varied from city to city, however. In Chicago and New York, for example, "Black Hand" became the preferred term and *mafia* fell into disuse, although in New Orleans the two terms were used interchangeably. [11]

After September 1903, and continuing into the 1920s, "Black Hand" came into general (although not exclusive) use to indicate extortion and blackmail among Italians. Such crimes were usually the work of individuals or small groups who came together only briefly to carry out a single job or a limited number of jobs. There were organized gangs specializing in typical Black Hand projects, and these followed set procedures. "Specialists" were also employed for certain functions.

The usual consequences of ignoring the demands of a Black Hand note (often delivered through the U.S. mail) were the kidnapping of a loved one (especially a child), the bombing of property, the wounding or slaying of the victim, or the murder of a member of the family. Such activities were not limited to any one economic class; no one living in an Italian district was exempt. Bankers, barbers, and beggars were potential victims of extortion; people of differing means were asked to pay according to their known or suspected resources. Criminals, some as prominent as James ("Big Jim") Colosimo, who domi-

10. Ruins of grocery store in Brooklyn destroyed by Black Hand bomb. (*Everybody's Magazine*)

nated prostitution and gambling in Chicago's Near South Side Italian district for two decades, received Black Hand notes. Colosimo decided in 1909 to import outside help against Black Hand threats, and brought his wife's nephew, John Torrio, from New York. Torrio had a reputation for dealing successfully with New York's Black Handers, and fulfilled his uncle's expectations in Chicago. He eventually succeeded Colosimo and became the dominant figure in Chicago syndicate crime in the early 1920s.[12]

Black Handers, unless dealt with efficiently and severely (in the Torrio fashion) fattened off the financial resources of prominent criminals in every American city. Ignazio Saietta ("Lupo the Wolf" to associates, the police, and newspaper readers) was the chief of one of the most successful counterfeiting gangs in New York and thus one of the city's most notorious Italian criminals. In 1909 Lupo filed a petition of bankruptcy. During the proceedings it was divulged that he had received numerous Black Hand threats over the years. Although he ignored most of these threats, he had turned over $10,000 to various extortionists. "He made the announcement . . . as a thing to be taken for granted," noted a newspaper reporter, and seemed surprised "at the interest his announcement aroused." Like most Black Hand victims, Lupo had received threatening letters, and like many other Italian residents fearing for the lives of their loved ones, he had paid.[13]

Giosue Gallucci, another New York crime leader, dubbed "King" of the East Harlem Italian colony, was known to have been "the prey of Black Handers." When he was murdered in April 1915, police immediately theorized that he was the victim of a Black Hand gang, though it is more likely that he was the casualty in a war between East Harlem Sicilian gangs (the killer was never caught). Nevertheless, events connected with this confrontation—which culminated even more violently two years later in Brooklyn—suggest that Italian gangs of this era used the Black Hand reputation and known techniques as covers, eliminating rivals in such a manner as to suggest Black Hand operations to the police and to the public.[14]

Although Black Handers worked on all levels of immigrant society, they limited themselves geographically to Italians living or working in the colonies. Non-Italians also attempted to use the notoriety of the name in order to obtain easy money. Evidence suggests that every instance of non-Italian Black Hand activity took place during a flurry of newspaper interest and publicity focusing on Italian Black Hand activities, or during and after sensational and well-publicized cases. It is important to note that the Italian population in American cities was not static; a great deal of residential mobility occurred constantly. In the decades of *Mano Nera* activity, immigrants and second-generation Italians who could manage to do so moved out of Italian districts, at the first opportunity shifting to less crowded and more pleasant environments. Those who moved away from Italian districts also left the Black Hand behind. A computer-assisted study of 141 Black Hand cases that took place during 1908 in New York, Boston, Philadelphia, Baltimore, Chicago, Pittsburgh, Cleveland, New Orleans, Kansas City, and San Francisco, uncovered the fact that not one Black Hand case reported in the press took place outside an immigrant district. Those who had left the colony were unmolested, and for good reasons:

they usually comprised the immigrants who were adjusting to American customs and standards, they might seek police protection, and in general they were far less pliable than the newcomers to the various "Little Italies." The Black Handers themselves remained in the immigrant community, where there was an almost limitless supply of compliant, hard-working victims; the territory was familiar, and the Black Hander blended in with other residents. In a non-ethnic neighborhood he would be a conspicuous alien if he delivered a note at the home of an intended victim or attempted to observe the reaction to demands sent through the mail. He would find it more difficult to apply pressure on the victim or to punish him for non-compliance.[15]

Blackmail letters were straightforward, explicit, and often crude:

[New York City]

This is the second time that I have warned you. Sunday at ten o'clock in the morning, at the corner of Second Street and Third Avenue, bring three hundred dollars without fail. Otherwise we will set fire to you and blow you up with a bomb. Consider this matter well, for this is the last warning I will give you.
    I sign the Black Hand.[16]

St. Louis, Mo., Aug. 9

Dear Friend,

This is your second letter. You did not answer or come. What have you in your head? You know what you did in Brooklyn and that you went to Italy and then returned to Dago Hill [St. Louis' Italian colony] to hide yourself. You can go to hell to hide but we will find you. It will be very bad for you and your family if you do not come to an understanding. So come Thursday night at 10 o'clock. If you do not come we will cut you up in pieces. How will that be, you dirty false face. So we will wait for you. With best regards, good-by. [Beneath the words were two pictures, one a skull and crossbones, and one a man in a coffin. There was also a postscript.]
    So this will be your presentment if you do not do as we tell you. The way the blood flows in my veins is the way the blood will flow from your veins.[17]

New York, May 24, 1911

Mr. Tano Sferrazzo
307 East 45th Street
City

Various men of my society as you know well will demand some money because we need it in our urgent business and you finally have never consented to satisfy us to fulfill your duty. Therefore today finishes your case. In a few words I will explain the matter. You must know that in cases of this kind as your own when they are handled by useless persons the matter can be easily dropped or in other words neglected, but in your case we are men of high society and of great importance, and therefore the matter cannot be dropped, or in other words we cannot neglect this matter because the society will inflict a severe penalty. Therefore to-day talking with the chief I have decided that you must do your duty otherwise death will take you and you must not worry over it because these are our rules, so you are warned which road do you wish to choose, do what you please, it is immaterial to us. Money or death. If you want to save your life to-morrow May 25th at 10 p.m. take the Third avenue train, go to 129th street, walk toward Second avenue. Walk as far as the First avenue bridge that leads you to the Bronx, walk up and down the bridge for a while; two men will then present themselves and will ask you, where are you going? to them you will give not less than $200.

Signed Black Hand [18]

Pittsburgh, Pa.
May 27, 1908

Mr. G. Satarano:

You please you know the company of Black Hands. I want you to send $2,000, all gold money. You find some friend to tell you about it. Send it to head man, Johnstown. We don't want you to tell no person that talks too much. If you report about this letter we will kill you. We will kill you with a steel knife. You and your family. Give me money right away, for I want to use it. And remember, keep it quiet.

Black Hand [19]

Phila., Pa.

You will never see Italy again if you do not give $1,000 to the person that pinches you after he salutes you.

(I say one thousand.)

Carry it with you always and remember that I am more powerful than
the police and your God.

                                                          Black Hand.[20]

Financial success aroused the envy of less successful Italian immigrants and alerted those who made a career of extortion. Black
Hand letters could come from envious neighbors or professional criminals, or both. As a case in point, Carmello Cannatella, who owned a
fruit stand at 322 West Camden Street in Baltimore, bought a house on
South Paca Street in 1906, and this sign of prosperity brought forth a
Black Hand letter. Cannatella took it to the police. With detectives following him, he brought the required amount of money to the designated place, but no one appeared to take it. Subsequently he received
other letters, and on November 10, 1908, his fruit stand was burned.
The police never discovered who had set the fire, but they speculated
that Cannatella's prosperity had aroused local envy, fanned undoubtedly by the ostentatious manner in which his son Lawrence displayed
the family's wealth—dressing expensively, exhibiting jewelry, and at-
tending the theater regularly. Cannatella's wife was in favor of buying
additional property, but he feared that this would only arouse more
jealousy; so instead they kept their money in the bank.[21]

While Cannatella's problems were probably caused by envious
neighbors, those of New York's Domenico Gumina were the work of
an organized and highly professional extortion gang. Gumina operated
a small grocery store at 305 East 71st Street, where he and his family
(a wife and five children) also lived. At about one o'clock on the afternoon of April 28, 1914, his five-year-old son Giuseppe disappeared
while playing in front of the store. At six or seven o'clock that evening Gumina received a Special Delivery letter stating that if he
wanted his son returned he must raise $2,000, then go to his "influen-
tial and confidential friends," who would help him. Gumina immediately talked to the police, who advised him to do as directed in the letter. Officers were assigned to the case. Gumina then went to his
"friends" and reported the kidnapping.[22]

A few days later, a friend of eight years, Benedetto Randazzo, and his brother-in-law Matteo Pallazzolo offered to contact "people." In a second meeting a few days later, Pallazzolo dickered with the grocer over the price necessary to get Giuseppe back. Gumina complained that he was a poor man, that business was bad, and that although he wanted his son back he could never raise $2,000. Pallazzolo offered to negotiate. Talks drifted on for two weeks, and finally it was agreed that Gumina should pay $125. Since the grocer could not scrape together even that much, the police assigned to the case contributed $45. The money was handed to Randazzo and Pallazzolo at Gumina's house. Police followed the two men when they left, and shortly thereafter rounded up five men and a woman comprising a Black Hand gang that specialized in kidnapping children.

The pattern was typical of Black Hand techniques. At the trial the prosecution proved that each stage of the operation, from taking the child to the arrangements made for his return to his parents, had been carefully planned. As Assistant District Attorney Royal H. Weller stated, "Each one of these people played his or her own particular part, each one doing a particular thing which none other did, and each one filled the entire circuit." This gang was unusually well organized and professional, and prior to its abduction of Giuseppe Gumina, unusually successful. The grocer by his action proved that not all Sicilians were afraid to turn to the authorities for aid. In this instance the machinery of justice also functioned effectively, finding all the accused guilty and sentencing them to jail terms of from ten to thirty years.[23]

Sometimes Black Hand gangs or techniques became the means by which Italian-colony businessmen reduced the effectiveness of business rivals, or eliminated them entirely. Shortly after midnight on December 10, 1907, the rear of Joseph Di Giorgio's home in Baltimore was wrecked by a dynamite explosion. A native of Sicily, Di Giorgio had become, through hard work, one of the leading Italian fruit dealers on the East Coast. He was president of the Atlantic Fruit Company, the Di Giorgio Fruit Company, the Baltimore Fruit Exchange, and the Mediterranean Fruit Importing Company of New York, and vice-president of the Connolly Auction Company of New

York, and through these companies controlled the importation and sales in the Baltimore area of fruit from California and Italy, and of bananas from Central America.[24]

During the month before his home was bombed, Di Giorgio had received three blackmail letters, all bearing Pittsburgh postmarks, and demanding $10,000—but none indicated where or how the money was to be delivered. In January 1908 eight men—among them Di Giorgio's old business rival Antonio Lanasa—were arrested and charged with attempted murder and conspiracy to extort money. Prior to Di Giorgio's arrival in Baltimore ten years before, Lanasa had been the leading fruit merchant in the city. Within the decade the positions were reversed: Di Giorgio, who had started his career penniless, was rich, and Lanasa was deep in debt. In addition to his financial problems (and apparently at least partly responsible for them), Lanasa had been victimized several times by Black Hand extortion gangs. The obvious objective of the operation was to eliminate Lanasa's rival, using the Black Hand as a cover. Extortion as a major factor seemed to be ruled out by the fact that none of the letters named a place or date to hand over the money demanded. According to a police authority, some prominent Italians in Baltimore regularly employed Black Hand gangs within their businesses to extort money from rivals.

The State's case was based primarily on the testimony of two of Lanasa's co-defendants, Salvatore Lupo and Joseph Tamburo. In the trial, which began on March 8, 1908, Lupo disclosed that Lanasa had traveled to Pittsburgh the previous November to arrange with Philip Rei, an alleged Black Hander, to have extortion letters sent to Di Giorgio, and had at the same time hired Lupo to bomb Di Giorgio's house: Lupo had attended a meeting held on December 8 to plan the bombing, and Lanasa and the other accused participated also. As Lupo testified, he then departed for Pittsburgh, intending to return to Baltimore on the tenth, but was delayed and appeared only after the explosion. Thus he claimed to be an accessory to, but not guilty of, attempted murder. Tamburo, another of the accused, agreed with Lupo's testimony. On April 28, 1908, the jury found Lanasa guilty and he was sentenced to ten years in prison. Lupo received a 15-month term.

Two members of the dynamite group hired to blow up Di Giorgio's

home were hired outside Baltimore—Lupo in Pittsburgh, and John
Scarletta in Cleveland—comprising only one of many instances in
which Black Handers traveled to different cities to practice their trade.
"Diamond Jim" Colosimo's problems with *Mano Nera* extortion letters in Chicago were solved by John Torrio, who tracked down three
Pittsburgh residents who, believing that Chicago would be their city of
opportunity, tried to blackmail Colosimo. They discovered that they
had chosen the wrong victim. Torrio ordered the trio murdered and
saw to it that the news of their fate was publicized. Unlike many victims, Colosimo had no further trouble from Black Handers.

Most Black Hand threats and payments went unreported. New York
Italian-American police officers, quoted in a June 1909 *Cosmopolitan
Magazine* article, estimated that for every extortion case reported to
police in the New York area there were "probably two hundred and
fifty of which nothing is said." If this assessment is accurate, the extent of Black Hand activity in the city was staggering, for police
department records disclosed that 424 Black Hand offenses were reported during 1908.[25] Yet only a small proportion of these crimes
found their way into the pages of the city's newspapers. A careful
reading of every issue for 1908 of the New York *Times, Il Progresso
Italo-Americano,* and *L'Araldo Italiano* (the last-named being two of
the country's leading Italian-language journals) discloses that only 33
Black Hand offenses were reported in one or another of the papers
during the year.

Although the situation in other cities was less serious than that of
New York, with its huge population from Southern Italy, it is clear
that countless extortion letters were sent in every city containing Italian colonies. Some victims paid quietly without the knowledge of
neighbors or friends; there is much evidence to indicate, however, that
many recipients simply ignored threatening letters and were not bothered further. The cases reaching the papers tended to include violence
or arrests, and hence might be more sensational than the vast numbers
of unreported incidents; yet these newspaper stories formed the lurid
picture that the general public, both Italian and American, had of the
Black Hand.

Although both contemporaneous and more recent writers have provided ample literature on the Black Hand, none has attempted to examine systematically the Black Handers' activities, either over a period of time or in a number of cities. Thus the extent of Black Hand operations remains unknown, and variations in patterns of operation remain isolated. Since the period from the turn of the century to the end of World War I formed the era of *Mano Nera* activities, a single year, 1908, was selected for intensive examination, as being the mid-point in the development and functioning of the Black Hand as well as in the efforts of law-enforcement agencies and concerned citizens to subdue it. Seventeen newspapers published in ten major cities containing a sizable Italian immigrant population and located in different parts of the country—New York, Boston, Philadelphia, Baltimore, New Orleans, Pittsburgh, Cleveland, Chicago, Kansas City, and San Francisco—were read to determine the nationality of senders and recipients of *Mano Nera* threats, methods used (oral, written, pictorial), number of threats made, type of threat (e.g., death, bombing, abduction, robbery, physical violence), demands made and the amount of money involved, and the result (e.g., arrest or other police action, action taken by Black Handers against the recipient).

A total of 141 Black Hand cases appeared in the seventeen newspapers. (Several cases were reported in more than one paper, and some papers—notably the New York *Times* and *Il Progresso*—reported not only offenses that occurred in their own area but also those of other sections of the country.) Examination of these cases indicated that Black Handers operated in the "Little Italy" of every city examined, although the greater part of the action was localized on the East Coast, since most of the new immigrants, who provided the most malleable victims for extortionists, landed there. Of the hundred cases involving Italians reported during 1908 in the seventeen newspapers, exactly half were committed in the three eastern Italian nuclei (New York, Philadelphia, Boston); 33 per cent occurred in New York alone. The smallest amount of Black Hand activity was in the settled and predominantly Northern Italian community of San Francisco, where only one offense was reported during the year—and that the work of a recent arrival from New York who needed money and decided (as he told police after his capture) to take it from a San Franciscan Italian who "had plenty." A wealthy Berkeley merchant of Italian background received a blackmail note in May 1908, but the extortionist turned out to be a non-Italian, Harry Tiesel.[26]

Perhaps the best publicized Black Hand case in San Francisco involved Antonio, Antonio Jr., and Joseph Pedone. The Pedones operated successfully in the Bay Area from 1914 until their involvement in a shoot-out with Gaetano Ingrassio on November 30, 1916. Late in 1915 Ingrassio received the first of several Black Hand threats. The letter, postmarked San Mateo, read:

> Dear Friend:
>   Some of our friends in our society wish you to carry $2,000 in gold. Then we want you to go from San Francisco by the electric car to San Mateo on a Saturday afternoon. When you get there, walk back on the railroad track and some good friend is going to approach you. He is our friend, and you give him the money. Otherwise it will be very bad for you.

Subsequent letters threatened bodily injury to Ingrassio's family; yet he refused to submit to the threats. On November 30, 1916, he encountered the Pedones (who were, as he believed, responsible for the letters) on Columbia Avenue between Filbert and Greenwich streets. In an exchange of gunfire, Ingrassio wounded both Pedone brothers, Joseph and Antonio, and was in turn killed by Antonio, Jr. The Pedones were indicted for the killing and found guilty, and the Bay Area's most notorious Black Hand gang was destroyed.[27]

While Black Hand threats were sent every month of the year reviewed, the highest incidence was during the mid-winter months of December (when 15 were sent), January (14), and February (14), representing 43 per cent of the total for the year. As Lieutenant Joseph Petrosino of New York's Italian squad explained, "The winter is the hard time of the year with all Italians, and naturally the collections come harder." Consequently, "men who have given up a few dollars now and then for months suddenly decide that, come what may, they will pay no more. According to the laws of the 'trade,' this means punishment, and there you have your outrages." [28] It is likely that this is an accurate analysis; it is also possible that the high winter incidence was due in part to the fact that many Italian immigrants were engaged in seasonal labor—especially on the railroads, on construction sites, or in maintenance work. Such men either returned to Italy for the winter months or holed up in a tenement in the Italian section of an American city until the following spring. By December or January the money saved during the preceding season had been used up. Many borrowed (often at exorbitant rates) from a padrone or labor agent, and then worked on his railroad or construction gang the following season to pay off the winter's debts. Others among the unemployed resorted to sending *Mano Nera* letters to obtain enough money to tide them over.[29]

The hundred cases reported in 1908 in the press were distributed as follows:

TABLE 3
BLACK HAND CASES INVOLVING ITALIANS
REPORTED IN THE PRESS IN 1908

CITY	NO. OF CASES AND % OF TOTAL
New York	33
Chicago	12
Boston	9
Baltimore	5
Cleveland	4
Pittsburgh	6
Philadelphia	9
Kansas City	5
New Orleans	9
San Francisco	1
Others *	7

Total 100

* Pottsville, Pa.: 2 Export, Pa.: 1; Richmond, Va.: 1; Elkins, W. Va.: 1; Punxsutawney, Pa.: 1; Berkeley, Calif.: 1.

All but eight of the one hundred reported cases involved use of the mails. In two of the exceptions, Black Handers pinned the note to the victim's apartment door, and in the other cases made the demands

11. Group of prisoners awaiting trial on charges of Black Hand activities in New York. (*McClure's Magazine*)

orally. In nearly all the cases reported in the press, the victim received more than one threatening letter.

The most frequent demand was for money: $500 in twelve instances, $1,000 in seventeen; in thirteen cases, the letters simply made a general demand for money. The most frequent threat was that of death—in 35 per cent of the cases, that of the victim, and 29 per cent, some form of bodily harm to the recipient's family, generally his children.

Apparently the newspapers tended to publicize the more violent and sensational cases, for in one-fourth of the cases involving Italians reported by the press, bombs damaged the victim's house, business, or other property. Bombings had the effect not only of intimidating the entire colony but also of attracting the attention of reporters and leading to the public's demands that the police take action. This public pressure resulted in greater police effort to find the bombers, although such effort did not necessarily have positive results. Only seven of the bombings ended in arrest; only twenty-one cases in all culminated in arrest.[30]

Eight of the bombing cases occurred in New York. The most sensational and frightening concerned Francesco Spinella, a successful interior decorator, who owned two tenement houses and leased a third on East 11th Street in Manhattan's Lower East Side Italian district. On May 7, 1908, Spinella received a Black Hand letter demanding $7,000, with the alternative that his "entire property" would be destroyed. Spinella had immigrated twenty years before, had worked hard to earn his prosperity, and meant to keep for himself and his family the money he had accumulated. The Black Handers were just as determined to take it from him, or to ruin him in the attempt. On May 19 a bomb explosion damaged the front of the two buildings, 314 and 316 East 11th, though no one was injured. Spinella still refused to give in. Over the following ten weeks he received twenty blackmail notes, and during the same period ten explosions destroyed his and surrounding buildings and drove away all his tenants.[31]

As Frank Marshall White reported five years later in *Outlook Magazine,* Spinella was a ruined man. "He has not paid anything to the Black Hand, but his decorating business has failed, his houses are mortgaged up to nearly their full value, and he and his wife and children are working out by the day to pay the interest on the mortgages." The unfortunate man, White noted, had "almost given up hope of being able to pull through financially." Although the publicity given this case should have provided an object lesson for other victims on the futility of trying to withstand the Black Hand, yet, as court records show, many Italians in New York and other cities successfully opposed the Black Hand.[32]

In Chicago, Black Handers sent extortion letters not only to individuals but also to schools. On April 24, 1908, the Jenner School, an elementary school in Chicago's (predominantly Italian) Near North Side, received a note which, translated, read: "The Jenner school and two other schools will be blown to pieces at 2 o'clock today." At the foot was the picture of a black hand and a dagger. Similar notes were delivered to two nearby schools, Adams and Two Sisters, a Protestant

institution. Staff workers at nearby Eli Bates settlement house advised
parents that the letters were probably written by "hoodlums merely to
frighten the residents of the Italian neighborhood," a theory supported
by the fact that the note made no monetary demands. Nevertheless,
parents and pupils panicked. The results apparently so satisfied the
writers that they sent notes to other schools. Fortunately, this form of
terrorizing lasted only a short time. With the exception of a letter sent
on April 8 to the largely Italian Seventh Avenue public school in Newark, New Jersey, these Chicago letters were the only Black Hand notes
directed to institutions rather than individuals.[33]

Violence and alleged Black Hand activities were not limited to the
urban areas. The 1908 trial and conviction of a reputed Black Hand
leader, Rocco Racco, for the murder of Seeley Houk two years before
in rural western Pennsylvania received considerable publicity in the
American and Italian-language press. It was a widely held belief that
western Pennsylvania's Mahoning Valley was "a hotbed for the society." In the years after 1900 violence prevailed among Italians in the
limestone quarry towns stretching from New Castle, Pennsylvania, to
Youngstown, Ohio, and the numerous beatings, knifings, and murders
were attributed to the Black Hand. The violent situation reached its
climax on April 24, 1906, when the body of Seeley Houk, a fish and
game warden, was discovered weighted down with stones in the Mahoning River a short distance east of Hillsville, in Lawrence County.
Houk's watch, money and other valuables remained on the body—an
indication that robbery had not been a motive for the killing. Suspicion
turned at once to Rocco Racco, allegedly the Black Hand Society
leader in Hillsville. Seven months earlier, the warden had killed a dog
belonging to Racco, and the owner reportedly vowed that "just as my
dog died in the woods, so shall this man die." Although it was never
proved in court that Racco had identified Houk as his dog's killer,
nonetheless, since an American official had apparently been the victim
of a foreigner's vengeance, authorities swung into action. Local police
and inspectors from the State Board of Game Commissioners called in
the Pinkerton Detective Agency to help.[34]

At William Pinkerton's direction, Frank Dimaio, superintendent of the Pittsburgh office, had in 1905 formed a group of agents of Italian birth or extraction in anticipation of his Agency's inevitable involvement in Black Hand cases. Following Houk's murder, operatives traveled to New York to pose as newly arrived immigrants; they were to manage to be transported to the Mahoning Valley. Early in 1907 they descended on Hillsville, New Castle, and other mining towns, where they set about making friends, infiltrating local organizations, and collecting evidence that would lead to the arrest of Racco later that year. The trial in 1908 rested on this evidence, and Racco was found guilty. After an appeal failed, the Italian was executed.[35]

More significant than the evidence collected against Racco was the light shed on secret societies in the mining towns. Thus, although these groups were called Black Hand societies by outsiders and by many Italian residents of the towns, they did not operate like the groups in New York, Baltimore, Chicago, and other large cities. As Agent No. 89, who centered his activities in Hillsville (called "Helltown" by residents), reported to the Agency on May 22, 1907, "I have not heard of any threats being made by the members of the Society or any other Italians in the shape of a letter." Individual members might engage in blackmail "unknown to the head man," but "if they are found doing this by the head man, they are likely to be severely punished by him." Two days later No. 89 stated that "the so-called black hand letters are not the work of the Society." Further data collected by the Pinkerton agent revealed that an autonomous organization existed in each of the towns; members consisted entirely of Calabrians; and each member referred to his group as "the Society." Moreover, residents of the town believed the organization to be *mafia*-like, although the various leaders with whom he had talked could not agree "as to the formation of the Society and the reasons for its existence." The agent's letters pinpointed extortion as a general group motive; such extortion victimized the organization's weaker and more vulnerable members for the profit of the stronger.

Many concerned people within the Italian community and in American officialdom wrestled with the problem of crime among the newcomers—a problem increasing over the years in importance and impact, according to newspaper accounts as well as official reports. "Sooner or later, if the Black Hand is not checked," commented Lindsay Denison, "it will be a menace not only to Italian-born Americans but to all of us." [36] In fact, non-Italians did receive Black Hand threats, but in every case the senders as well as the recipients were non-Italians. Some would-be extortionists attempted to profit from the fear fostered by publicity accorded Black Hand violence. Thus, George Boljer, a prosperous butcher and owner of several tenements who resided at 412 Henry Street in Brooklyn, received a Black Hand letter threatening death if he did not deliver $700 to a designated place. When the police set a trap for the expected Italian brigands, the aspiring extortionist turned out to be one Mrs. Mary Peters, a tenant of Boljer's who believed that he should share some of the wealth that he displayed so ostentatiously. In a similar situation, W. J. Snow, owner of a tenement on Vivian Place in Lynn, Massachusetts, received a Black Hand letter on February 14, 1908, demanding that rents not be raised; his death would be the price of non-compliance. Not surprisingly, the police conjectured that tenants had sent the letter.

In March 1908 Harry Reik, a farmer's son who hoped to capitalize on Black Hand notoriety, sent dairyman Albert Snedeger, who lived just outside Wheeling, West Virginia, a Black Hand letter demanding $1,000 on pain of death. When caught by the police, Reik stated that he had heard of other people's obtaining money in this way, and he wanted his share. Others sent perverse or callous letters. In the wake of the Di Giorgio bombing in Baltimore, George Savage of 115 Park Avenue, Baltimore, received a letter demanding $500 and threatening to kidnap his daughter. According to the police, the threat, dated December 12, 1907, was the work of "some youths with rather a peculiar sense of humor." Miss Henrietta Trippe of the same city received a note on January 19, 1908, demanding $25. The perpetrator turned out to be a "mischievous boy." [37]

Non-Italian- as well as Italian-Americans applauded the formation in early 1904 (shortly after the press had identified and publicized the Black Hand) of the 28-man Italian squad in New York City's Detective Bureau under the leadership of Sergeant (soon to be Lieutenant) *fight back hand.*

Joseph Petrosino. Similar units were formed in other cities. Non-Italians also approved of measures taken by the "better elements" within the Italian communities to fight the Black Hand. In one such undertaking, Italian leaders in Chicago joined together and on November 11, 1907, organized the White Hand Society, amid much fanfare and the full support of the city's leading Italian-language newspapers, *L'Italia* and *La Tribuna Italiana Transatlantica,* as well as of the Italian Ambassador in Washington and the Italian Minister of Foreign Affairs in Rome. Organizers expressed the hope that a glorious new era would begin with this "war without truce, war without quarter" against the Black Hand, and looked forward to the day when there would be White Hand (*Mano Bianca*) groups "in all the cities which contain large Italian colonies, which suspect the existence of *mafiosi* or *Camorristi* in their midst." By the end of the month *Mano Bianca* units existed in Pittsburgh, New Orleans, Baltimore, and other cities, but the early hopes were not fulfilled. White Hand groups, however, realized some successes: Giuseppe Sunseri and E. Bisi, rich Pittsburgh merchants and members of that city's White Hand, and friends of Baltimore Black Hand victim Joseph Di Giorgio, fought a battle with Black Handers in the Pennsylvania Railroad yards on December 9, 1907. In the exchange of gunfire Sunseri was wounded, but he killed one of his assailants, Philip Rei.[38]

Despite good publicity and some support in other cities, the *Mano Bianca* remained primarily a Chicago operation, and clearly its success or failure would be determined in that city. By January 1908 it claimed to have driven ten of Chicago's most dangerous Italian criminals out of the city, and in February it announced additional successes. During the same month, however, the *Mano Nera* counterattacked. On February 28, Dr. Carlo Volini, president of Chicago's White Hand Society, received a letter informing him that

Black hand fought White hand

the supreme council of the Black Hand has voted that you must die. You have not heeded our warnings in the past, but you must heed this. Your killing has been assigned and the man waits for you.

Volini professed to reporters that he was unafraid, and that he and his organization intended to continue the fight. "They may kill me," the reporters quoted him, "but the cause for which I live will go on." [39]

Dr. Volini was not killed, but the fortunes of the White Hand declined rapidly after that—not so much because of Black Hand pressures as of lack of Italian immigrant support for the White Hand. The instinct of self-preservation, rather than apathy or indifference, lay behind this lack of support. Immigrants knew that crime pervaded their community; they knew also that authorities could or would do little to eliminate it. They believed that the White Hand was powerless in the face of official corruption or tolerance of corruption, and they had no desire to get involved in a lost cause. [40]

The murder of Lieutenant Petrosino in Palermo on March 12, 1909, sent tremors of terror through the Italian communities and the American community as well. Joseph Petrosino seemed to epitomize the American success story for many within and outside the Italian colony. The son of a tailor, Petrosino migrated to New York with his parents from Padula, province of Salerno, when he was nine. He supplemented the family income first as a newsboy and later as a bootblack, while he attended school. Before entering the police department in 1883 (when he was 23), he worked as a tailor, clerk in a bank, and a "white wing" (Sanitation Department employee). Dependable, hard-working, loyal, and physically brave, the short, husky Petrosino formed a model police officer—though his rise through the ranks was slow, in part because of prejudice against Italians, in part because he was not noted for an incisive or probing mind.

His greatest opportunity came in 1904 when, in the midst of the city's first Black Hand scare, he assumed command of the newly formed Italian squad, and shortly thereafter received promotion to lieutenant. On February 19, 1909, less than a month before his trip to Italy, he was named head of the new secret service branch of the police department, a high-powered super-secret agency whose function was to crush anarchists and the Black Hand. (In the public view, and apparently also that of Police Commissioner Theodore Bingham, the two were in-

12. New York City Police Detective Joseph Petrosino (*left*) arresting Tomasso Petto ("Petto the Ox") for murder of Benedetto Madonia. (*Everybody's Magazine*)

tertwined.) As head of this powerful unit, Petrosino was in line for a captaincy.[41]

With the approval of the Italian government and the Italian police, Bingham sent Petrosino to Italy to gain information on several of the (estimated) five thousand Italians in New York who—Petrosino believed—had Old World criminal records. During his 26-year career with the police, Petrosino was credited with returning more than five hundred criminals to Italy to serve jail sentences they had eluded by emigrating. He was to gain further information in Italy so that even more criminals could be returned to Italian jail cells.

Petrosino's murder, like that of Hennessy in New Orleans nineteen years before, inflated the reputation of *mafia* power in Sicily and Black

Hand power in America, and confirmed the widespread belief that if
the *mafia* decided to "get" someone, sooner or later that person would
die violently, despite any precautions he might take. This belief pre-
supposed, of course, that Petrosino's trip to Italy was a tightly guarded
secret, and since it was a secret (the public reasoned), that the *mafia*
found it out and killed him meant that the *mafia* had informers within
the Italian government and the police force, probably in both Palermo
and Rome. But Petrosino's trip was common knowledge before he
left America. Thus, on February 5, 1909, New York's *L'Araldo Italiano* carried an announcement of Petrosino's departure for Italy on the
9th; the announcement outlined his itinerary. The purpose of his trip
was described, and the writer wished him well in his information-
gathering mission. Any person with access to the Italian-language
press of New York knew of Petrosino's plans and itinerary. English-
language newspapers also discussed Petrosino's forthcoming trip. A
Herald editor on February 20, 1909, told of his presence in Italy to
"procure important information about Italian criminals who have
come to this country." New York police sought this information,
explained the writer, because they knew of "many criminals in the
city whom they would like to deport, . . . [but] lack definite information about their records in Europe necessary to prove their case."
Hence, anyone who could read—particularly one with money and contacts—could travel to Italy, or send the information to friends or relatives there. Petrosino's death could easily have been arranged.

So great was the prestige attendant upon accomplishing the murder
of a law enforcement officer of the status of Petrosino that criminals in
both Italy and the United States competed for responsibility. Don Vito
Cascio Ferro, the dominant *mafia* leader in Sicily from the turn of the
century to the 1920s (when the Fascists broke his power), allegedly
admitted publicly of only one murder, that of Petrosino. After arrang-
ing an alibi at the home of a friend who was a member of the Chamber
of Deputies, Don Vito drove to the center of Palermo—in his friend's
carriage—and waited for Petrosino. According to Michele Pantaleone,
he then "killed him with one deadly shot" and returned to the dep-

Mafia
leader
killed
him

uty's house. When he was charged with the murder, Don Vito "easily got away with his crime through the testimony of his authoritative friend who swore that his guest had never left his home." [42]

Michael Fiaschetti, an associate of Petrosino on the Italian squad and his successor as its head, later claimed that on an undercover trip to Italy in 1921 he learned the identity of the murderer. Friends he made among the Neapolitan *Camorra* openly discussed the activities of their Sicilian counterparts. According to Fiaschetti, the killer had emigrated to the United States several years after Petrosino's death. "The man who killed Petrosino is still somewhere in the United States," Fiaschetti wrote in 1930, although he never learned the assassin's name. This man could not have been Don Vito, who at that time resided in a Fascist prison. Reporter Ed Reid maintained that "the murderer of Joseph Petrosino, or rather the man who plotted that infamous crime," was New Orleans crime figure Paul Di Cristina. *L'Araldo Italiano* claimed the dubious honor for those New York criminals who were potential targets of Petrosino's fact-finding trip. Regardless of who pulled the trigger, Petrosino's death was an important victory for the underworld. Information leakages to the press made the assassination attempt possible. Petrosino made the murderer's task easier by traveling alone, although he knew that he was in enemy territory and had made many enemies by virtue of his effective (if rough) handling of Black Hand and other Italian-descended criminals in New York. [43]

The New York Italian squad continued to function after Petrosino's death. Anti-crime groups (like the White Hand) and Italian squads organized to battle the extortion gangs contributed to the decline of the Black Hand during the late 1910s and the virtual disappearance of the gangs in the 1920s, but neither citizen committees nor police squads were primarily responsible for the end of the Black Hand era. At least three factors contributed to its demise. First, the supply of vulnerable victims dwindled with the termination of immigration after 1914 and the onset of hostilities in Europe. Second, there existed the potential for effective federal action, as pointed out in June 1915 in the Chicago *Herald:*

The fact that the "Black Hand" criminal can hardly operate without sending his letters through the mail—as personal delivery of any sort would leave dangerous clues behind—gives the Government practical jurisdiction of the greater part of these offenses.

In 1915 federal officials enforced the laws prohibiting the use of the mails to defraud, and Black Handers did indeed have to resort to personal delivery of notes. Since the risk of being recognized rose drastically, many would-be extortionists were undoubtedly discouraged

13. Alleged pre-World War I Chicago Black Hander Vincenzo Cosmanno, who became a syndicate gunman during the 1920s. (Chicago *Tribune* Photo)

from taking this approach. As journalist Frank Marshall White accurately predicted in 1918, "There is every reason to believe that the words black and hand in conjunction will soon cease to have a sinister connotation in this country." [44]

These two factors limited the opportunities for criminals in the ethnic colony. The third factor involved a vast new field of endeavor that presented itself when federal laws (enacted originally as a wartime measure) prohibited the manufacture and sale of alcoholic beverages. American tastes and habits did not adjust to the new regulations, and enterprising young men found themselves in a position to reap immense profits. Many well-qualified Black Handers like Frank Uale (Yale) of Brooklyn, "Scarface" Di Giovanni of Kansas City, Vincenzo Cosmanno and the Genna brothers of Chicago left the less profitable extortion rackets of the Italian quarter in order to move into the more lucrative work of producing and distributing illicit alcohol. Indicative of this shift, and also one consequence of it, was the decision of the New York City Police Department in 1924 to disband the Italian squad, then headed by Mike Fiaschetti. The reason, wrote Edward Dean Sullivan in 1930, was that "the top calibre blackhanders were all in the booze game. No work—slight risk—vast remuneration." Although some Black Hand bands continued to operate in the 1920s, especially in New York, which continued to receive a trickle of new immigrants even after the restrictive immigration laws of 1921 and 1924 were passed, prohibition marked the end of the Black Hand era. It also introduced many local Italian criminals into the mainstream of American gangsterdom. But the *Mano Nera* was only one of several sources of personnel for prohibition-era syndicates. During the same decades in which the Black Hand thrived, ambitious young Italian-Americans were in the process of making their way in various other criminal activities. [45]

5

Early Ventures in Syndicate Crime

In the early decades of the century, rich financial returns attracted young Italian-Americans to prostitution, gambling, counterfeiting, labor racketeering, and the budding narcotics traffic. More than Black Hand activities (which victimized Italian immigrants), these areas of operation threatened the wider American public, besides serving as an attractive means of upward socio-economic mobility for ambitious and ruthless immigrants. Similarly, the second-generation Italians who absorbed the American emphasis on material success also used criminal activities as a training ground. Most of those who advanced to positions of leadership after the passage of the Volstead Act and who helped forge the powerful illicit business organizations, or criminal syndicates, of the prohibition era got their start before 1920.

Manpower for these syndicates came from a number of sources: some "graduated" from Black Hand and Italian-colony "Mafia" groups; others had served as whorehouse proprietors, gambling-house operators, labor goons, counterfeiters, narcotics dealers, and a wide range of petty crooks and thieves. Former juvenile-gang members who grew to maturity in time to participate in the scramble for wealth made possible by enactment of the Eighteenth Amendment provided the new recruits who emerged by the 1930s as a dominant element in the syndicates of Chicago, New York, and other cities.

The ambitious young men from youth gangs who had moved into minor positions in the syndicates rapidly learned techniques and gained experience at the same time that they established contacts, especially with politicians and police, that became invaluable in succeeding years, for one of the most important lessons of their apprenticeship years before 1920 was the value of friends in local government and law enforcement agencies. Such contacts, which served them so well during the prohibition era and after, were forged before the Dry Decade began.

During these pre-prohibition years, Italians began to enter the lines of illegal enterprise that provided managerial techniques, contacts, guidelines, and proof that huge amounts of money could be made with small danger of punishment. The more able and intelligent Italian criminals learned also that both the risks and the rewards varied with the type of activity engaged in. Cunning neophytes like Frank Costello (Francesco Castiglia) noted that armed robbery, for example, required more effort, involved greater danger, and resulted in smaller financial gain than other means of acquiring money.

Costello was born in Laropola, a small town near Cosenza in Calabria, on January 26, 1891, and emigrated to the United States with his parents when he was four. The Castiglias settled on East 108th Street in Manhattan's East Harlem Italian district. Frank's first brush with the law came in 1908 when he was 17 and was arrested for assault and robbery. The case was dismissed, since it was a first offense. In 1911 he was again arrested and charged with assault and robbery; again the case was dismissed. Three years later, after an attempted robbery, he was arrested and charged with carrying a concealed weapon. He gave his name as Frank Saverio.

By this time, when he had a reputation as a "tough guy" and gunman, Costello was sentenced to a year in jail. He was released after ten months, receiving two months off his sentence for good behavior, and emerged from prison a changed man. In 1914 he had married a non-Italian, Loretta Geigerman, and soon had family responsibilities. His prison term impressed on him the values of working away from public scrutiny, the need for a legitimate cover, and the advantage of having powerful and influential friends. Immediately Costello began to cultivate local politicians. He moved into gambling activities, and with

Capone.

a partner, Henry Horowitz, a small manufacturer of novelties, formed a legitimate business, the Horowitz Novelty Company, to produce kewpie dolls, razor blades, and (as the real purpose of the firm, and its money-maker) punchboards and other gambling devices.[1]

During the 1920s and 1930s, the small, debonair, politically well-connected Costello, along with other able and highly ambitious young Italians, Irishmen, Jews, and members of other ethnic groups, helped to revolutionize crime in America. Individuals played a vital role. Bright, ruthless, upwardly mobile youths like Costello, Charles ("Lucky") Luciano, and Meyer Lansky in New York; Frank Milano and Moe Dalitz in Cleveland; Hyman Abrams and Charles ("King") Solomon in Boston; Daniel Walsh in Providence; "Boo Boo" Hoff in Philadelphia; Dion O'Banion and Al Capone in Chicago; and John Lazia in Kansas City were convinced that opportunities for personal advancement and material success were not available through legitimate means, and so turned to crime as a profession.

The majority of America's Southern Italian and Sicilian immigrants arrived between 1890 and 1914, at a time when the fluid political, social, and economic patterns that had speeded the advancement of Northern and Western European immigrants in the decades after 1840 were in the process of growing more unyielding as the nation emerged from its frontier stage of development. As the earlier immigrant elements became acculturated, they, like the native population, isolated the newcomers, and set up barriers to prevent later arrivals (from other ethnic backgrounds) from challenging their own position. The situation, of course, remained more fluid in the western, more recently settled sections of the country than in the longer-established East. In effect, both the economic opportunities in legitimate lines of activity, and the social acceptance of Italians increased as the newcomers traveled westward across the nation.[2]

Whether born in a Southern Italian hovel or in an American tenement, the children grew to maturity in a period when education began to emerge as an increasingly important qualification for both public and private employment. And yet, lacking the social graces and often unable to speak or understand standard middle-class English, many of

14. Sicilian native Frank Milano arrived in Cleveland's Mayfield Road Italian district as a boy. After an apprenticeship in youth gangs, he and his brother Tony headed a lucrative counterfeiting ring until 1911, when they were apprehended. Tony went to prison. During the 1920s the brothers emerged as leaders among Cleveland's Italian bootleggers. (1930 Cleveland *Plain Dealer* photograph)

these children found school, with its regimentation and its middle-class teachers and traditions, a strange and often frightening experience. Moreover, school discipline emphasized the sublimation of desires and ambitions for long-term, deferred goals—an attitude that seemed unreal in the tenement world of immigrant children, where one seized material gratification whenever it was available. Even to more ambitious and intelligent children, school too often seemed a waste of time and effort, filled as it was with difficult exercises completely irrelevant to their needs and interests. To slum area youngsters like Salvatore Lucania (Charles "Lucky" Luciano), John Torrio, and Alphonse Caponi (Al Capone), excitement and economic opportunity seemed to be out in the streets rather than in the classroom. As soon as they reached the legal withdrawal age of fourteen, they left school.

Lucky Luciano was one such dropout. Born the third of five children of Rosalia and Antonio Lucania in Lercara Friddi (in the sulphur-mining area of western Sicily) in November 1897, he arrived in New York City with his family early in 1907. The family settled on First Avenue near Fourteenth Street, on Manhattan's Lower East Side, in an ethnically mixed but predominantly Jewish neighborhood. Luciano entered school (P.S. 10), shortly after his arrival in New York.

15. New York's Lower East Side Italian colony on the eve of World War I. (Community Service Center, New York)

Though his conduct in school was satisfactory, his academic record showed the results of chronic truancy, and he was committed to the Brooklyn Truant School on June 25, 1911, for a four-month period. He left school the following year, when he reached the age of fourteen and could legally apply for working papers. At that time he was in fifth grade.[3]

In 1936, when Luciano was on trial as head of a city-wide prostitution ring, Irving W. Halpern, Chief Probation Officer, Court of General Sessions, reported to the courts on his investigation of "Charlie Lucky's" boyhood experiences:

> During this phase of his life, the defendant was reared in an impoverished environment in the lower East Side, and at an early age he was beyond the control of his parents. His behavior patterns and social attitude during this formative period were largely conditioned by the influence of unwholesome associates, with the result that by the time he was eighteen years old he had acquired a definitely criminalistic pattern of conduct.

After leaving school, Luciano took a job as shipping boy in a hat factory, but one week of work and a $7 paycheck convinced him that he wanted something more from life: This type of work was for—in his words—"crumbs." A "crumb," according to Luciano, was one "who works and saves, and lays his money aside; who indulges in no extravagance." Luciano wanted "money to spend, beautiful women to enjoy, silk underclothes and places to go in style." For a short time he was a member of the Five Points Gang, and an habitué of Fourteenth Street pool-halls. He became a drug user and pusher, and on June 26, 1916, at the age of eighteen, was found guilty of unlawful possession of narcotics. He spent six months in a reformatory.

Slum-area youngsters joined gangs and turned to delinquent behavior at an early age. Unlike most of their contemporaries, who also belonged to corner gangs and were involved in occasional mischief-making, the criminals-in-the-making had little or nothing to do with legitimate labor, which they believed was only for "suckers," men who worked long hours for low pay and lived in overcrowded tenements with their families. It appears that all the prohibition-era racketeers, whether born in the United States or brought here as infants or children, started their careers in one or another gang. The corner gang became their school.[4] Slum-area ethnic neighborhoods in the decades before 1920 abounded in such youth gangs. One of the most notorious (and also the one Luciano joined) was the Five Points Gang. Its leader, Neapolitan Paolo Antonio Vaccarelli, had taken the name Paul Kelly when he became a prize fighter in the late 1890s. Kelly was a complex, multi-faceted man, soft-spoken and urbane, who (as Herbert Asbury described him) had a "well-bred manner" that "could have moved at ease in relatively cultured society." He also was the uncontested leader of a vicious and violent gang of young thugs who engaged in robbery, mayhem, and prostitution. Through alliances with other gangs, Kelly commanded the allegiance of 1,500 youths— chiefly Italian, but including Jews, Irish, and other "ethnics"—and literally controlled the area between the Bowery and Broadway, Fourteenth Street and City Hall Park. Besides Lucky Luciano, his followers included Al Capone and John Torrio, himself leader of a neighborhood gang, the James Street Boys.[5]

The Five Point Gang's principal rival was another huge Lower East Side gang (totaling some 1,200 men) led by Monk Eastman, a vicious, ape-like psychopath. The Eastmans and the Five Pointers engaged in a series of bloody battles between 1898 and 1904 when, on February 2 of that year, Eastman was arrested for robbery and firing at police officers at Sixth Avenue and 42nd Street. The evidence was too strong for his numerous and powerful friends in Tammany Hall to tamper with; and he received a ten-year prison sentence. "Kid" Twist, who succeeded him, continued the war against Kelly's gang until the night of May 14, 1908, when the Five Pointers ambushed and killed Twist as he enjoyed the pleasures of Coney Island. It was a hollow victory, however, for the years of fighting had sapped the manpower of both gangs. The disarray of Kelly's forces combined with the increasing activity of reform groups working to curb the power of the urban political machine to persuade Kelly that it was time for him to move on to bigger and more remunerative projects. Accordingly, he transferred

16. Former Five Points Gang leader and Vice President of International Long-shoremen's Association Paolo Vaccarelli (Paul Kelly) (*left*), photographed in October 1919. (United Press International)

his base of operations to Harlem, where he moved into a lucrative new field, that of labor racketeering, though he maintained many of his Lower East Side connections and remained a power there for years to come. From Harlem he organized the ragpickers and served as their business agent and walking delegate. He used the threat of the strike to extort money from Upper East Side real estate and property agents. Later he became a power in organized labor as vice president of the International Longshoremen's Association (ILA), a member union of the American Federation of Labor until September 1953, when it was expelled on charges of "racketeering and accepting bribes from employers."

Kelly's history reflected the fact that by 1920 Italians were threatening the Irish control of the waterfront. In 1880, according to Charles B. Barnes's pioneering study, *The Longshoremen*, 95 per cent of New York City's longshoremen were Irish, the remaining 5 per cent being German, Scottish, English, and Scandinavian. By 1912, although the Irish were still more numerous, Italians ranked a close second, comprising one-third of the total. Seven years later, according to a New York Inter-Racial Council survey of immigrant group location and economic activity in the city, Italians comprised 75 per cent of the city's longshoremen. At that time, and since then, Irish and Italians worked in ethnically exclusive groups: Irish stevedores led Irish longshoremen, and Italian stevedores led Italian longshoremen. The Irish kept control of the West Side docks; Italians appropriated the East Side and the piers in Brooklyn and New Jersey.[6]

A major reason for the attractiveness of the waterfront was the high pay. As the Inter-Racial Council study disclosed, Italian longshoremen in New York averaged between $65 and $100 per month, a figure that compared very well with the wages of other workmen surveyed, such as Italian carpenters ($75 to $100) or tailors ($50). Moreover, work on the docks offered opportunities for lucrative illegal activities; even before Italian criminals gained control, crime was a way of life on the waterfront. The very process by which dock workers were selected by hiring agents—the so-called "shape-up"—created vast opportunities for bribery, kickbacks, loan-sharking, and other corrupt practices, besides resulting in inefficiency of operation and a demoralized, insecure labor force. Italian criminals brought organization and greater ruthlessness and violence than had been known before, and made possible huge profits from large-scale pilfering, loan-sharking, gambling, and the smuggling of drugs and other illegal products from overseas. The presence on the docks of a union, the ILA (which was organized in the 1890s but did not gain full control of the waterfront until 1914), did not reduce or curb crime, but rather introduced additional methods of extorting money from workers and employers alike.

Although Italians became a dominant force on the New York docks, they never achieved such pre-eminence in other ports. In Boston, New Orleans, and San Francisco, for example, the Irish retained tight control over the waterfront and effectively excluded Italians (and blacks). In Boston, according to Barnes, first- and second-generation Irish comprised about 85 per cent of the longshoremen engaged in foreign commerce; the remaining 15 per cent included Germans, Scandinavians, a few Portuguese, and a scattering of other nationalities. Boston was entirely a union port with regard to foreign commerce, and the union refused to accept either Italians or blacks to membership. The coastwise trade, a much less important and less lucrative operation, was unorganized; Italians found work here.[7]

Criminals worked for businessmen in highly competitive fields during the two decades before prohibition (although the full flowering of labor and business racketeering would not come until the late 1920s and the 1930s). An early example of the use of underworld elements to neutralize business opposition was described to the Kefauver Committee in 1951. In 1913 the Cleveland *News* and the *Leader*, both owned by Daniel R. Hanna, Sr., were engaged in a fierce circulation war with the city's two other newspapers, the *Plain Dealer* and the *Press*. Arthur B. McBride, already at 24 a veteran of similar newspaper wars in Chicago, hired on as circulation manager to head the *News* circulation forces.[8]

In answer to a question from Assistant Committee Counsel Joseph L. Nellis as to the nature of the trouble caused by the *Plain Dealer* and the *Press*, McBride replied, ''Well, they were chasing our boys off the corner; wouldn't let them handle it in Cleveland.'' The method employed to deal with the problem was that of hiring a group of young toughs to push the sales of the *News* and the *Leader* and to make the work of competitors more difficult. Among those used by the Hanna newspapers were several future Cleveland syndicate leaders, including Alfred ("Big Al") Polizzi, John and George Angersola, and Morris "Mushy" Wexler. (In the 1930s McBride went into the taxicab business, and one of his trusted followers in the taxicab wars that plagued Cleveland in 1933 and 1934 was Anthony "Muscle Tony" Civetta.) [9]

Although newspaper wars raged in other cities as well during the early years of the century, perhaps the most violent occurred in Chicago in 1910 between the *Tribune* and the *Examiner*. In the view of Hearst biographer Ferdinand Lundberg, from the Chicago newspaper war "the personnel for Chicago's future gangs was assembled." The circulation battles offered a training ground for *"the system of gang warfare and racketeering"* (italics in the original) that would emerge in the city during the 1920s and 1930s. Newspaper wars formed only one source of personnel and techniques. Even more significant was the early experience gained in gambling and prostitution, although it must be emphasized that the prohibition-era gangsters came from a variety of criminal backgrounds. [10]

Both sides in the war hired young, capable thugs and gunmen, none of them Italian, who later rise to prominence during prohibition years. Among these were Maurice ("Mossy") Enright, "Red" Connors, and Frank McErlane. The *Examiner* circulation manager was Moses Annenberg, who, during the conflict, switched his allegiance to the rival *Tribune*. He was later to amass a fortune from the wire service, the publishing business (including horse-racing papers like the *American Racing Record*), and city dailies like the Philadelphia *Inquirer,* real estate, insurance companies, and other enterprises.

Machine politicians as well as businessmen and union leaders made use of the services of underworld thugs—generally to the profit of both gangsters and politicians. An effective, enduring political machine provided a variety of services and favors for constituents. In order to win and hold immigrant support, bosses made available to a succession of ethnic groups patronage positions and jobs with private companies. Work included street cleaning, garbage collecting, custodial jobs in public buildings, building and road maintenance, and assignments in public transportation networks and sewage systems, besides construction work on tenements, bathhouses, and parks. This employment generally offered unskilled workers relatively steady incomes and job security, and to the immigrant groups gave tangible proof of the benefits to be gained from local politics.

Professional police and fire-fighting forces, which emerged during the middle decades of the nineteenth century, quickly fell under the control of local politicians, to provide additional sources of patronage for the machine. By the 1870s this connection had evolved into a working relationship among criminals, politicians, and the police, and it has plagued American cities ever since.

In addition to jobs, the successful political boss obtained exemptions from city ordinances for core-area businessmen; arranged bail and obtained pardons; sponsored dances, parades, picnics, social and athletic affairs, bazaars, and community church functions; distributed turkeys at Christmas; gave food and fuel to needy residents; sent flowers to the sick, and attended funerals. Those who received patronage positions or favors were obligated to vote for the machine, and although they seldom formed a majority of a ward's eligible voters, they provided a loyal and disciplined nucleus. The high degree of residential mobility displayed by immigrants discouraged many from taking an active interest in ward politics. Bosses encouraged this general apathy in order to increase the value of the votes of their loyal followers; hence, the ballots of the patronaged few could determine election outcomes. Members of the underworld were among the most loyal supporters of the machine.[11]

In exchange for a free hand in operating houses of prostitution, saloons, and gambling halls, criminal elements not only helped get out the vote on election day but also kept as many opposition voters as possible from reaching polling stations. In addition, through hoodlum muscle and cash, bosses used intimidation, bribery, violence, and trickery to prevent the rise of effective competition.

The intimate and mutually beneficial working relations between the

political machine and criminals, both juvenile and adult, was emphasized by muckraker George Kibbe Turner in an article "Tammany's
Control of New York by Professional Criminals," in the June 1909
issue of *McClure's Magazine*. Turner described the Bowery as being
(at that writing) "the recognized metropolis of American criminals,"
and traced this situation to the promotion by Tammany Hall boss Richard Croker of Timothy D. Sullivan to Bowery Assembly district leader
in the early 1890s. (New York, which at that time meant Manhattan
and the Bronx, was divided into 35 Assembly districts, each containing from 40,000 to 80,000 inhabitants and in turn subdivided into
Election districts. The Assembly district leaders constituted the governing body of the Democratic Party organization, Tammany Hall.)

Before Sullivan's arrival the Bowery Democratic organization had
not efficiently organized the vote or effectively tapped the Assembly
district's major business, which was to furnish residents and visitors
with a variety of illegal services. "Big Tim" quickly changed this situation by giving leading criminals important functions in his political
machine. As Turner relates, "The head gamblers and the merchants of
prostitution, then [the mid-1890s] as now, were election district captains, who brought out the vote; and the vagrants, minor gamblers,
and thieves furnished the voting 'repeaters,' that is, men using false
names, who cast as many votes as they could get away with." As a
result, Turner continued, "the Bowery Assembly district was very
soon the banner Democratic district of New York. Its peculiar business
interests grew in direct proportion to its vote." By the turn of the century, Italians predominated in the Bowery, and Sullivan cultivated
their support by submitting and helping to secure the passage of a bill
making Columbus Day a state holiday. Furthermore, he accepted the
takeover by Italian criminals of illicit activities in his district, in exchange for their getting out the vote on election day.[12]

A similar process took place in other core-area Election and Assembly districts in New York. That process occurred also in the precincts
and wards of other cities where Italians, Eastern European Jews, and
other "new" immigrant groups had moved into neighborhoods previously inhabited by Irish, Germans, and other natives of Northern and

Western Europe. Knowledgeable political bosses dating from the earlier immigrant waves hung on to their positions and power by the shrewd distribution of patronage and political favors, and by accepting the dominance, or at least the equality of, the new arrivals in their political domains.

Often uncouth and nonconforming to middle-class standards of behavior and political morality, urban political bosses and the organizations they directed nevertheless fulfilled vital functions. During the last decades of the nineteenth century and the early decades of the twentieth, American cities underwent rapid expansion in area as well as in population. Among the newcomers were millions who were strangers not only to city life but also to the United States. From Italy, Poland, Greece, Hungary, Russia, Austria, and elsewhere in Southern and Eastern Europe, they streamed into the United States, and nearly all of them settled in cities, generally in the major urban-industrial states of the East and Middle West. Of necessity as well as of self-interest, machine politicians were not concerned with the long-term interests of constituents, but rather devoted their attention to short-term needs such as jobs, handouts of fuel during harsh winters, and a variety of personal favors.

Middle-class reformers reacted strongly and negatively to core-area politicians, the system they directed, and the people they represented. Failing to recognize and deal with the underlying problems that engendered corrupt political machines, many reformers generally reacted to, as Turner put it, the "decadence in the popular government of great cities." They saw the boss system as a cancer eating at the vitals of the democratic system upon which the greatness and the survival of the nation were based. An evil that particularly infuriated them was prostitution, which existed with the acquiescence (sometimes the active support) of politicians and law enforcement agencies. Prostitution, like liquor, repelled and at the same time held a fascination for many reformers.

At the turn of the century, prostitution in urban America operated on a widespread and open basis. Although not sanctioned by law, segregated vice districts flourished in large and small cities. The general public was shocked, horrified, and titillated when the extent of prostitution, its relation to local politics and to police corruption, and the effects of the life on the prostitutes themselves were described in federal studies and local vice-commission reports as well as in popular magazine articles, newspapers, and books. Historian Allen F. Davis noted Jane Addams's decision in 1911 to write on prostitution with the comment that "she was also aware that anything written on prostitution would sell." [13]

During the decade before World War I, twenty-one cities appointed vice commissions. As historian Egal Feldman has observed, "In no period of American history did the custodians of American morality direct more serious attention to the eradication of prostitution than they did in the few years preceding World War I. . . . Ministers, social workers, men and women of medicine, science and letters all joined in the unusually massive assault." Investigations drove home the enormity of the problem through the use of statistics. Thus in 1897 New York was estimated to have more than 30,000 public prostitutes. The famous 1911 Vice Commission of Chicago proclaimed that "prostitution in this city is a *Commercial Business* of large proportions with tremendous profits of more than Fifteen Million Dollars per year" (emphasis in the original). The Commission estimated that five thousand full-time professionals plied their wares in the city's Red Light district, but refused to hazard a guess as to the number of "clandestine and casual groups made up of immoral girls and women, married and otherwise," who operated on a part-time basis. Using a Federal Department of Justice enumeration, Howard B. Woolston concluded that American brothels between 1911 and 1913 employed nearly a hundred thousand women (the U.S. population in 1910 was nearly 92 million). Other estimates were far higher. In 1912 Stanley W. Finch, Chief of the Bureau of Investigation of the Department of Justice, placed the number at "not less than 250,000." Sociologist Walter C. Reckless quoted sources—which he believed to be inflated—giving a total of 250,000 minimum, and more likely closer to 300,000 or 500,000; R. N. Wilson placed the total at over 500,000. [14]

Although prostitution in general formed one concern of the progressives, "white slavery" was a particular source of fear and indignation. "Hysterical Americans," social-welfare historian Roy Lubove noted, worried "that no woman was safe from the human 'fiends' who used drugs, alcohol, and physical violence to force or deceive unsuspecting females into a life of immorality and bondage." In an address presented before the World's Purity Congress in Louisville on May 7, 1912, Stanley W. Finch maintained that "not less than 25,000 young women and girls are annually procured for this traffic and that no less than 50,000 men and women are engaged in procuring and living on the earnings of these women and girls." Clifford G. Roe, counsel for the American Vigilance Association, observed that "an America commercialized has commercialized its daughters. Who would have prophesied a century ago that today like hardware and groceries the daughters of the people would be bought and sold?" U.S. District Attorney for Chicago Edwin W. Sims added to the statistics and the voices of alarm by likening the " 'Business' in the ruination of girls" to the business "the great packing houses do in the sale of meats." Sims believed that at least 15,000 young women were imported each year into the country for immoral purposes and that these were "but a mere fraction of the number recruited for the army of prostitution from home fields, from the cities, the towns, the villages of our own country." [15]

Although reformers liked to believe that these girls were held in bordellos against their will, most appear to have found the houses at least no worse than the lives they had left behind and to which they would return if they departed the urban Red Light district. In Chicago, on February 16, 1912, teenager Josephine Walker swore out a complaint against three Italian men who had forced her into a life of sin. The trial took place the next day, the men were found guilty, and on the 19th Josephine was placed in a good middle-class home, where she was "cleaned up and given a hat and coat and clean underwear." In two days the quiet life had worn thin and Josephine ran away. On February 27 she was picked up by police in Chicago's vice district. [16]

Reformers were misled by the fact that the girls constantly complained about their forced entry into prostitution, how much they hated the life they led, and how much they wanted to leave. In fact, most had no intention of leaving. A number of people wrote Jane Addams after the publication of her book, *A New Conscience and an Ancient Evil*. Among these were self-confessed former prostitutes and pimps. One day, according to historian Allen Davis, a letter arrived at Hull House from a young Toledo woman who confessed that she was still in the life. She asked whether she could correspond with Miss Addams. The woman lived out of the city, and Dr. Alice Hamilton, a personal friend of Miss Addams and a Hull House resident, began a correspondence with her. During the following months the girl, Davis related, "pictured herself as a captive bird beating herself against the bars." Finally Dr. Hamilton had an opportunity to see her during a visit to Toledo. As she recalled years later, "It was a sadly disillusioning experience." Rather than being an unwilling white slave of primitive masculine passions, "the woman had come into the house of her own free will and had no intention of leaving unless she found a man to support her." Dr. Hamilton completely changed her thinking about prostitution. One exposure to the reality of "the sporting life" convinced her that the girls were more guilty than their customers. For the men, a visit to a House was a brief interlude for which they paid, but for the prostitute, "it was her sole preoccupation and at the same time it brought her money." [17]

In an age that glorified the ideal of womanly purity and innocence and generally ignored the reality of women's needs as human beings, the idea was unthinkable that young girls might be attracted to lives in prostitution by the money, clothes, and hopes of escaping the drudgery of factory work and the hopelessness of tenement life. Stories of innocent country girls (and many of their city sisters) forced against their wishes to live and work in bordellos were more numerous than tales of those who went willingly, hoping thereby to escape poverty and deprivation; but they were also farther from the truth. Mrs. Ophelia Amigh, Superintendent of the Illinois Training School for Girls, sadly observed in 1910 that "in this day and age of the world no young girl is safe.'' Mrs. Amigh probably did not recognize (or refused to accept) the fact that many girls, for one reason or another, did not want to be "safe." [18]

Prostitution was a money-making business. Since a social stigma was attached to the so-called second oldest profession (pimping), members of the most recent immigrant groups, especially Frenchmen, Italians, and Jews, procured and managed the prostitutes and the resorts of the cities of the East and Middle West. In this business the French influence dominated. By the 1860s, during the reign of Louis Napoleon, the French procurer (*maquereau,* "mackerel") was operating a highly developed and very profitable business in Paris and elsewhere in France—so much so that the operators adopted a costume of their own: black velvet trousers, a blouse, and a silk cap called a *bijou.* With the downfall of the Second Empire and the advent of the more austere and equalitarian Third Republic, the procurers fell into disrepute. Many were exiled to the penal colonies of New Caledonia and French Guiana. Others emigrated, and the exodus beginning in the 1870s witnessed their dispersal across the entire globe. (Those who remained behind and directed the home business discarded the traditional costume and went underground.) [19]

By the turn of the century the French dominated the business of importing young girls from overseas for use in American brothels. One gang, centered in Chicago and headed by Alphonse and Eva Dufour, was the distributor of European prostitutes to various cities in the Middle West, including Minneapolis, St. Louis, and Kansas City, as well as New Orleans. According to federal authorities, who uncovered their operations in June 1908, the Dufours had operated in Chicago for at least three years, and headed an organization that imported at least three thousand girls and cleared approximately $200,000 each year. Frenchmen were also proprietors of some larger resorts in other cities. French involvement continued down into the 1920s and 1930s. As late as 1937, a grand jury empaneled to determine the extent of vice, gambling, and "the rackets" in San Francisco reported that the French still played an important part in prostitution in that city. Edward Atherton, a former FBI agent who directed the investigation and uncovered much of the information upon which the grand jury based its conclusions, found "the French group" in that city to be "the most highly organized unit in the entire graft setup." Most were in the country illegally, and lived in constant fear of being extradited. The same situation existed in the pre-World War I years when French *maquereaux* played a prominent role in the prostitution business in New York, New Orleans, Chicago, and other cities. Because of their profession and illegal entry into the country, most led a precarious daily existence and survived at the mercy of law enforcement officers whose acquiescence in their presence, while it could be bought, was at best tenuous. Pressure from reformers could bring crackdowns and arrests or the demand from authorities for larger payoffs. For this reason the French tended not to be permanent residents of the United States, but they moved constantly among American cities and between the United States and France (and other countries as well). Thus their role in American prostitution, though prominent and continuing, focused mainly on supply and coordination.[20]

As a group, the French remained outsiders and—unlike their Eastern European Jewish and Italian associates—generally did not develop the essential ties to ward and city political machines that facilitated the continued smooth functioning of criminal syndicates. In contrast, Jewish and Italian gangs on New York's East Side assured Tammany-supported candidates huge majorities at each election, and in exchange enjoyed unlimited protection that literally permitted them to commit offenses up to and including murder. This protection also guaranteed the smooth and—except under most unusual circumstances—uninterrupted functioning of the whorehouses. A grand jury investigation of vice in Chicago's First Ward in 1914 found, according to State's Attorney Maclay Hoyne, that "three rings are ruling in the South Side levee, which have been collecting money from the little fellows and splitting it with the police and politicians." The first and largest prostitution ring or "syndicate" was the Colosimo-Torrio outfit, headed by James Colosimo and his lieutenant, John Torrio. Until 1909 a Frenchman, Maurice Van Bever, had been Colosimo's partner, but after his conviction on charges of running a white-slave ring, Tor-

17. Chicago syndicate leader James Colosimo, who laid the foundations of prohibition-era Torrio-Capone empire. (The Chicago *Sun-Times*)

rio took charge. Julius and Charlie Maibaum bossed a second syndicate, with the assistance of Ed Weiss, Jakie Adler, Harry Hopkins, and Jakie Wolfsohn. The Marshall brothers headed the third ring. Despite the existence of these powerful organizations, some independents still prospered, including Joe ("Jew Kid") Grabiner and Harry Cusick (or Guzik), who, with his brother Jack, would become prominent in the Torrio and Capone organization in the 1920s). The political protectors and patrons of Chicago's Red Light district were First Ward political bosses and city aldermen John ("Bathhouse John") Coughlin and Michael ("Hinky Dink") Kenna, the so-called "Lords of the Levee." [21]

Since customers constantly demanded fresh talent, prostitutes were moved periodically from bordello to bordello and from city to city. Thus, an investigation by local and federal authorities in 1909 uncovered evidence of a system involving the procuring and exchange of prostitutes between the Colosimo-Van Bever ring in Chicago and gangs in New York, Milwaukee, and St. Louis. The capture of Joe Bovo destroyed Van Bever and brought the existence of the vice network to light. At the time of his arrest, Bovo was bringing two prostitutes, Pearl Hendren and Hazel Elbe, from St. Louis to work in the Colosimo-Van Bever-operated houses in the South Side levee. The attorney of Jim Colosimo himself, Rocco De Stefano, represented Bovo, but the prostitutes provided evidence against him and refused to change their testimony in Municipal Court trial, which had begun on December 3, 1909. Found guilty of pandering, Bovo was sentenced on January 5, 1910, to a six-month jail term and fined $300. The sentence, however, was only a part of Bovo's problem. In March 1910 he was returned to St. Louis to stand trial for wife and child abandonment. Several other members of the vice network were tried and convicted, including Maurice Van Bever and his wife Julia. Evidence of their direct involvement provided in court resulted in sentences for each of a year in prison and fines of $1,000. Colosimo's name received frequent mention in the press and by law enforcement officers in connection with the case, but the prosecution could not produce evidence linking him to the accused. John Torrio, who had arrived from New York earlier in the year to help Colosimo deal with troublesome Black Handers, was picked up by the police and indicted. On December 6, 1909, Torrio (who at the time managed the Saratoga for his Uncle Jim) and Sam Hare, manager of The Victoria (another Colosimo resort), came before Municipal Court Judge Henry M. Walker to demand a jury trial. The trial was postponed to December 20, when the case was dismissed because of insufficient evidence. The prosecution's witnesses could not testify to the fact that Torrio and Hare had employed Bovo to bring them to Chicago to work in the houses they managed; they had the clear impression that such was the case, but had no proof to offer. Bovo could have provided the proof, but he refused to do so. Torrio and Hare escaped without punishment.[22]

During the pre-prohibition decade, Italians reaped great profits from vice operations in Philadelphia, Boston, Milwaukee, Denver, San Francisco, and elsewhere. Anthony ("Black Tony") Parmagini, who became a major bootlegger and narcotics dealer in San Francisco during the 1920s and early 1930s, operated a disorderly house in that city during the decade before 1920. In Denver members of the Mauro clan, which played an important role in the city's criminal underworld during prohibition, exploited the prostitution business in the years prior to World War I.[23] Despite widespread and lucrative vice operations in these and other urban centers, in no other city during this period—including New York—did Italians attain the degree of success that Colosimo and Torrio enjoyed in Chicago. Nearly all of Colosimo's estimated yearly income of $600,000 accumulated from prostitution and gambling. In the years after 1910 Torrio efficiently expanded the business established by "Big Jim" a decade before. The innovative Torrio demonstrated how a new means of transportation, the automobile, could be adapted to the use of whoremongers. Because of a police crackdown in 1912 on Chicago's segregated vice district—the result of church and civic group pressures—resort owners and prostitutes found it expedient to disperse. Torrio opened a roadhouse in Burnham, the first of a string of suburban resorts and gambling halls that thrived on customers from Chicago, who made use of the mobility provided by the automobile. During the 1920s Al Capone greatly expanded the suburban vice and gambling operations pioneered by his mentor, John Torrio.[24]

Numerous prostitution rings existed in almost every large city in America. Some, like the Colosimo-Torrio gang, were well-organized and cooperated in exchanging prostitutes with organizations in different cities. No evidence is available of the existence at that time of a national or international vice syndicate (or of several syndicates), despite the fears of contemporaries. To those who fought vice—clergymen, honest law enforcement officials, and concerned citizens—it seemed that their opponents succeeded only because of tight and efficient organization, perhaps the leadership of an evil genius. Although there was no "Big Chief," as alleged by District Attorney Edwin W. Sims in 1911, vice was organized and proved extremely profitable for the criminals involved. Even during the not-so-dry years following passage of the Volstead Act, prostitution remained a huge money-maker for criminal syndicates. After Repeal, narcotics, labor and business racketeering, and gambling helped make up for revenue lost from the liquor trade.[25]

In the decades before World War I, a budding drug culture existed in the United States, and by 1919, according to City Health Commissioner Royal S. Copeland, New York contained as many as 200,000 drug addicts. Italians, however, apparently did not gain prominence in, or reap extensive financial returns from, the narcotics business until the 1930s. Lucky Luciano (who engaged in narcotics traffic as well as numerous other moneymaking ventures at a later time) in the decade after 1910 was a small-time drug pusher and user in New York City.[26] Typical of the small-scale narcotics operations of Italians during these early years were the activities of Alexander De Meo, which came to light in the course of a murder trial in New York during 1913. According to Assistant District Attorney Frank Moss, De Meo and his partner Rocco Viola were in the business of "getting hold of opium and selling it to these places, which we call opium dens." On April 14, 1913, De Meo and Viola contacted a sailor, Edward Hobson, who had smuggled in a small quantity (the amount was never specified) of opium purchased from Chinese suppliers in Panama. When Hobson arrived in New York, his brother Leo and a friend, both sailors for the Munson Steamship Line and also active in drug smuggling, contacted another friend, Michael Lazarus. Lazarus worked for the Munson Line as well, but had once managed a lunch room on Third Avenue near 116th Street, and there had developed connections with opium dealers. He arranged a meeting on April 14 between the Hobson brothers, Viola, and De Meo. De Meo, in turn, brought the Hobsons to Abraham Lewis (*alias* Abie Harris) and Morris Klein (*alias* Green), who ran an opium den on East 100th Street. Edward Hobson had six cans (size undisclosed) of opium and asked $40 per can. Klein refused, and they finally settled on a total price of $132, or $22 per can. De Meo then demanded a commission. When Klein refused to pay, Hobson offered $2, but De Meo refused this insulting amount. After they left Klein's place, De Meo talked Hobson into meeting him again on the evening of the 15th with the promise that he would help sell the remainder of the smuggled opium. When they met, De Meo and Viola led the Hobson brothers to a tenement house at 424 East 116th Street, shot them, and fled. Viola was never located, but De Meo was arrested, tried, found guilty of murder, and sentenced to life imprison-ment. Evidence presented in the De Meo trial indicated that even those opium dens located in the Italian neighborhoods of New York were not, at least in 1913, owned and operated entirely by Italians. Jews handled at least some of the business. In fact, the role of Italians dur-ing this decade appeared to be rather insignificant.[27]

Narcotics became a more lucrative line of activity during and after prohibition. Long before that time, counterfeiting had attracted nu-merous Italians. One of the most prominent early Italian counterfeiters was New York's Ignazio Saietta ("Lupo the Wolf"). Following his arrival in 1899 from Italy, Lupo organized a gang of counterfeiters in Manhattan's East Harlem Italian neighborhood. The gang specialized in two- and five-dollar bills, which were produced in Salerno and shipped to New York in crates and boxes supposedly containing olives, olive oil, spaghetti, macaroni, wine, cheese, and other Italian products. The bills were allocated to wholesale dealers, who paid from 30¢ to 40¢ per bill, and then distributed the bogus money throughout the country. As related in Chapter 4, the gang was impli-cated in the "Barrel Murder" case in 1903, but escaped punishment for the gory crime (although some members, including the vicious psychopath Petto the Ox, were arrested and tried). Finally, in No-vember 1909 the U.S. Secret Service considered that it had an "air tight case." The Service was ready to move against what New York Bureau Chief William J. Flynn described as "one of the biggest bands of counterfeiters which has ever operated in this country." Lupo, his brother-in-law Giuseppe Morello, and the other gang member were brought to trial in federal court and were found guilty of counterfeiting activities. Lupo received a thirty-year sentence and served twelve years before being paroled in 1922, just in time to participate in the opportunities presented by the Eighteenth Amendment.[28]

Italian counterfeiters operated lucrative activities in other cities as well. Anthony "Tony" Milano, who returned from federal prison to become a major power in the Cleveland underworld from the prohibi-tion era to the 1950s, functioned during the first decade of the twen-

tieth century as a successful practitioner of the counterfeiting art, until
the Secret Service halted him temporarily in 1911.[29]

Another notorious criminal whose early ventures included counterfeiting was Chicago's Anthony D'Andrea. D'Andrea, whose jail sentence on bogus-money charges was commuted by President Roosevelt
in 1908, was a political-criminal leader to be reckoned with. His base
of support, on Chicago's Near West Side, included Italian fraternal organizations and labor unions. In early 1908 Boston was flooded with
bogus silver coins, mostly dimes and half-dollars, that the local office
of the Secret Service determined were the product of an Italian group
of counterfeiters dubbed "The North End Gang" by the newspapers,
since most of the money appeared in the Italian district located in the
city's North End.[30]

Counterfeiting continued unabated into the second decade of the
twentieth century. In New Orleans, a gang led by Sam Geraci plied a
lucrative trade producing and distributing bogus money under the legal
cover of his fruit and vegetable peddler license until his arrest in

18. New Orleans Police Department mug shot of local counterfeiter Sam Geraci. (In author's possession)

March 1914. Counterfeiting did not disappear after the passage of the
Volstead Act. Like other criminal specialists, counterfeiters found
their skills in demand during the prohibition period. During the 1920s
they turned their talents to faking liquor labels, an activity that generally elicited little more than mild concern from police officers.[31]

Gambling, which since the 1930s has been the largest single source
of income for the nation's crime syndicates, brought immense profits
before prohibition. Organized gambling had its origins in the 1850s
and 1860s. John ("Old Smoke") Morrissey, who played an important role in professionalizing gambling operations in both New
York and New Orleans during the 1850s, in the following decade
showed how to use organization, political allies, and large outlays of
money to short-circuit the efforts of reformers. In 1867 the Anti-
Gambling Society of New York staged successful raids on several of
the city's "better" gambling houses. Morrissey arranged and commanded the counterattack. The city's gamblers contributed money,
and Morrissey "prudently doled [it] out to the special agents of the
reformers and the police," in the words of Henry Chafetz. "For some
years there were no further raids." It was Morrissey's policy to collect
"substantial tribute money" from gambling-house proprietors before
each election. Although some of this money stuck to the fingers of
Morrissey and his politician friends, most of it collected in the Tammany campaign fund, where it bought protection for the gambling interests from machine-controlled police. Morrissey's political career
and his gambling career complemented each other, as Herbert Asbury
has demonstrated, and each made the other possible. "Old Smoke was
the most powerful gambler of his time because he used his political
strength to dominate and levy tribute upon his fellow-gamesters."
Conversely, he was "politically important for so many years because
of the great following he had acquired as a gambler and a prize
fighter." By 1870, as Chafetz has noted, Morrissey "held a position
almost equal to that of Boss Tweed and Honest John Kelly." [32]

The concern of reformers over the widespread gambling and the
bribing of police officers to permit these operations formed the subject
of an investigation and exposé in New Orleans by the city press in

May 1870. This investigation, far from eliminating the problem, entrenched it by making the gamblers even more dependent upon the goodwill of the guardians of the law. By this time at least, a formalized system apparently existed in New Orleans whereby the gambling interests pooled their resources to provide sufficient cash to satisfy police officers at all levels, from patrolmen to commissioners. Thus a New Orleans *Times* editorial of June 9, 1870, complained that "this is the day set aside every month by the Metropolitan Board of Police for collection of its $1400 blackmail, in return for which it grants immunity and support to the gamblers." The paper also described an additional problem that frustrated efforts in New Orleans (and other cities) to deal with gambling and other forms of "victimless" crime: the connivance and cooperation of politicians. "As not the least notice has been taken of the exposé made recently, it is to be now taken for granted that both the State and city administration endorse the outrage as regular."

A similar situation existed at about the same time in Chicago, with the added dimension of capable leadership that made the most of every opportunity. Chicago's syndicate crime first appeared in the 1870s. In the years before the Great Fire, gambling dens operated openly with police protection, some of them twenty-four hours a day. Joseph Medill, elected mayor in 1871 on a "Let's rebuild Chicago" platform, openly fought gamblers, liquor interests, and the criminal elements of the city. Michael Cassius McDonald, Harry ("Prince Hal") Varnell, the Hankins brothers, and other prominent Clark Street gamblers retaliated by organizing the underworld for political action, and they succeeded in electing Harvey D. Colvin mayor in 1873. The gambler-supported candidate went down to defeat in 1876, but this setback proved to be temporary. With Carter Henry Harrison's mayoral success in 1879, the gambling interests regained their influence at city hall. In the 1880s McDonald, Varnell, and the Hankins brothers developed a highly profitable bookmaking syndicate that soon monopolized gambling at the Chicago and Indiana race tracks.[33]

By the turn of the century most of the early leaders either had retired, died, or moved on to seek opportunities elsewhere, but police-

and-politician-protected syndicate gambling still flourished in the city. Mont Tennes gave orders on the North Side and Alderman Johnny Rogers on the West Side. James O'Leary reigned, in John Landesco's words, as "the chief gambler on the South Side." First Ward political bosses Kenna and Coughlin, together with Tom McGinnis, Pat O'Malley, and John F. O'Malley, controlled the gambling houses and handbooks located in the Loop, Chicago's business district. At this time, with his network of hundreds of small handbook agencies, Tennes was "the most extensive gambling operator in Chicago" with the exception of O'Leary. Tennes then gained control of the wires carrying racing news from the race tracks; this control made possible the operation of an illegal handbook syndicate behind the legitimate front as a racing news-distribution service. As a result, by 1909 Tennes was "in absolute control of race track gambling and handbooks in Chicago," a position he enjoyed until the reform administration of William E. Dever in 1923 closed two hundred downtown handbook "joints" that produced for Tennes an estimated $364,000 per year. At this time Tennes's gambling operations were concentrated in the Loop, and the city administration's actions forced his retirement from race-track gambling. Tennes retained control of the wire service and continued in the following years to sell his service to handbook operations run by the Torrio-Capone organization as well as those of its chief rival, the North Side mob.[34]

Prior to prohibition, Italians functioned throughout the nation in big-time or syndicate operations in the larger American community, but in no city did they comprise the dominating force before the 1920s. Gambling, in the form of Italian lottery, was popular in every "Little Italy"; with the exception of New York, however, nowhere was the Southern Italian and Sicilian population sufficiently large and concentrated to make it a worthwhile field for syndicate gangs to fight over. The circumstances surrounding the struggle that took place during the World War I years between Upper East Side Manhattan and Brooklyn-based gangs for monopoly of crime within the Italian community of New York suggest that the Italian criminal experience in that city, although exhibiting many of the characteristics found elsewhere in the nation, was in important respects unique. This uniqueness grew out of the size of Gotham's Italian population, which by 1920 was approximately one million. The high population densities (the highest in the country) in the tenement neighborhoods and the high proportion of recent arrivals from overseas in core-area Italian districts resulted at least in part from New York's role as the nation's principal seaport. This role meant that most Italians who migrated to the United States made at least a short stopover in one of New York's immigrant colonies. In other cities, such as Chicago, Boston, and Cleveland, criminals found it necessary to turn to the wider community for the big money-making opportunities.

The New York Italian colony contained a sizable population and offered rich economic opportunities. As early as 1909 Frank Marshall White stated, on the basis of information provided by the Italian Chamber of Commerce, that "today in New York City alone the estimated material value of the property in the Italian colonies is $120,000,000, aside from $100,000,000 invested by Italians in commerce, $50,000,000 in real estate, and $20,000,000 on deposit in the banks." [35] Hence even before the "Prosperity Decade" following the end of World War I, New York's Italian community offered a lucrative market for illicit activities, particularly gambling and prostitution. It also provided a huge market for products from the homeland and from the West Coast, such as artichokes and olive oil, the distribution of which the criminal elements attempted to control. All of this emerged in what Eric Hobsbawm has termed the second struggle between the *mafia* and the *Camorra* in the United States (the first being, in his view, the Provenzano-Matranga feud in New Orleans). Nicholas Gage maintains that this struggle was "the first major Mafia war, in 1917," against the *Camorra,* "for control of the profitable New York rackets." Gage is mistaken on at least two counts: that the war began in 1917, and that it involved territory and riches outside the Italian community. [36]

A long-simmering feud between East Harlem-based Sicilians and groups of Neapolitans from Brooklyn broke into the open after the assassination of Giosue Gallucci and his son Luca in May 1915. The elder Gallucci, who had migrated from Palermo twenty years before as a poor man, at the time of his death held $350,000 worth of real estate and was reputedly a millionaire. Following Ignazio Saietta's imprisonment on counterfeiting charges in 1909, Gallucci became the undisputed "King of Little Italy," and controlled several small industries, the coal and ice business, cobblers' shops, the olive oil business, and the lottery in the Italian neighborhoods of the city. He maintained a tight hold over these activities until the time of his murder. His position and his various activities were protected, and he gained virtual immunity from the law through his mastery of machine politics. Gallucci, who was also known as "The Boss," headed several political organizations. The New York *Herald* observed on May 18, 1915, "He certainly was the most powerful Italian politically in the city, and during campaigns was exceptionally active." An additional and vitally important result of his successful ventures in local politics, the paper observed, was "a certain measure of immunity from police interference." [37]

His relatively secure position with relation to the police, Tammany Hall, and the outside community was, within the Italian criminal community, precarious. Perhaps the most powerful and influential Italian resident of the city, Gallucci was the frequent recipient of Black Hand threats. He was often shot at and "had been wounded many times." Working for Gallucci provided a precarious way to make a living, as ten murdered bodyguards (too late) discovered. "The Boss" became fatalistic. A week before his assassination he predicted that "I know they will get me yet." The identity of "they" was never officially determined, but the Morello family profited the most by Gallucci's death. It regained the control over the East Harlem criminal empire which it had lost following the federal government's successful prosecution of the Lupo-Morello counterfeiting ring in 1909.

After Gallucci's death, war broke out between the East Harlem and Brooklyn gangs for control of the businesses and illegal enterprises that had constituted the realm of the "King of Little Italy." These became the spoils of war. The competing groups were the Morello (or East Harlem) gang, composed of men of Sicilian birth or parentage, and the largely Neapolitan Navy Street gang and its ally, the Coney Island gang. The East Harlem leaders were Nicholas and Vincent Morello, their half-brother Ciro Terranova, Charles Ubriaco, Giuseppe Verrazano, and Steve La Salle. A brother-in-law of the Morello and Terranova brothers, Ignazio Saietta organized and led the gang before his sentencing in 1909 to a thirty-year term in federal penitentiary on counterfeiting charges.[38]

The Navy Street gang leaders were Alessandrio Vollero, Eugenio Bizzaro, Andrea Ricci, and Leopoldo Lauritano. Pellegrino Morano bossed the Coney Islanders from his restaurant, the Santa Lucia. The gang's meeting place and base of operations was a coffee house owned by Vollero and Lauritano at 113 Navy Street. Although they were reputedly successful cocaine procurers and dealers, they and the other Navy Street leaders decided to expand their criminal activities in order to take advantage of the lush monetary opportunities offered by New York City's huge Italian population. Specifically, they wanted to take over the artichoke business, betting on the Italian lottery, the numerous and lucrative *zicchinetta* games (this was a card game), and the coal and ice business in Italian neighborhoods. In the process they challenged the East Harlem Sicilians, who had controlled these activities for years.

The struggle continued into 1916, with casualties on both sides. During the summer of 1916, the Neapolitans decided upon a bold move, one that they believed would eliminate the enemy leadership and assure their control of Gallucci's former empire. The plan, worked out in a series of meetings over a three-week period between August 15 and the day of the murder, was to lure the Morello gang chieftains to a peace conference at the Navy Street coffee house. September 7 was the day decided upon to carry out the plan. Although the Neapolitans hoped to kill all the rival leaders at one time and place, only two of them, Nicholas Morello and Charles Ubriaco, arrived. They were murdered a short distance from the designated meeting place on Navy Street.

During the following weeks, the Brooklyn gang tried to eliminate the other East Harlem leaders, but they were only partially successful.

On October 6 Verrazano, a gambling kingpin known in the under-world as "The Big Man," was shot and killed while sitting at a table in the Occidental Restaurant at 341 Broome Street in Manhattan. Steve La Salle, in prison during the autumn months of 1916, was safe for the time, since no Vollero gang members or friends were in that prison. In November 1916 the Navy Street leaders made unsuccessful efforts to arrange the murder of the remaining Morellos. The Morellos kept close to their East 116th Street home, and attempts to flush them out or to rent a room across the street (from which to shoot at them) failed.

In the meantime, with the opposition leadership either dead, in prison, or in hiding, Vollero and his associates moved in on the Morello operations. The Brooklyn gang looked forward to obtaining the equivalent of a gold mine. The returns they actually gained, while substantial, did not reach their expectations. In their efforts to control the city's artichoke business, they learned that the dealers did not readily accept new masters. An initial effort to establish a monopoly over the artichoke trade in Brooklyn failed when wholesale dealers refused to give in to threats from the Vollero gang. The Navy Streeters abandoned this plan and decided to settle for a portion of the artichoke dealers' profits. They demanded that the wholesalers pay the gang $50 for each carload of artichokes to arrive in the city (most of them came from California). The dealers responded that this amount was much more than they could afford; they countered with an offer of $15 per carload. A compromise of $25 was finally reached. Even at this figure the Volleros were unable to bring all the dealers into line.

Italian gamblers in the city also resisted monetary demands of the Navy Street gang. Coal and ice dealers proved to be recalcitrant. As with the artichoke venture, results in these enterprises were mixed, and the money extorted in every case was far below the gang's expectations. Although the bosses may have done better, ordinary gang members did not grow rich from the new sources of income. As the prosecuting attorney disclosed at the trial of Alessandrio Vollero, married gang members received a flat rate of $20 a week; single men received $10. "Members of the gang who just did odd jobs, and did not work regularly on these different jobs that they were sent out to do, would get seven dollars a week and different sums of money." These wages continued until the spring of 1917. At that time the Navy Street leaders and several gang members were arrested for the Morello and Ubriaco murders.

The arrests came as a great shock, for although the murder had been carried out in the open during the day, Vollero and his associates had little fear of the police. Not only did they pay graft to various members of the force, but also they believed that no trouble with the law could befall them in their own territory. Vollero was quoted as saying, "The police cannot get any witness down there where we are. We can take care of the witnesses down there, we can get witnesses to prove anything we want down there, and they dare not come forward to testify against me." For months this confidence seemed justified, but in the spring of 1917 a grand jury in Brooklyn returned indictments against Vollero and his associates. At that time the authorities and the grand jury received information that a Navy Street gang member named Ralph Daniello had been picked up by the police in Nevada, where he was in hiding, and was being returned to New York. Daniello, whose role in the case had been unknown to the police up to this point, turned out to be the central figure in solving the murder. Although he was only an ordinary gang member, Daniello had been present at all the conferences leading up to the Morello and Ubriaco murders and had participated in the Manhatten killing of Verrazano. Daniello decided to tell all, thereby destroying the hopes and plans of the Navy Streeters. At the same time, he strengthened the Morello control of Italian-colony crime.

During the trial several of the Brooklyn criminals used the name "Camorra" to describe the Navy Street and Coney Island gangs, and "Mafia" to identify their Manhattan rivals. The so-called "Code of Silence" did not function in this trial. Daniello and other gang members freely revealed the inner secrets of their organizations. A member of the Coney Island faction, Tony Notaro, even described the gang's initiation rites. Although the gangs did not function as effectively as the stories of the *mafia* and *Camorra* would indicate, some carryovers from Sicily and Naples operated in New York. They did so both because of the vast potential market provided by Southern Italian residents in that city, and the huge pool of manpower for gangs composed of members from specific provinces in the homeland. Even these gangs, it must be noted, represented an expansion of attitudes in the homeland, where criminals in one town or rural district looked with suspicion on their fellows from neighboring towns and provinces. In addition, not all the Southern Italian criminals in New York continued to operate in bands composed entirely of Sicilians or Neapolitans. Others, among these the more ambitious and aggressive younger men like Luciano and Torrio, functioned well in the larger, more challenging, and more lucrative non-Italian gangs, in the company of Jews, Irish, and other ethnic groups. In many cases, young Italian gangsters preferred to operate outside the ethnic community.

The factors that made possible the large Neapolitan and Sicilian gangs of New York did not exist in sufficient strength in any other part of the country. There were, indeed, "Mafia" gangs in other cities, but these were pale imitations of the New York groups, which themselves were not the omnipotent organizations that journalists and gang members pictured them to be. In Chicago, which ranked second to New York in the size of its Italian population, Anthony D'Andrea (identified by Nicola Gentile as the city's *Capo Mafioso*) was singularly unsuccessful in bending the city's Italians to his will, and specifically in using them to further his own political ambitions. Gentile, himself a prominent Italian-American crime figure in Pittsburgh, Cleveland, New York City, and Kansas City for more than twenty years prior to 1937 (when he fled the country to escape a prison sentence for drug charges), lived in Chicago during 1919 and 1920, the years when D'Andrea's power was at its height.[39]

In his autobiography, Zio (Uncle) Cola Gentile recalled D'Andrea as a man "so savage and so fierce" that he was "greatly feared in all the United States." This description, while an accurate assessment of his standing among fellow "Mafiosi," is ironic because D'Andrea was at this time in the midst of a violent struggle—which he lost, along with his life—against the Irish machine boss, John Powers. The con-

19. Chicago Italian-colony political-criminal leader Anthony D'Andrea prior to his murder in 1921. (Chicago *Tribune* Photo)

test arose over control of Chicago's Nineteenth Ward, which contained the city's largest Italian colony. Powers gained dominance over the ward in the early 1890s, when its population consisted chiefly of Germans and Irish. Over the years the ethnic composition of the ward changed as earlier residents moved away, to be replaced by Italians and Eastern European Jews. By 1920 the ward was largely Italian. D'Andrea, who had built a powerful base of support through his position as business agent for the Sewer and Tunnel Miners' Union, president of the Hod Carriers' and Laborers' local, and president of the *Unione Siciliana* (the largest, most influential Italian fraternal group in the city), organized and directed an Italian revolt against the Irish ward boss. In a series of confrontations beginning in 1915, D'Andrea challenged Powers's position. The struggle culminated in 1921 in a violent aldermanic campaign between the two men. Gangs terrorized ward residents, threatened and carried out bombings and muggings, made charges and countercharges. The contest ended with Powers's victory over the Italian. Significantly, and contrary to the myth of "Mafia" power and invulnerability, not even a *Capo* with the alleged strength and influence of D'Andrea could win political office when faced by a man of equal cunning, ruthlessness, and power. Recognition as an ac-

knowledged "Mafia" chieftain was no guarantee in itself of electoral
success even in a ward where 70 per cent of the voters were Italian. In
the test of strength, D'Andrea failed to control the Italian vote, receiving 3,603 votes to Powers's 3,984. He died from a gunshot blast less
than three months after his defeat.[40]

D'Andrea's successor as *Capo*, Michael Merlo, remained in the
background and, until his death (from natural causes) in 1924, was said
to be a powerful figure in Chicago machine politics as well as in
crime. There is no way to verify this belief, since Merlo, unlike
D'Andrea, purposely kept himself as a shadowy and enigmatic per-
sonage; he operated behind the scenes and carefully cultivated his
image as a powerful, all-knowing leader of his people. He nurtured,
that is, the image of a *mafia* leader in Sicily. In the United States,
however, this image would not stand the test of an electoral campaign,
and Merlo, unlike D'Andrea, was realistic enough to recognize the
fact.

"Mafia" leaders exerted a great deal of power and influence in the
Southern Italian communities of American cities. They found it un-
wise to venture outside or to attempt to master American urban politics
or urban crime. Although they provided very useful manpower and,
during prohibition, reaped huge profits through this manpower, they
did not provide leadership outside their colonies. As we shall see in
Chapters 6 and 7, leadership for the struggle during the 1920s and
1930s to take over American entrepreneurial crime came from the second generation, either those born in the United States or those who arrived as children and hence grew up in the American urban environment.

Every city with a Southern Italian population contained a "Mafia"
feeding off the common laborer's honest toil and claiming to serve as
a means of easing adjustment to American society. With rare exceptions (most of which were in New York), none of these had been a
member of the Sicilian *mafia* or a similar organization in the Italian
South before he left the homeland.

It was understandable that criminals in Italian-American neighborhoods would try to re-create familiar institutions, just as their more

law-abiding counterparts attempted to establish homeland institutions through mutual benefit societies and newspapers. It proved impossible to reproduce homeland institutions exactly; subtly and often unrecognized by the criminals themselves, the patterns and character of the institutions—in this case, criminal organizations—were altered by conditions, opportunities, and limitations present in the new environment. In the process, the illegal organizations became combinations of the familiar Old World models adapted to New World needs. Despite what the criminals themselves claimed, and what contemporary and more recent observers have accepted almost without question, the pre-prohibition era immigrant area *"Capos"* and the "Mafia" did not have the prestige and influence in American cities that the original models enjoyed in the Old World villages. Even in relatively isolated western Pennsylvania mining towns, the criminal societies lacked the vitality and strength of homeland counterparts.

In Hillsville, New Castle, and other mining towns in Mahoning Valley of western Pennsylvania, the "Mafia"-like organizations (called "the Society" by members) were divided into branches, each of which had a head man and a second man who were elected by the majority of the membership, and could also be removed from office at any time. The chief concern of the group appears to have been to increase the membership. Everyone from the leaders to the lowliest members talked openly and readily to strangers about the innermost secrets of the Society—hence the Pinkerton agents' fund of knowledge. Not only did members work hard to increase the membership; they applied heavy pressure to potential members. The major reason for this membership drive was the initiation fee, which was not a fixed amount; the soliciting member determined the figure, and then split the fee with the head man. The initiate knew that he also could profit by obtaining new members. Members therefore applied pressure on potential members. "There are very few who refuse to join," states a Pinkerton report, "and those who do refuse understand it is necessary to move from the district." [41]

Membership, however, did not mean safety from extortion, as Dominick Tuttino, a New Castle restauranteur, discovered. In June

1907 Tuttino was tried by the Society and found guilty of certain transgressions. As a result, his standing in the Society was reduced. He indicated his anxiety to do whatever was necessary "to get in good standing" once again. Pinkerton Agent 89 viewed the events as "simply another scheme on the part of the leaders of the Society at New Castle to blackmail Tuttino of some more money." Apparently they had already extracted more than $2,000 from the man and, "as they know he has money, they will continue reducing him and later on elevating him in the Society, until they get the bulk, if not all, of his money from him." The agent assumed that Tony Pancalli, head man at New Castle, had ordered the extortion, but a later communication negated that assumption. Pancalli complained to the Pinkerton man that he could do nothing, "for Joe Catrone reduced Tuttino; that Joe Catrone, Trepepi, Lofare, Juti and others are the gang and everyone is afraid of them, and what they want to do is all right." The head man's power lay in his ability to control the members of his gang and to direct their activities and desires. Pancalli discovered that, until he could establish his domination over the organization, a head man could not go against the will of the powerful members of the Society if he hoped to remain in office. Members could vote an unpopular and weak leader out of office, as Mike Portoghese was reduced in rank and replaced by Sam Esposito as head man by the Sharon (Pennsylvania) Society membership in June 1907.

Whether in rural western Pennsylvania or a major urban center like New York, Chicago, or San Francisco, "Mafia" organizations served important social as well as financial functions. The group provided a sense of belonging and of security in numbers. This function was achieved at least in part through the use of initiation ceremonies, passwords and rituals, and rules of conduct with which members must abide. In addition (and like the Old World models), the groups were run (in theory, at least) along democratic lines, each member having a voice in specifying the (illegal) activities of the organization and also a vote in the election of leaders. In practice, shrewd, effective and ruthless *Capos* and others in the gang's hierarchy, once entrenched, came to view their positions as permanent and not subject to the whims of an electorate. Over time, subordinates also came to share this view. Rank-and-file members accepted their lot as inferiors, at least in part because of economic realities: whether in New York, Chicago, or Hillsville, Pennsylvania, they received fixed weekly or monthly wages, with the promise that when they got into trouble with the law, the organization would look after them, providing also for the needs of their families. In this respect, the "Mafias" bore some resemblance to legitimate fraternal insurance societies. Yet these "Mafias," unlike legitimate fraternal insurance organizations, were criminal gangs composed of vicious men who did not hesitate to employ any means necessary, including murder, to get what they wanted. Moreover, the wages that these members received to pay for the needs of their families came from illegal activities of the organization and its members.[42]

While the rank and file received fixed amounts, the leaders took percentages; a leader's share was based on all the group's activities. Any money that a member might make on his own initiative from an illegal venture had to be shared with the leader. Thus, as the gang's operations became more lucrative, the leader's income became ever larger. As the bosses became wealthier, the followers became more deferential and dependent on their largesse. The home-brewing industry during prohibition increased the income of the leaders far beyond anything enjoyed before and also widened the gap between them and their followers. This gap also made the leaders somewhat vulnerable when they were challenged in the late 1920s and early 1930s by the "American" (second generation) criminals.

For the second generation—the younger men who decided, even in the decades before 1920, to pursue criminal careers outside the colony in the American underworld—concern with the social wellbeing of members was old-fashioned and simply irrelevant. Part of their adjustment to American values became an effort to apply certain big-business practices—such as efficiency, specialization, monopoly through elimination of competitors—to the conduct of criminal activities. Thus the syndicates developed by John Torrio, Charles Luciano, and their associates and contemporaries placed an emphasis on eco-

nomic or monetary factors rather than on social values. Common
sense, however, dictated that they not move too fast. Thus, when
Luciano eliminated Salvatore Maranzano, the last of the New York
"Mafia" overlords, in September 1931, his objective was to rationalize proceedings and organize crime as an efficient business operation.
Luciano was careful, however, not to change things greatly at first; nor
did he move quickly, in order that the Old World types still in the organization would continue to feel comfortable with him as the new
overlord.

The turning point in the development of the powerful business-like
Italian-American syndicates in New York, Chicago, Denver, and other
cities came with the passage of the Eighteenth Amendment. And the
syndicates were ready. . . .

PART 3

FLOWERING OF THE ITALIAN SYNDICATES

❦ 6 ❦

Prohibition: Consolidation of the Syndicates

On January 16, 1920, the Eighteenth Amendment and the Prohibition Enforcement Act (Volstead Act) went into effect, forbidding "the manufacture, sale or transportation of intoxicating liquors" for beverage purposes, and granting to the Congress and the states the concurrent power to enact enforcement laws. (The personal possession or use of such beverages was not prohibited; hence, although the supplier was subject to legal action, a consumer who wanted a drink and could pay for it was free to indulge.) This legislation brought to fruition a series of successes by anti-saloon and anti-liquor forces during the first two decades of the twentieth century—the so-called progressive period—although anti-saloon and anti-liquor sentiment had been an integral part of urban reform sentiment since at least the 1870s.

Contemporary writers presented the struggle to outlaw the liquor trade during the years to 1920 as a rural *versus* urban confrontation, but this view does not give the whole story, and perhaps not even its most important aspects. Prohibition, in fact, formed an important element of the urban progressive mentality, and found its strongest urban support in peripheral areas of cities and in the suburbs—that is, in the middle-class neighborhoods. Indeed, it was essential to reformers to regain control over the city's core area, with its heavily immigrant population, and to defeat the corrupt political machine, which brazenly used the immigrant vote to remain in power. Most urban reformers believed—often correctly—that the ward boss, corrupt politics, and the saloon were bound up together. The most effective way to smash the boss system, therefore, seemed to be through the destruction of his base of operation and support, the saloon.[1]

Reformers hoped, through their program of enforced abstinence from alcohol, to uplift the lower classes, to make working men more moral (many perceived a connection between prostitution and alcohol), to improve the racial stock, and to increase industrial efficiency. Social workers, women's groups, and other reformers of the period maintained that drink was the major cause of poverty, and made much of the widely-held belief that, in cities where prohibition had been adopted (Denver, Spokane, and Des Moines, for example), social problems seemed to decline.[2]

After the turn of the century, a number of cities had moved in the direction of prohibition by designating "no license" areas—areas where saloons, beer gardens, breweries, and distilleries were prohibited—usually in the middle-class sections of town. The core remained unswervingly loyal to the saloon. This arrangement guaranteed the availability of alcoholic beverages for affluent adults who wanted them, but removed from their children the temptation occasioned by liquor stores or saloons. The problem of saloons in the central city therefore remained. The poorer classes were still subject to temptation and, according to the middle class, needed to be saved, whether or not they wanted redemption. The Eighteenth Amendment took care of this problem.[3]

Members of the working class might not be able to afford the price of bootleg booze during the 1920s, although middle- and upper-income consumers certainly could. Thus middle-class support of prohibition during the progressive era seems ironic in retrospect, since the most damaging blows to the Eighteenth Amendment were dealt by a segment of the same middle class. Through an open contempt for the law, a flaunting of the Amendment in the name of personal liberty, this segment undermined authority and indicated that one should obey laws only when it is personally convenient to do so.

Unrecognized or down-played by reformers was the fact that the passage of legislation comprised only the first step in making America dry. Of at least equal importance were the official machinery created for enforcement, and public willingness to comply with the laws. A major source of future frustration and controversy was the joint sharing of enforcement responsibility between the federal government and the states, which resulted in a long legal battle between Washington and the State houses. In addition, the use of the term "intoxicating" rather than "alcoholic" affected numerous court cases brought to trial under provisions of the law, since it was more difficult to prove intoxication, as defined by the Volstead Act, than the presence of alcohol.

The Volstead Act, named after Congressman Andrew Volstead of Minnesota but apparently written in large part by the Anti-Saloon League's general counsel, Wayne B. Wheeler, fleshed out the Amendment by defining "intoxicating" liquor (one-half of 1 per cent of alcohol by volume) and by authorizing machinery for the enforcement of the law. Thus, the continued manufacture and sale of alcoholic liquor was authorized for industrial, medical, and sacramental purposes. The production of light wine and cider at home was permitted. Observers maintained that these provisions (as intended by supporters) provided for the continued drinking habits of rural dwellers and at the same time protected city workers from temptation. Beer, the beverage supposedly preferred by urbanites, was prohibited under the law, although the manufacture of a terrible-tasting and non-intoxicating drink (called "near-beer") with an alcoholic content up to one-half of 1 per cent was allowed. A federal enforcement unit, the Prohibition Bureau, was established, with the responsibility of regulating the legitimate use of alcohol and of preventing violations of the law. Violators faced a maximum fine of $1,000 and six months in jail for a first offense. For second offenders the penalties included fines of not less than $200 nor more than $2,000, and jail sentences of not less than one month nor more than five years. Persons found guilty also faced the loss of personal property. Thus automobiles, airplanes, and boats used for the illegal transportation of liquor could be seized and sold at public auction to help pay the cost of enforcing the law, and bars and other places used to sell alcoholic beverages could be padlocked by court injunction for the period of one year.[4]

Although the Volstead Act set up strict guidelines, the machinery created to enforce the law was totally inadequate. Effective enforcement would have required an army of dedicated public servants. Instead, as Prohibition Commissioner Roy A. Haynes recorded in 1923, the maximum number of employees in the Prohibition Unit during its first two years was 3,996, including an office staff of more than 700 in Washington. Thus the force in the field during these crucial early years when the pattern of enforcement was set did not exceed 3,300 agents to police a population, in 1920, of nearly 106 million people. The manner of recruitment of Prohibition Unit agents further hindered effective enforcement. Instead of being selected on the basis of merit and under the provisions and protection of Civil Service regulations, these agents were political appointees, many chosen or recommended by machine politicians who themselves had little interest in the proper enforcement of a law that most of them opposed on general principle and personal preference. (Their followers, most of them of immigrant background, had, of course, always opposed prohibition.) [5]

Progressive-era reformers had not anticipated still another basic problem when they pushed prohibition legislation through the states and finally the House and Senate. The general public's craving for alcoholic beverages did not disappear just because alcohol was not readily available; indeed, the drinking of liquor and beer became more popular than it had ever been before, particularly among the younger members of the middle class and among newly liberated women. Largely because it was something frowned on by society, a flaunting of convention—and relatively safe, since the law did not make it a crime to purchase or consume liquor, only to produce or sell it—frequenting a speakeasy and drinking bootleg "booze" became for many a symbol of independence.

The legislation had been intended, at least in part, to help those of the working class who, reformers believed, had little control over their appetites or their ability to resist temptation. Although the evidence is not complete on this point, it appears that prohibition did slightly curb working-class drinking. One objective of reformers became realized:

20. Al Capone (*right*) during a 1926 court appearance in Chicago. To many
Americans Capone symbolized the lawless era that grew out of passage of the
Eighteenth Amendment. (Courtesy Chicago Historical Society)

the old-time saloon, the working man's social club of the pre-World
War I decades, disappeared.[6]

But while blue-collar workers were apparently consuming less alcohol than before, a large number of the middle and upper classes were
behaving in ways previously identified with "lower-class" conduct.
For years before prohibition there had been speakeasies (or unlicensed
saloons), where liquor of inferior quality was sold to the dregs of the
poorer class. During the 1920s the financially solvent, not the poor,
frequented speakeasies, and drank their liquor fresh out of the bath-
tub.

Members of the working class and particularly those of immigrant
background benefited from prohibition in ways never anticipated by
reformers. Someone had to produce and distribute the alcohol, which
was still consumed in large volume. Many ethnics and their offspring

were willing to pay the price of possible imprisonment, personal injury, and even death in order to reap the money to be gained from supplying the public—that is, the middle and upper classes—with what it wanted, in contrast to what in the pre-war years it had proclaimed that it wanted.

One of the major tragedies and unanticipated consequences of "the noble experiment" was that it opened the way to the full flowering of entrepreneurial crime in America, under the guidance of ambitious younger ethnic-group members, a flowering that was aided and encouraged by the "better classes." The emergence of bootlegging gangs should have caused little surprise because bootlegging had existed in dry states before the enactment of national prohibition. In Denver, to illustrate, many Italians and other ethnics—the men who would become conspicuous local gangland figures during the 1920s—developed a market and tested techniques during the six years after 1914, when Colorado became a dry state. In Detroit, Italian gangs were actively bootlegging at least as early as 1919, and by that time were engaged in violent internecine warfare for the lion's share of the illegal liquor market.[7]

In a statement released to the press on January 15, 1920, the Anti-Saloon League of New York observed that "at one minute past midnight tomorrow a new nation will be born." It predicted that "to-night John Barleycorn makes his last will and testament. Now for an era of clean thinking and clean living! The Anti-Saloon League wishes every man, woman and child a happy Dry Year." This optimistic outlook died almost immediately. Within hours after John Barleycorn was supposedly laid to rest in the United States, Volstead Act violations were reported in New York, Chicago, Des Moines, Detroit, Peoria, and other cities, large and small, across the nation. Within days police departments were carrying out raids in an effort to break up budding bootlegging gangs and to end the emerging, and highly profitable, traffic in illicit alcohol. Dry laws or not, Americans wanted their drinks, and were ready to do business with anyone who could supply them.[8]

The network of contacts with police, politicians, and members of the

21. The huge profits to be made from bootlegging led to gang warfare and a typical prohibition-era scene—the gangster funeral, in this case, that of Chicago bootlegger Angelo Genna in 1925. (Courtesy Chicago Historical Society)

legal profession developed during decades of illegal gambling activities, prostitution, and labor racketeering, readily adapted to the new situation. For all involved, violation of the Volstead Act was more acceptable to the public, as well as "cleaner," than prostitution or the narcotics traffic. Much of the general public accepted and condoned law-breaking when it involved the manufacture and distribution of liquor and beer. Even the murder and maiming of rival gang members in the scramble to create monopolies and gain larger profits seemed, to many Americans, to be a modern version of the old Wild West shootout; such events stirred remarkably little anger or dismay. The professional and private activities of gang leaders like Al Capone, "Legs" Diamond, "Dutch" Schultz, Frank Yale, and Hyman Abrams became front-page items in the newspapers. A thrill-seeking public enjoyed vicariously the sensational, luxurious, and dangerous lives of the "booze Barons" as a respite from ordinary lives as dishwashers, bookkeepers, dentists, teachers. Only when non-combatants, especially children, were shot or killed did public opinion demand action against the gangsters.

Such a situation developed in New York in 1931. A former Dutch Schultz gunman, Vincent ("The Mad Mick") Coll, decided to go into business for himself as a hijacker of beer trucks belonging to his ex-boss. On July 28, 1931, Coll and his ethnically mixed gang (which included Italians) went machine-gunning for Joey Rao along East 107th Street in East Harlem. They did not kill any of the Rao group, but they hit four children playing in the street, instantly killing five-year-old Michael Vengali and seriously wounding three-year-old Michael Bevilacqua; the other two received minor bullet wounds. The press instantly labeled Coll "the baby killer." Fellow gangsters, the public, and the authorities viewed him as a mad animal. After the Vengali killing, Coll began kidnapping gangsters for ransom and murdering others for pleasure. The underworld reportedly placed a price of $50,000 on his head, a move dictated by its own interests. All the gangs in the city hunted for the killer, and finally Schultz's men tracked him down and machine-gunned him to death while he was talking in a telephone booth in a 23rd Street drugstore. In this instance as in others, attention soon shifted to other problems. Public indignation and outrage cooled, and the gansters re-emerged to flaunt their power, wealth, and political influence.[9]

Illicit alcohol provided the principal underpinning and major source of income for crime groups from 1920 until the repeal of the prohibition amendment in 1933. It is impossible to determine precisely how much money syndicate criminals made from the manufacture, transportation, and sale of liquor and beer during these years, but from Internal Revenue Service and Prohibition Bureau records it is clear that liquor income ran into hundreds of millions of dollars. According to a 1925 Department of Commerce report, smuggling alone brought in $40 million a year, and this estimate was admittedly "low." The Torrio-Capone organization of Chicago during the late 1920s and early 1930s showed an annual gross from beer and other alcoholic beverages of at least $60 million and perhaps as much as $240 million.[10]

Criminal syndicates obtained their supplies from a number of sources. One, medicinal liquor, comprised, as Charles Merz noted, "the least important source but the most obvious." Since the Eighteenth Amendment permitted the use of liquor for medicinal purposes, doctors could prescribe and druggists could dispense intoxicating liquors. By July 3, 1920, before prohibition was six months old, more than 15,000 physicians and 57,000 pharmacists had applied for the license to prescribe and dispense liquor. Many of these men were honest and attempted to obey the law. Others—numbering in the thousands—welcomed the wording of the amendment as an opportunity to collect a windfall.[11]

A major source of alcohol during the early years of prohibition was the stock of liquor on hand in warehouses at the time the Volstead Act went into effect. Like other means used to obtain alcohol, the "burglarizing" of liquor warehouses occurred very early in the game. Just hours after the Volstead Act went into effect, prohibition officials in Peoria reported the first arrests growing out of enforcement of the new law. At two o'clock in the morning on January 17, 1920, Internal Revenue and Prohibition Bureau agents "pounced on two truckloads of whisky which were being removed from a warehouse by 'burglars.' " The warehouse was owned by Woolner & Co., "formerly one of the foremost distillers in the country." Prohibition officers also reported a discovery that would prove to be part of the pattern in this form of obtaining liquor illegally: officials of the distillery owning the warehouse were implicated in the robbery.[12]

During the initial period, some pre-prohibition brewery owners likewise conspired with criminal interests to violate the law. Thus, in November 1924 the Chicago press reported that John Torrio's silent partner in his bootlegging enterprises was a leading brewer in the city, Joseph Stenson, who lived at 1218 North Astor Street on Chicago's fashionable Gold Coast. As the Chicago *Daily News* stated, Stenson's earnings from "the syndicated beer 'racket' he works under political protection, have been reckoned at $12 million a year since 1920. Nobody has ever risked a guess at the clearings of the many-sided Torrio." [13]

Other brewery owners employed underworld leaders as "fronts" while continuing to operate their companies in apparent compliance with legislation prohibiting the manufacture of alcoholic beverages for general consumption. In short order the criminal elements took control—at least in part because of the unwillingness of legitimate owners to continue their involvement when police enforcement became more effective and the prospect of jail terms more likely.[14]

The production of illegal beer became a huge business. Between 1920 and 1933 in Detroit alone, local and federal officials raided one thousand illegal brewery operations and "poured nearly three million gallons of mash down the city's sewers." Brewers who had never come under gangster influence as well as those with criminal connections found themselves sorely tempted to circumvent the law. Cereal beverage plants (as breweries were called) were prohibited by the Volstead Act from producing beer containing more than one-half of 1 per cent of alcohol. The process by which this "near-beer" was made, however, required the prior manufacture of the genuine pre-prohibition product. Hence the entire process by which genuine beer with an alcoholic content of 3 to 4 per cent was produced had to be followed to completion; the product was then de-alcoholized until it reached the legal limit. This process provided excellent opportunities for bootleggers and dishonest brewery owners to siphon off quantities of beer before it went through the final stage of de-alcoholization. Even after the legal produce had left the brewery, it could be altered to become a more potent beverage. It was, in fact a common practice of "less scrupulous breweries" (as Charles Merz labeled them) to supply distributors with alcohol which could be "shot" or "needled" into the near-beer after it had passed government inspection and was on its way to a thirsty public.[15]

America's wine drinkers had no difficulty satisfying their thirst during prohibition. As early as 1920 those who could not or would not manufacture their own wine at home could buy a "harmless grape jelly" placed on the market by the California Wine Association. By adding water, the purchaser could make this jelly into a wine beverage. By 1931 with the introduction of Vine-Glo, produced by a grape growers' cooperative named Fruit Industries, Inc., California wine producers apparently felt secure enough to adopt a bold, hard-sell argument. According to Vine-Glo advertisements,

> Now is the time to order your supply of *Vine-Glo*. It can be made in your house in sixty days—a fine, true-to-type guaranteed beverage ready for the Holiday Season.
>
> *Vine-Glo* . . . comes to you in nine varieties, Port, Virginia Dare, Muscatel, Angelica, Tokay, Sauterne, Riesling, Claret and Burgundy. It is entirely legal in your home—but it must not be transported.[16]

Prohibition thus gave impetus to the wine industry, which was centered in California. According to Gilman Ostrander, it proved to be "a period of wild prosperity unparalleled in the history of the wine industry." The immigrant populations of the nation's large cities apparently consumed most of the wine grapes. Home production of wine reached a huge volume and was "the one branch of the bootleg trade which remained in the hands of small businessmen." Because it produced an immigrant-group beverage that did not have wide appeal among members of the larger American community, wine-making did not attract the attention of criminal entrepreneurs.[17]

An example of entrepreneurship that strongly attracted the syndicates involved the conversion of alcohol produced for industrial purposes. The onset of prohibition coincided with the rapid expansion of the chemical industry. Under provisions of the Volstead Act, alcohol could be produced for industrial use in the preparation of photographic film, smokeless powder, and hundreds of other products. Production of denatured alcohol expanded from 7 million gallons in 1910 to 28 million gallons ten years later. During the 1920s this figure shot up to more than 180 million gallons a year, of which an estimated 50 to 60 million gallons found its way into bootleg channels. After it was doctored and watered, each gallon of industrial alcohol produced three gallons of scotch or gin, "fresh off the boat." To discourage illegal use of industrial alcohol, the government attempted to render the product undrinkable by insisting on the addition of denaturants, some of them poisonous. Unfortunately for many users, bootleggers did not always remove the denaturants. A "drinker beware" attitude evolved, whereby the customer paid a premium price to obtain bootleg booze that might kill him.[18]

Smuggling comprised another source of illicit alcohol. By the late 1920s this activity had been perfected into a big-business operation involving importation of more than 5 million gallons a year. Alcohol purchased from foreign sources was brought in by sea, by air, and by land. Every form of transportation that could be thought of was utilized, including steamships, motor boats, airplanes, automobiles, motorcycles, and in at least one instance a converted World War I German submarine. Smuggling activities flourished along all coasts of the United States, from Maine to Florida, from Florida to Texas, from California to Washington, and across the Canadian and Mexican borders. U.S. Coast Guard Intelligence Division agents reported that, whatever the means employed and regardless of the point of entry, "most of the distilled spirits smuggled into the United States originate in Canadian distilleries." [19]

The American market became, in fact, crucial to the economic wellbeing of the Canadian liquor industry. In 1929, for example, more than 80 per cent of the entire production of the Canadian industry found its way, either directly or indirectly, to the United States. Although consumption of alcohol by Canadians dropped by approximately 50 per cent during the twenties, liquor revenue received by the Canadian government during the same period increased some 400 per cent. Of the decreased amount of alcohol sold to the Canadian drinking public, over 80 per cent arrived from overseas, almost all of it from Great Britain.[20]

One Canadian firm that existed almost exclusively to cater to the tastes of the American drinking public was Consolidated Distilleries, Ltd., a subsidiary of Canadian Industrial Alcohol, Ltd., of Montreal. According to Internal Revenue Service records, Consolidated Distilleries was organized as a Canadian corporation in 1920. It manufactured "American type whiskey, such as Bourbon and Rye, for the American trade and sold it to bootleggers in the United States." Brands included Old Crow, William Penn, and Corby's Special. Consolidated Distilleries employed several representatives (salesmen), who supplied American bootleggers with alcohol. One salesman, Tom Pestolasi, operating out of the British West Indies, sold at least 150,000 gallons (worth more than $2 million) of Consolidated products for the American market between January 1927 and July 1929. This alcohol was smuggled in along the Gulf Coast. Counted among Consolidated's customers was a Boston-based syndicate headed by Mario Ingraffia and Hyman Abrams which dealt with the parent organization in Montreal and not its subsidiary in Nassau. This organization, according to an IRS memorandum, "kept fairly accurate accounts of its business," and "from an examination of its bound sheets, stock records, etc.," agents concluded that during the years 1931 and 1932 "approximately 55,971 gallons worth nearly $800,000 of liquor landed along the New England Coast which was purchased from Consolidated Industries." [21]

The La Penna gang of New York City was another Consolidated Distilleries' customer. According to a confidential Prohibition Bureau report of June 22, 1928, prepared for the Commissioner of Prohibition by Special Agent Eugene R. O'Brien, this gang was "involved on a large scale in the traffic in intoxicating liquors which were being smuggled into the United States from Canada." Like the Ingraffia-Abrams organization in Boston, members of the La Penna "combination" (to use Agent O'Brien's term) came from a number of backgrounds, including Italian, Irish, Jewish, German, and Anglo-Saxon. The gang chieftain, James La Penna of 150 West 50th Street in Manhattan, reputedly a millionaire, had formerly owned a number of cabarets. [22]

La Penna had been an acquaintance of former Chicago syndicate leader John Torrio since the turn of the century, when their rivalry as neighboring saloon owners on James Street in Lower Manhattan and as prize-fight managers developed into a lifelong friendship and intermittent business relation. In 1925 Torrio left Chicago for an extended stay in his native Italy. He apparently returned to the United States and New York in 1927, but few definite facts are known about his activities in the late 1920s. Considering his organizational genius and his long friendship with La Penna, it seems likely (but not certain) that Torrio was associated in the smuggling business with La Penna in 1928, perhaps as the brains and power behind the organization. It is known that the two worked together in the smuggling business in the 1930s, and when Torrio's complicated dealings were unraveled to a degree sufficient to pin something on him, "the Fox" was indicted on charges of income tax evasion. When Torrio was indicted, La Penna was charged as a co-defendant, since their connections were amply documented for the years 1931–35, the period under investigation by the Internal Revenue Service.

During the preceding decade, as O'Brien's report stated, La Penna "operated, on a large scale, in the illicit handling of liquor through a Canadian connection and landing large quantities of it at different points on Long Island, New York." The "Canadian connection" was Maurice Haupt, a resident of Montreal and sales representative of Canadian Distilleries, Ltd. Three schooners, the *Patrick,* the *Michael* and the *Bettina,* were apparently used to transport the hundreds of thousands of gallons of illicit liquor to the United States. Jimmy's brother, Brooklyn resident John La Penna (of 1105 East 19th Street), took an active part in the operation. John's "principal duty was to locate landing spots, arrange for trucks to transport, and dispose of the liquor after its arrival in New York City." Two other men identified as leading members of the combination, Charles Smith, of 393 Avenue T, Brooklyn, and Lou Steinberg, of 112 West 59th Street, Manhattan, apparently helped handle sales and distribution, which, as the Prohibition Bureau agent indicated, were extensive. The La Pennas sold part of their stock to other wholesalers and to retailers in the New York area and shipped the rest by truck throughout the East.

The disposition of the La Penna case in many respects echoed results of most other cases involving the activities of large-scale prohibition era groups when federal, state, or local authorities intervened. That is, operations continued as though nothing had happened. O'Brien and his fellow agents traced the La Penna combination's activities for months, followed gang members when they traveled to Montreal, tapped their phones, and recorded seemingly incriminating conversations. On February 28, 1928, they caught six La Penna gang members "with the goods," at Mattituck, Long Island, seizing 430 sacks of a dozen bottles of whiskey each, along with three automobiles, and arresting Harry Cox, Thomas Gerardo, Mike Pellico, Jerry Lundin, Jerry Marino, and John Massino.

The La Penna case never came to trial. The Attorney General's office rendered an opinion on October 1, 1928, that "this case could not be successfully prosecuted in its present status." Not even the Mattituck seizure was prosecuted. The case was closed and everyone involved released. Continued investigation by Prohibition Bureau agents "for the purpose of obtaining additional information to enable the charges to stand up if presented for trial" ended after an October 30, 1928, memorandum labeled it "a waste of time as those involved are no longer operating together in their former location, and are believed to be disbanded and broken up and out of the business, making it impossible to obtain any additional evidence in connection with this charge." Internal Revenue Service records of La Penna's activities in the 1930s show the inaccuracy of this judgment. In 1931, for example, bootlegging paid La Penna nearly a million dollars in net income.

The La Penna group comprised only one of several syndicates operating along the Eastern seaboard and was far from the largest. Nearly a hundred foreign vessels engaged exclusively in the contraband trade on the East Coast. Furthermore, as reported by the Coast Guard, "hundreds of specially constructed high-speed motor boats, fishing vessels, and coastwise vessels are employed in the traffic along the South Atlantic, Gulf, and Pacific coasts. Once ashore, the alcohol was transported inland, generally by automobile or truck, sometimes to destinations hundreds of miles from the landing place.[23]

The same process took place along the land border and across the waterways between Canada and the United States, and, to a smaller degree, across the Mexican border. Detroit provided the major port of entry for smuggled alcohol along the porous Canadian border. At the end of 1926 a special Royal Commission estimated that over $40 million worth of liquor moved annually across the Detroit River from Windsor to Detroit. Whiskey imported through Detroit traveled on railway freight cars and by automobile to Chicago and from there throughout the entire Middle West.

Police estimated that during the 1920s at least a hundred carloads of liquor a day traveled in convoys over major highways through Michigan to Chicago. The ordinary load per car was fifteen to twenty cases, although some loads were as small as four to six cases. The business was lucrative for, Larry Engelmann has pointed out, in Chicago "one bottle of Detroit whiskey was cut into three bottles, and the product was then sent to Minneapolis, St. Louis, and smaller cities of the midwest." [24]

In 1930 the Canadian Parliament passed a law making it illegal to export liquor to the United States or to any country that had adopted prohibition. This law put a severe crimp in the smuggling business but did not end it. Instead of shipping booze directly to the United States, Canadian companies routed it to a Caribbean port and then to the United States. Smugglers, of course, still carried liquor across the Canadian-American border. [25]

The Internal Revenue Service determined in investigations conducted in 1935 that Canadian distilleries figured prominently in the liquor-smuggling business; not only had the distilleries been "manufacturing liquors of a type designed only for the American trade" but also they "had established depots at smuggling bases on the French islands of St. Pierre et Miquelon, in the Bahamas, in British Honduras, at Ensenada, Mexico, at Papeiti, Tahiti, at Vancouver, British Columbia, and at other points. . . . [and] thereby almost completely encircled the United States with liquor smuggling depots." The investigations resulted in a compromise arrangement with the Treasury Department whereby four Canadian concerns—Distillers Corporation-Seagrams, Ltd.; Hiram Walker-Gooderham and Worts, Ltd.; Canadian Industrial Alcohol, Ltd.; and United Distillers, Ltd.—agreed to pay a $3 million fine. This was a small penalty compared with the hundreds of millions of dollars in profits the companies had made by exploiting the American market during prohibition years. [26]

In the late 1920s, the domestic liquor industry (which had competed successfully with imported alcohol throughout the decade) became the principal source of liquor consumed in the United States. Illicit stills produced most of the domestic variety. In January 1930 the Prohibition Bureau estimated that the ratio of moonshine to diverted industrial alcohol in circulation in the nation during the preceding year reached seven or eight gallons to one. This calculation, based on a low estimate of industrial alcohol of 9 million gallons, meant that stills produced in excess of 63 million gallons of alcohol in 1929. Stills ranged in size from the portable one-gallon-capacity home equipment to huge factory operations that could produce more than two thousand gallons daily.[27]

Urban moonshining was widespread during the prohibition era because homemade alcohol was easy to produce and relatively difficult for authorities to discover. The portable one-gallon home still could be bought on the open market for as little as six or seven dollars. Instructions for setting up and using a still could be found in most public libraries, or obtained directly from the federal government. A number of Department of Agriculture bulletins described in detail and in simple language, as Charles Merz has observed, how to manufacture alcohol "from such familiar ingredients as apples, oats, bananas, barley, sorghum, sugar beets, watermelon, and potato culls." [28]

Countless native as well as foreign-born Americans in cities and on farms made use of information prepared and disseminated by the government to produce enough alcohol for individual and family drinking needs. Some criminals, like Chicago's Genna brothers, saw a rich potential for profit in organizing the home industry. In the mid-1920s the Gennas distributed hundreds of portable home stills to residents of the Near West Side Italian community with orders to "produce or else." This particular enterprise resulted in a highly lucrative operation with gross sales of $350,000 a month and total assets valued at $5 million.[29]

The bootlegger who organized home stills in the Italian community of Brooklyn's Bay Ridge section was former Black Hander Frank Yale. In addition, Yale was a leading figure among the bootleggers who smuggled liquor along the Long Island coast. The anger and frustration of ordinary citizens over the wealth and power flaunted by

22. Brooklyn syndicate boss Frank Yale. (Courtesy Chicago Historical Society)

liquor barons like Yale is reflected in a letter sent to Attorney General Harry Daugherty:

July 10, 1923

Attorney General Daugherty,

Dear Sir, Over two weeks ago I sent you full information about the ring-leader of a Rum Running Gang of Italians in the Bay Ridge Section of Brooklyn. I gave you his monstrous record. I refer to *Frank Yale* or *Uale* (Italian way of spelling it) of #6605—14th Avenue, Brooklyn. I have never learned if the Federal men got the goods on him in his enormous Bootlegging transactions which covers 2 States and many near-by cities; at any rate here is one more cowardly nick in the handle of Yale's murdering gun, for he must have had this young chauffeur named Frank Forte murdered. an honorable war veteran and an innocent victim of this murdering gang of dago rum runners. It is noised about that this chauffeur knew too much and was riddled with bullets.

Uale or Yale is pulling the "baby act" to throw the Police off his own trail. It is an awful joke for him to try and pose as a charity worker among the people of his district. He has no regard for the rights of anyone but himself and he is the most vicious gangster at large. In the name of common justice Mr. Daugherty won't you put your Prohibition sleuths on this scoundrel's trail and expose him as Forte's murderer. He was an eye witness and still claims he can give no description of the car number or occupants. His Rum Running will go on until he is in jail and he will have killed every man that knows too much of his criminal acts. This latest murder shows his defiance of law and life. The local authorities are unable to get him, he has them fooled to the eyes and he can't even read or write English. Guard this letter, Mr. Daugherty or I too would be riddled with shots. Respectfully

Tony Franzel

Written along the side of the page:
Important—Do not allow this letter out of your Department for anything that the poor boobs here in Brooklyn or New York get hold of, they show to the accused and then another life is taken by the gangsters.[30]

Apparently mistaken for Yale by the gunmen, Forte, who was employed as chauffeur for Yale's wife and children, was shot and killed while sitting in the driver's seat of a touring car in front of Yale's home. Questioned by police, Yale could not account for the murder and had no idea of the identity of the killers.

For those involved, "alky cooking" for a criminal syndicate represented a substantial supplement to the regular family income. The Gennas, for example, paid $15 a day. As John Kobler pointed out, the family's job was to keep the fire burning under the still and skim the distillate. A home still yielded an average of 350 gallons of raw alcohol a week, at a cost ranging from 50 to 75 cents a gallon. Even though a stench of fermenting mash hung over whole neighborhoods, the "alky cookers" ran a small risk of arrest because their syndicate protectors and directors lavishly dispensed graft money to the police to ignore what their noses and eyes told them was going on.[31]

In addition to home stills, urban moonshiners used commercial stills, popular because of the quick return they provided on the investment. A commercial still representing an investment of $500 (for the equipment, raw materials, labor, protection) could produce from 50 to 100 gallons of liquor a day. The liquor cost 50 cents a gallon and sold for $3 or $4 a gallon. Operating at full capacity, the still would pay for itself in four days. Operation beyond that time produced pure profit. Danger of its being discovered by authorities could be reduced by moving it periodically. If the still was confiscated, a new one cost only four additional days' effort.[32]

"Prohibition is a business," maintained "Scarface" Al Capone. The early 1920s comprised a period of intensive competition of entrepreneurs attracted by prohibition's economic opportunities. The low capital outlay required to become a minor bootlegger, and the potential for high financial return, became strong inducements for formerly law-abiding citizens as well as small-time criminals to try their luck in a highly competitive but—at least in the early years after the Volstead Act—a wide-open field of enterprise. Prohibition fitted almost naturally into the nation's capitalist tradition of commercial enterprise. In addition, criminals could talk of their value to society and the business world because the liquor trade provided a service that Americans wanted and willingly paid for. Large numbers of otherwise law-abiding citizens demonstrated their eagerness to become law-breakers and at least occasionally to give in to their craving for alcohol.[33]

Prohibition, John Landesco observed in 1932, "opened up a new criminal occupation, with less risk of punishment, with more certainty of gain, and with less social stigma than the usual forms of crime, like robbery, burglary, and larceny." Although for many bootleggers, fear of legal punishment might have been negligible, arrest was only one of the risks bootleggers faced in their scramble for profits. Competition in the bootlegging business differed from that in other developing fields in that unsuccessful operators often did not live to regret their decision to compete in this line of work. The method developed to eliminate competition was direct, pragmatic, thorough and final. It was "the one-way ride." [34]

During the 1920s and early 1930s intense competition and a great deal of bloodshed occurred, but the trend over the years was toward consolidation, organization, and even cooperation. This tendency varied somewhat from city to city, but the general direction lay away from an open-market situation with its unbridled competition (and the resulting uncertainty of supply and distribution). Although shoot-outs, murders, and hijackings made sensational copy for newspapers, they provoked little public concern or outrage; nevertheless, they were bad for business because of the element of uncertainty injected into operations. As a result, although considerable violence (by normal business standards) continued to characterize bootlegging, certain individuals or groups emerged as dominent forces by the end of prohibition. These men encouraged cooperation rather than cut-throat competition, in cities from Boston and New York to San Francisco and Los Angeles.

In the huge market area represented by Chicago, cooperation among bootleggers came early, largely by reason of the farsightedness, diplomatic skills, and organizational genius of one man, John Torrio. "As an organizer and administrator of underworld affairs," observed a U.S. District Attorney, "Johnny Torrio is unsurpassed in the annals of American crime; he is probably the nearest thing to a real mastermind that this country has yet produced." IRS agents who investigated Torrio's illegal activities during the 1930s in New York and looked back upon his long career as a master of crime viewed "this mild-mannered, quiet-spoken little man" with awe and wonder. They felt that an appropriate nickname for him was "The Fox" because he "showed all the wile, slyness and cunning of the marauder of the forests."

Between 1920 and 1923, Torrio brought a measure of peace to warring criminal factions, and elevated himself to a position of dominance by convincing his fellow gangsters of the advantage of cooperation as opposed to uncontrolled competition. He presided over the city's division into spheres of influence, keeping most of the South Side under his personal control. This mutually beneficial arrangement broke down, however, because of two interrelated factors. One was the desire on the part of many of the gang bosses, conspicuously Dion O'Banion, to operate unencumbered by restrictions imposed by one of their number. The other was a change in the local political situation.[35]

Compliant politicians were vital to the smooth operation of bootlegging enterprises (as well as to other forms of syndicate crime such
as gambling, prostitution, and narcotics). Torrio's power and the basis
of his success rested on his ability to provide protection from the law
to his bootlegging associates. With lavish outlays of money he purchased the cooperation of local politicians and police officers. "Immunity from punishment," John Landesco pointed out in 1929, "appears
to be an almost indispensable element in maintaining the prestige and
control of a gangster chief." [36]

The relative calm of the corrupt William Hale Thompson administration (1915–23) ended abruptly when the election of William E.
Dever as Mayor of Chicago in April 1923 upset Torrio's harmonious
arrangement. The refusal of Dever and his chief of police, Morgan A.
Collins, to cooperate with Torrio destroyed the old system of official
protection and damaged the prestige and control of the syndicate chieftain. On May 19, 1924, Chief Collins directed a secret and highly successful raid on the Sieben Brewery. Along with the usual small-time
crooks (truck drivers, gunmen, workmen), the raid netted three major
gang leaders including Torrio himself. Torrio's arrest and indictment
proved beyond any doubt that the syndicate did not have the power to
control the new city administration. Ambitious underlings like O'Banion and Hymie Weiss promptly challenged the established criminal hierarchy. [37]

The "union of each for the good of all" under the guidance of Torrio gave way to the "war of each against all" in which yesterday's
ally often became today's enemy. Between September 1923 and October 1926 gangsters murdered an estimated 215 of their colleagues in
the struggle to gain control of local booze and beer businesses. Police
accounted for another 160 outlaw deaths. One casualty was former
altar boy Dion O'Banion, boss of the North Side gang at the time of
his death on November 10, 1924, in the flower shop he owned and
operated on North State Street across from Holy Name Cathedral. Although the killers were never identified, general gossip assumed them
to be either members of the Genna clan, which had long feuded with
O'Banion, or paid assassins employed by the Torrio-Capone organiza-

23. John Torrio following unsuccessful attempt on his life by members of Chicago's North Side Gang. Scarf was deliberately placed so as to hide bullet scars. (Chicago *Tribune* Photo)

tion. Dion's successor, Polish-American Hymie Weiss (born Wajciechowski), vowed to avenge his Irish friend's death. On January 12, 1925, unknown assailants tried to kill Capone; later in the month Torrio suffered a nearly fatal wound from unidentified gunmen. In February a thoroughly shaken Torrio appeared in U.S. District Court to face charges growing out of his part in the Sieben Brewery affair. The former overlord of crime meekly accepted a verdict of guilty and the temporary safety of a nine-month prison sentence. Following his early release from jail, Torrio hastily departed from Chicago, leaving the organization to his hand-picked successor, Brooklyn native Al Capone.[38]

Capone, who assumed control of Torrio's empire while he was still in his twenties, continued the war for control of Chicago's underworld. His methods were in keeping with his own personality and differed radically from those of his predecessor. In contrast to the small, quiet, conservatively attired Torrio, the bulky, loud, and uncouth Capone

24. Chicago North Side Gang boss Hymie Weiss, murdered October 11, 1926, by members of Capone syndicate. (Courtesy Chicago Historical Society)

fitted the gangster stereotype. A womanizer and lavish spender, he preferred direct action to diplomacy when faced by a problem. The major problem for him, as it had earlier been for Torrio, was the powerful North Side organization led (until November 1924) by Dion O'Banion. Capone utilized a number of techniques against O'Banion's successors, including even an attempt at diplomacy. In early October 1926, Capone made peace overtures to North Side boss Hymie Weiss, but was turned down. At approximately 4 P.M. on October 11, Weiss returned from a day at the Criminal Court building to the North Side gang's headquarters at 738 North State Street, in the same building as the old O'Banion flower shop. As he crossed the street, Weiss was caught in a barrage of gunfire and died almost instantly. Ten days later, on October 21, Capone participated in a peace meeting with leaders of the North Side and other local gangs. As a result, the city was divided among rival organizations, and these agreed not to operate outside the allotted territories. The truce lasted until April 4, 1927, when police officers killed Vincent "the Schemer" Drucci. As boss of the O'Banion gang, Drucci had abided by the terms of the October agreement. His successor, the Polish George ("Bugs") Moran, refused to honor the peace settlement. After a relatively quiet interim period, the gang war progressed toward a bloody conclusion. On February 14, 1929, four men—two dressed as police officers—entered a garage at 2122 North Clark Street and murdered seven members of the North Side group. This event, the so-called St. Valentine's Day Massacre, did not eliminate Moran, who by chance did not stop by the garage that particular morning. The shaken Moran, however, left the city for the East Coast. Although he later returned to Chicago, neither he nor the North Side organization regained their former preeminence. Ten years after his arrival in Chicago to serve as Colosimo's bodyguard, Capone, through what one writer has termed the underworld's "most gory act of terrorism," brought relative peace to Chicago's underworld. This period of quiet also brought a closed market for criminal activities, which lay under the control and supervision of "The Big Fellow's" organization.[39]

Neither Capone's conviction in 1931 on charges of income tax evasion nor his imprisonment until 1939 (first in Atlanta Penitentiary

25. St. Valentine's Day massacre of seven members of Chicago North Side Gang. (Courtesy Chicago Historical Society)

and then, after 1933, in Alcatraz) could loosen the syndicate's grip on Chicago, for during his tenure as syndicate chieftain Capone had not operated in isolation. According to a written statement dated September 20, 1930, prepared by Al Capone's lawyer Lawrence P. Mattingly in behalf of his client for submission to the Internal Revenue Service, three associates helped "the Big Fellow" guide the syndicate's operations. These were Frank Nitto (or Nitti), Jack Guzik, and Ralph Capone, Al's brother. Guzik, a former whorehouse proprietor, directed gambling and vice activities; Ralph saw to the mob's bootleg liquor interests; Nitti, at this time the syndicate's "enforcer," later displayed a flair for business, and along with Guzik became the financial expert. The lion's share of the profits from these enterprises went to the four leaders, each of whom received one-sixth of the organization's net income. The remaining one-third was divided among the rest of the syndicate's members, or, as Mattingly described them, "a group of regular employees." Following Capone's departure from Chicago, Nitti and Guzik directed a dynamic and rapidly expanding enterprise. After Nitti's suicide in 1943 and Guzik's death in 1956 of natural causes, the mantle of leadership was transferred to lesser men. Nevertheless Colosimo, Torrio, and Capone had built well. The organization was so powerful that weak leadership seemed to have little harmful effect on it. The business of crime continued to prosper.[40]

The syndicate that established its hegemony over Chicago's underworld by the end of the 1920s, although containing large numbers of Italians, was not limited in membership to any single ethnic group. Among the non-Italians in the organization's hierarchy were Jack Guzik, the "so-called brains of the Capone organization," his brother Harry, Murray ("the Camel") Humphreys, Sam ("Golf bag") Hunt, Dennis ("Duke") Cooney, Hymie Levin, and Edward Vogel.

Ethnic diversity characterized many of the criminal syndicates that emerged during the prohibition era. Italians did not constitute the dominant criminal force during prohibition, although they operated in all the major cities across the country.

In the late 1920s and early 1930s, Boston syndicate crime was headed by Jewish criminals, first by Charles "King" Solomon and after his murder in 1933, by Hyman Abrams. Italians played important roles in these organizations, but were not the stars. Mario Ingraffia, Louis D. Fox, W. J. Bradley, and Richard I. ("Duke") Bailey served as prominent members of Abrams' group which, according to a U.S. Bureau of Customs report, comprised the largest bootlegging outfit operating along the New England coast from the late 1920s to 1931. Solomon at the time of his death reportedly "directed the wholesale peddling of liquor for the wealthiest liquor syndicate ever built up in New England." In addition, he "was said also to control the sale of narcotics in Boston and the traffic in women." Michael ("Mike the Wise Guy") Rocco, an intimate of Solomon's, helped to provide the muscle for the latter's bootlegging activities. Solomon did not include the liquor traffic in his thriving narcotics traffic until 1930. He quickly became a major force, but even so was unable to prevent widespread hijacking (mainly by Irish gangs from Boston) of liquor cargoes at offshore drop points. Such hijackers regularly beat out the "legitimate" syndicate receivers.[41]

Gangland violence characterized Philadelphia during the prohibition era. Twenty-two bootlegging-connected murders during the two preceding years and accusations of police corruption prompted the calling of a special grand jury investigation in 1928. The grand jury found, among other things, that three syndicates dominated the liquor trade in the city. A former Jewish prizefight promoter named Max ("Boo Boo") Hoff headed the most powerful gang and became known as Philadelphia's "king of the bootleggers." [42]

The Italian gangs of South Philadelphia, which in later years established their control over the city's underworld, were in the late 1920's led by the six Lanzetti brothers, who dealt also in prostitution and narcotics. The third syndicate in Philadelphia's underworld triumvirate was that of Mickey Duffy. Born Michael J. Cusick, Duffy was one of the many Polish criminals of the prohibition period (others included Hymie Weiss [or Wajciechowski] and George ["Bugs"] Moran, both of Chicago) who, like other gangsters of Slavic origin, have been ignored by writers concentrating on three more prominent groups, the Irish, Italians, and Jews.

Poles as well as other Americans found the prohibition laws oppressive and irrelevant to their needs and feelings, and, like many fellow Americans, they seemed to feel little remorse about breaking those laws. This is seen in the large Polish community of Hamtramck, a city of 80,000 lying within the boundaries of Detroit. During prohibition, according to University of Michigan sociologist Arthur Evans Wood (who in 1955 published a comprehensive and insightful historical and sociological study of the community) Hamtramck had a widely held reputation for crime. "To the man on the street the very name, Hamtramck, connoted crime, delinquency and general disorder." Most of it related to bootlegging. Liquor was sold, Larry Engelmann has shown, "in candy stores, restaurants, pool rooms, brothels, private homes, and from automobiles that cruised the mainstreet. State police reported to the governor that there was no difference between the wild nights and the wild days" of Hamtramck.[43]

The best known and most feared extralegal organization in Detroit during the 1920s was the so-called Purple Gang, which apparently got its name from one of its founders, Samuel ("Sammie Purple") Cohen. This was a loose confederation of two Jewish gangs that merged in the early 1920s under the leadership of Abe Bernstein. Although the Purples engaged in a wide range of activities from shoplifting to murder, their major line of endeavor and principal source of income was bootlegging. For several years the Purples prospered as suppliers of Canadian whiskey for the Capone organization in Chicago. By 1931, however, the Purple Gang as well as other bootlegging groups had been elbowed aside by Italian gangsters spearheaded by Joseph Zerilli, Angelo Meli, and Pete Licavoli. Throughout the preceding decade Detroit's Italian criminals had been divided into two (and sometimes more) warring factions. In early February 1931, Zerilli succeeded in eliminating the last major leader of the principal rival Italian faction, Chester La Mare. La Mare's murder by two "close friends," who shot the unsuspecting "Capone of Detroit" in the kitchen of his own home, ended a year of bloodshed marked by eleven gang killings. Even while this internecine warfare took place, Italian criminals were busily engaged in killing rivals or potential rivals among members of

26. Funeral of Cleveland's Italian-colony gang bosses John and Joseph Lonardo, shot to death on October 3, 1927, by members of rival Porello syndicate. (Cleveland *Plain Dealer*)

other ethnic groups in the city. As a result, under Zerilli's command, they emerged as the dominant force in Detroit's underworld.[44]

Italian gangs in Cleveland, like their counterparts in Detroit, carried on a bloody, no-holds-barred war for control of the home-brew industry in the city's Italian neighborhoods. The struggle became known as the "Sugar War," since corn sugar formed the principal ingredient in the production of corn liquor. In the course of the war, which lasted through the 1920s, the leaders and many members of the Lonardo and the Porello organizations, as well as of lesser groups, died violently. By 1930 the Mayfield Road Mob led by Tony and Frank Milano, John Angersola (alias John King), Charles Colletti, and Alfred ("Big Al") Polizzi had emerged as leaders of the city's Italian syndicate.

While the Italians busily eliminated each other in order to win control of the home-manufacturing business—and occasioned widespread publicity and public concern—Jewish criminals, led by Moe Dalitz, Sam Tucker, Morris Kleinman, and Louis Rathkopf (later to be named the "Silent Syndicate" by journalist Hank Messick) imported liquor from Canada across Lake Erie by boat and plane. The Dalitz group made a fortune distributing high-quality Canadian liquor throughout Ohio and Pennsylvania and even New York, where they formed important contacts for the future with Meyer Lansky. Unlike the (Jewish) Purple Gang of Detroit, Dalitz and his associates operated quietly and behind the scenes and (like Torrio, Costello, and Lansky) left the limelight to the less intelligent and the publicity-hungry. Instead they concentrated on amassing power, and in the decades after prohibition expanded their influence beyond Cleveland—in the process increasing their wealth.[45]

In Denver, Kansas City, and Los Angeles Italians took a prominent part in booze wars of the 1920s and emerged triumphant by the end of the decade. In contrast, no one among the legion of bootleggers of the New Orleans underworld—whether Italians or members of other immigrant groups—was able to win undisputed control during prohibition. U.S. Senator Huey Long and state and local politicians controlled and channeled criminal elements and activities in the Louisiana metropolis. A similar situation existed in San Francisco, where the police held a tight rein over the local gangs. That is not to say that syndicates did not exist in these cities; rather, a combination of local factors and the absence of dynamic and intelligent criminals leaders made it possible for politicians and police to retain control over the criminal groups.[46]

The scramble for bootlegging revenue was far more vicious and complex in New York than in any other American city. With its numerous gangs and an enormous population providing the richest market for illicit alcohol, New York during the 1920s featured a bewildering maze of shifting rivalries, vendettas, and alliances. More than one thousand gangsters were killed in this urban jungle during the bootleg wars of the 1920s. Contemporaries Craig Thompson and Allen Raymond described the era in a book published in 1940:

Rum runners and hi-jackers were pistoled and machine gunned. They were taken for rides on the front seat of sedans and their brains were shot out from behind by fellow mobsters they thought were their pals. They were lined up in pairs in front of warehouse walls in lonely alleys and shot down by firing squads. They were slugged into unconsciousness and placed in burlap sacks with their hands, feet and necks so roped that they would strangle themselves as they writhed. Charred bodies were found in burned automobiles.

Bootleggers and their molls were pinioned with wire and dropped alive into the East River. They were encased in cement and tossed overboard from rum boats in the harbor. Life was cheap and murder was easy in the bootleg industry, and those men of ambition who fought their way to the top were endowed with savagery, shrewdness and luck. The killings by which their territories for trade were consolidated, and their competitors put out of the way, were not hot blooded affairs at all, but cold and calculated business practice.[47]

Arnold Rothstein, big-time gambler, businessman, politician, pawnbroker, fixer, and corrupter, attempted to bring order and reason to the extreme competition and chaos prevailing in the bootlegging business. "Rothstein's main function," according to his biographer Leo Katcher, "was organization. He provided money and manpower and protection. He arranged corruption—for a price. And, if things went wrong, Rothstein was ready to provide bail and attorneys." Beginning in the fall of 1920, Rothstein bankrolled the activities of Irving Wexler (better known as Waxey Gordon), Frank Costello, William V. ("Big Bill") Dwyer, Louis ("Lepke") Buchalter, Albert Anastasia, and John T. Noland (alias Jack "Legs" Diamond), whose gang contained such future luminaries as Lucky Luciano and Arthur Flegenheimer (Dutch Schultz). By 1923 it was clear to Rothstein that one man could not control bootlegging in New York City, and so he concentrated on other areas of illicit activity, such as narcotics, in which he invested his money.[48]

Following Rothstein's murder in 1928, John Torrio became banker and financier for underworld enterprises in New York. He also worked quietly behind the scenes to organize and rationalize the illicit alcohol business in New York and along the East Coast, just as he had done earlier in Chicago. In large part through Torrio's unrivaled talents as diplomat, the seven largest smuggling groups in the northeastern part of the United States settled their differences and agreed to share the liquor being smuggled in as well as to divide the market and its profits among themselves. The association included the Lucky Luciano forces (including Joe Doto, or Adonis, and Frank Costello), the Meyer Lansky-Benjamin (''Bugsy'') Siegel gang, Philadelphia's Nig Rosen, Longy Zwillman of Newark, Charles (''King'') Solomon of Boston, Rhode Island's Daniel Walsh, Yasha Katzenberg of New York, and the Torrio-Frank Zagarino group. Zagarino was a well-known New York bootlegger (and was murdered in the mid-1930s); Dutch Schultz headed one of the largest bootlegging gangs in the city, but refused to join with his competitors. This combination ''controlled the importation and sale of liquor in the New York metropolitan area, Boston and vicinity, Rhode Island, Connecticut, New Jersey, and the Philadelphia metropolitan area,'' according to an Internal Revenue Service investigative report. Furthermore, ''a commission had been formed in Canada by the various liquor interests and they only authorized the sale and export of liquors to these areas when it was destined to members of the Big Seven organization. As the combination grew it had eleven or twelve members, all big and substantial smugglers of liquor.'' The association functioned until 1933. During its existence ''it was all-powerful in its particular field, enforcing its rules by the most drastic racketeer methods.'' Prices were fixed by the association, which also limited each member as to the amount of liquor he could purchase in Canada and smuggle into the United States. Torrio's share was approximately five thousand cases of whiskey or its equivalent in bulk per month.[49]

Illicit liquor and beer offered money-making opportunities infinitely greater than those considered possible by Italian and other prohibition-era criminals prior to 1920. Many of the bootlegging gangsters also kept their hands in the narcotics traffic, gambling, and prostitution. A prime example of this diversity came to light in the middle of the prohibition decade of the 1920s as the result of a coordinated raid combining city, state, and federal law enforcement officers in Denver.

After three days of preparation, federal narcotics agents, "the entire state and city prohibition enforcement squads," deputy sheriffs, and assorted other officers arrested Joseph P. Roma and twelve members of his organization, and seized narcotics and whiskey in the possession of gang members.

Roma, who had come to Denver from New York in the early 1920s, by this time functioned as a major power in Denver's underworld, a man of great wealth with "a large house, an expensive automobile, and much property in various parts of the city." Roma's affluence derived from alcohol, most of it manufactured in Denver's "Little Italy," and narcotics, specifically cocaine and morphine. Federal agents determined that through Roma's activity Denver had become the distribution point for drugs into the Rocky Mountain states. The narcotics, manufactured at this time and into the 1930s in Swiss and German laboratories, were smuggled into the United States through New York, Tampa, and New Orleans and from there were transported to Kansas City. During the 1920s and 1930s Kansas City served as the distribution point for the entire Middle West, from Cleveland and Chicago to Denver and Laramie. Roma stood trial and on May 7, 1925, was found guilty of violating the Harrison anti-narcotics act; he received a prison term of three and one-half years and a fine of $2,000. When he left prison Roma returned to Denver and the boot-legging wars, but apparently kept out of further direct involvement in the narcotics traffic. He continued to rise in Denver gangsterdom and—following the murder of his chief rival, Peter Carlino, in September 1931—reigned supreme among Italian criminals until 1933.[50]

In Kansas City, rum-running and gambling ventures allegedly operated under the watchful eyes of Joseph ("Scarface") Di Giovanni, James Balestrere, and John Lazia. Lazia also emerged in the late 1920s as a major political force and an important part of the Pendergast machine after he organized the Italian voters of the city into a formidable bloc. Following Lazia's murder in 1934, his lieutenant Charles Carollo succeeded to Lazia's position of dominance over gambling activities in the city and to his political power and influence as well.[51]

27. Kansas City crime syndicate leader and political boss John Lazia. (Kansas City *Star*)

During the 1920s narcotics traffic, along with alcohol, figured prominently in the criminal operations of San Francisco's Anthony ("Black Tony") Parmagini, considered one of the city's most vicious and ruthless underworld leaders. Parmagini's involvement in the drug traffic antedated the prohibition period. "Black Tony" was born on San Francisco's Telegraph Hill in the 1890s and began his career as leader of a Barbary Coast juvenile gang. As a young adult he graduated to operating disorderly houses, and around the time of World War I became a drug dealer. During the 1920s he ranked high among the major bootleggers in the city and operated a fleet of rum ships between San Francisco and Los Angeles. His activity in importing narcotics from the Far East for distribution along the Pacific Coast was reportedly so lucrative that in itself it yielded Parmagini profits of at least a million dollars in the year 1929.[52]

Hundreds of prohibition-era gangsters added the proceeds from other forms of criminal business to those received from bootlegging. Among these were New Yorkers Lucky Luciano with his narcotics and gambling enterprises, and Frank Costello with his gambling empire. In Chicago both John Torrio and his successor, Al Capone, continued the gambling and prostitution activities begun around the turn of the century by "Diamond Jim" Colosimo. Records seized by Internal Revenue Service agents showed net profits in excess of $500,000 for a single Capone-controlled gambling house, The Ship, during an 18-month period in 1925–26. Capone gang-controlled gambling casinos and whorehouses flourished in Cicero, Burnham, Stickney, and other Chicago suburbs. One such operation was The Tavern, located in Stickney, which provided a bar and a horse parlor in the front and prostitutes in the back rooms. At The Tavern and other Capone resorts, a housekeeper supervised operations, providing linen and other requirements and receiving the money. The Tavern was a $2 house; and of this amount management (the Capone organization) received $1.10, the working girls, 90¢. The girls operated in shifts, "the same as a factory" as one observer noted at the same time, generally twenty-four

28. One of Al Capone's Cicero gambling houses, The Ship. (Chicago *Tribune Photo*)

hours on and twenty-four hours off. Capone obviously believed in maximum return on his investment, since each employee's work-day was carefully monitored. A girl who spent too much time with individual customers or who seemed unwilling to put in a full and enthusiastic work-day received a warning and then, if she did not mend her ways, was beaten up or turned out (or both).[53]

The Capone syndicate ran its operating units much as any efficient business organization now does. Each department was self-supporting and was expected to return a profit "or they raise hell with the one in charge." All individual expenditures as well as the sources of income were recorded in account books. The books provided the leadership with an accurate and current corporate picture so that any unprofitable ventures could be shored up and dishonest subordinates dealt with quickly. Financial records captured in raids on Capone-controlled Cicero gambling houses and speakeasies also provided the IRS with valuable information concerning sources of income for the Capone organization.[54]

With the passage of the Twenty-first Amendment in 1933, the highly sophisticated bootlegging business went into decline, and an era obviously had ended. Like good businessmen everywhere, however, Italian-American criminals were ready to abandon or sharply curtail their involvement in unproductive or declining fields of activity and concentrate on the sure moneymakers. The richest opportunities now were obviously in the traditional, so-called "victimless" crimes of gambling and prostitution—which entrepreneurs had continued to cultivate all through the prohibition years—and in business and labor racketeering. These operations, as well as narcotics, were the lodes that would be mined during and after the 1930s.

7

"The Americanization of the Mobs"

Successful and self-perpetuating institutions, both private and public, develop a history, often heavily laced with fiction, of how they became great and important. Over the passage of years certain events achieve significance as key factors in the eventual success of the organization. This tendency has been no less true for America's crime syndicates. For the Italian-American underworld, the date September 11, 1931, has taken on special meaning as the day the younger generation, led by Charlie Lucky Luciano, overthrew the "Mafia" oldtimers or, as they were called at the time, "greaseballs."

According to underworld lore, on September 11 Luciano ordered the assassination of Salvatore Maranzano in his Park Avenue office, and at the same time (or, according to some sources, within twenty-four hours, or forty-eight hours, according to others) the elimination of Maranzano's allies and friends all over the country. Thus "the Americanization of the mobs," as syndicate members termed the event, was planned and executed with deadly efficiency.[1]

This story contains at least two inaccuracies: that Maranzano's murder took place on September 11 (actually it occurred on the 10th); and that Luciano, leader of the anti-Maranzano forces, had ordered the liquidation of "greaseballs" (or "Moustache Petes") throughout America. The number of murdered "greaseballs" varied according to the writer, but apparently no writer verified his claims. The one correct point—and also the major point—of the story was the fact that

29. New York's "Joe the Boss"
Masseria. (New York *Daily News*)

Maranzano's death marked the victory of the "Americanizers" in New York over the "greaseballs." Even this matter needs qualifying. According to the story, the September "Americanization" took place throughout the United States. So far as can be determined, the process of elimination occurred only in the New York area, where it constituted the final step in Luciano's campaign to dispose of the two most powerful Italian-colony ("Mafia") leaders in the city—Joe Masseria and Salvatore Maranzano.[2]

Luciano's shrewd use of opportunities in 1931 to eliminate first "Joe the Boss" Masseria and then "Boss of Bosses" Maranzano resulted both in solidifying his own position of primacy and in completing the process of "Americanizing" criminal procedures among his Italian colleagues in New York City. In other cities this process, as well as the triumph of the Americanizers, had taken place during the preceding decade. Chicago's John Torrio and Al Capone achieved similar results in the years following "Mafia" boss Mike Merlo's death in 1924. In some cities the process was completed by the late 1920s, and in others—among them San Francisco and New Orleans

—conditions were not ripe for Italian-American criminals until well into the 1930s and sometimes even later.

In 1939 J. Richard ("Dixie") Davis, Dutch Schultz's former lawyer, related in *Collier's* the events and the significance of the day that the Americanizers disposed of "Mafia" overlord Maranzano at 230 Park Avenue. Davis's source, Abe ("Bo") Weinberg, a Schultz gunman held in high regard by his peers, claimed that he and three other Jewish gangsters had been loaned to Luciano for the murder because the potential victim did not know them. According to Weinberg, Maranzano's murder began a nationwide attack on the "oldtimers." In fact, "at the very same hour" as Maranzano's death "there was about ninety guineas [Italians] knocked off all over the country. That was the time we Americanized the mobs." [3]

The following year (1940) journalists Craig Thompson and Allen Raymond repeated (in their *Gang Rule in New York*) Dixie Davis's statements about the significance of Maranzano's murder in the "Americanization campaign." Although they personally could not vouch for its authenticity, they repeated Weinberg's statement to Davis that "scores of greasers" in the United States were slain on the same day as Maranzano. On the basis of their own inquiries among "several underworld sources," the newsmen offered "confirmation of the statement that September 11, 1931, was purge day" in the New York Italian underworld. [4]

In 1951 Burton B. Turkus, former King's County (Brooklyn) Assistant District Attorney, maintained that September 11 "has long been known as 'Purge Day' because of the elimination of the Greaser crowd . . . not only in New York, either—but all over the country." According to Turkus, the number of "Moustache Petes" eliminated during the forty-eight-hour period following Maranzano's death consisted of "some thirty to forty leaders of Mafia's older group all over the United States." Turkus presented this "mass extermination of Mafia executives" as "a remarkable example of planning" that neither law enforcement officials nor journalists recognized as being connected in any way. [5] Like the 1890 Hennessy murder in New Orleans and

Petrosino's assassination in Palermo nineteen years later, the Maranzano story strengthened the image of a deadly, evil society that
killed violently and without fear of retribution.

Other writers of the 1950s usually ignored Maranzano's death and
its significance. Italian syndicate member Joseph Valachi revived the
story in the following decade, first in his testimony before the McClellan Committee in 1963 and then in interviews with his biographer
Peter Maas. According to Valachi, Maranzano's murder was "part of
an intricate, painstakingly executed mass extermination" devised by
Lucky Luciano. Furthermore, "on the day Maranzano died, some
forty Cosa Nostra leaders allied with him were slain across the country." [6]

In the years since his revelations, Valachi has become the major
source of information (in some respects, misinformation) on the origins and early development of the organization he called "La Cosa
Nostra" ("our thing"). Sociologist Donald R. Cressey embellished
Valachi's recollections thus: on the day of Maranzano's death "and
two days immediately following, some forty Italian-Sicilian gang
leaders across the country lost their lives in battle. Most, if not all, of
those killed on the infamous day occupied positions we would now
characterize as 'boss,' 'underboss,' or 'lieutenant.' " [7]

Contrary to the remembrances of "Bo" Weinberg and Joseph Valachi, available evidence indicates that not ninety, or forty, or twenty, or
even five murders were carried out across the United States in conjunction with, or as a consequence of, Maranzano's death. The facts
do not support the theory that the Maranzano murder formed part of a
nationwide purge. The events that New York criminals recalled as taking place in September 1931 applied only to that city and were not
repeated elsewhere. Italian syndicate criminals did not at that time, or
since, kill quietly and unobtrusively when the purpose was not only to
eliminate rivals but also to impart a message. In the Maranzano case
the message stated clearly that any oldtimers still permitted to live had
better accept and adjust to the new order. According to legend, "several" associates and allies of Maranzano in the New York area were
eliminated at about the time of his death. Because of the bizarre man-

ner in which syndicate killers carried out their tasks, such murders would have quickly become known to authorities and newspapers. Although reporters have generally used the descriptor "several" to indicate the number of "Moustache Petes" eliminated on this occasion, they have cited only three victims as substantiation. The bound bodies of Louis Russo and Samuel Monaco were dumped into the Hackensack River, and James La Pore was shot in front of a Bronx barbershop; all died on September 10. These deaths, reported in the daily press, appear to have been the extent of the "Purge Day" bloodbath in the New York area.[8] A careful examination of newspapers issued during September, October, and November of 1931 in twelve large cities (Boston, Philadelphia, Pittsburgh, Baltimore, New Orleans, Cleveland, Detroit, Chicago, Kansas City, Denver, Los Angeles, and San Francisco) turned up evidence of only one killing that occurred at about the time Maranzano died and might have been linked to the death of the "Boss of Bosses." Denver, where this killing occurred, contained gangs that routinely used violence to settle disputes, so that the timing of the murder to coincide with events in New York might not have been intentional. Moreover, the leaders of the two rival factions were Calabrians, not Sicilians.

In late 1930 and early 1931, Pete and Sam Carlino of Pueblo, who dominated the bootlegging business in southern Colorado, made a bid to expand their operations and take over booze operation in Denver. Denver interests, led by Joe Roma, did not respond favorably to the Carlino gang's plans; nevertheless, gang members decided upon some sort of compromise (although the initiator of this solution is unknown) in order to avert possible bloodshed. On January 24, 1931, a meeting of approximately thirty of Colorado's leading bootleggers took place at a restaurant in Denver's Italian district. Police learned of the gathering and raided it. As a result, the participants never reached a compromise solution, and hostilities commenced.[9]

On the subsequent February 18, thugs shot at Pete Carlino from a moving automobile while he stood on a Denver sidewalk. On May 8, brother Sam and one of his lieutenants, James Colletti, were murdered in Carlino's home. Contrary to the code of silence, members of the

30. On June 23, 1931, Denver syndicate leaders Pete Carlino (*left*) and Joe Roma posed for photographers outside county jail after Roma had posted a $5,000 bond for his rival, arrested on charge of conspiracy to commit arson. Less than three months later Carlino was murdered, apparently on orders from his recent benefactor. (Denver *Post*)

family talked freely with the police and identified as the killer Bruno Mauro of Pueblo, whom they had believed to be a family friend. Open warfare continued through the spring and summer of 1931, and culminated in September. Carlino, the so-called "Al Capone of Southern Colorado," drove from Denver on the evening of the 9th en route to Canon City and was last seen alive on the 10th, when he visited a cousin who lived near Pueblo. On the 13th his "bullet-riddled" body was found on a lonely road near Pueblo. Apparently his killers placed the body beneath a bridge, but returned two days later to move it to a point where it would be more readily discovered.

After Carlino's demise, Denver criminal leader Joe Roma emerged as the dominant force in bootlegging operations throughout the state. "Little Caesar," as the five-foot-one Roma was called, retained this position until his murder on February 18, 1933, on the eve of repeal. Throughout the rest of the 1930s, and until the 1960s, relative quiet reigned in the Denver underworld under the direction of Anthony, Clyde, and Eugene Smaldone.

The succession process in cities other than Denver did not include slayings on or around September 10, 1931. Thus, in San Francisco, although a series of murders during the years between 1928 and 1932 involved several Italian booze gang leaders, no evidence exists that the local strife was connected with, or affected by, events taking place in

New York City during September 1931. In fact, none of the San Francisco killings occurred during that year.

Some measure of tranquility apparently existed among Bay Area Italian bootleggers until April 5, 1928, when one of the city's leading booze barons, Jerry Ferri, was shot to death in his Lombard Street apartment. This event initiated a four-year war among Italian underworld factions. Ferri's suspected killer, Alfredo Scariso, himself an alleged Italian syndicate leader, was "taken for a ride" on December 19, 1928, to a deserted road near Fair Oaks, in Sacramento County. Four days after Scariso's murder, one of his suspected killers, Mario Filippi, was shot to death. On July 30, 1929, Frank Boca, another who was "suspected of having participated in Alfredo Scariso's death ride in Sacramento valley"—to quote the *Chronicle*—"was found slumped over the wheel of his expensive automobile on Noriega street at Thirty-ninth avenue" with six bullets in his head and back. A lull in hostilities followed as the opposing forces regrouped. On October 13, 1930, rivals eliminated Genaro Broccolo, the so-called (and short-lived) "Capone of the West." The final event in the violent competition for control of bootlegging operations took place on May 18, 1932, when Luigi Malvese, "hijacker, bootlegger, racketeer and gun runner," was shot to death in mid-afternoon on a crowded sidewalk in the center of the city's Italian community. In the aftermath of this killing, no one leader emerged to dominate bootlegging activities in the Bay Area during the last months of National Prohibition.[10]

This series of murders involved gang leaders who before 1928 had been, if not friends, at least business allies; they had reached an understanding that they would share the opportunities offered by the area's thirsty citizens. Apparently this arrangement became unacceptable to at least some of the men involved. The subsequent struggle reflected a concern over profits rather than a generation gap, since all the men involved were in their late twenties or thirties. Nor was the struggle a showdown between Italian-colony-oriented or colony-based criminals and the "American" generation, since all the combatants came from the latter group. More importantly, the battle did not arise in order to determine who would control syndicate crime in San Francisco. The city's Italians profited handsomely from bootlegging, prostitution, and narcotics, but they did not dominate these activities during the 1920s and 1930s. Neither Italians nor members of other ethnic groups managed to establish control over illegal activities in San Francisco. Local police, who determined which illegal activities would be permitted as well as which criminals would be allowed to operate, frustrated cooperative efforts. As a result, gambling, prostitution, and other forms of entrepreneurial crime were carried on extensively by individual organizations that were small and fragmented.

San Francisco police not only drove "undesirable" individuals out of the city; they also prevented out-of-town criminals from entering the city. According to a grand jury investigation begun on November 21, 1935, however, this action did not result from a desire to enforce the law, but rather to protect the police position of dominance over the underworld and to guarantee the flow of graft money.[11]

The grand jury released its final report (which was named after the jury's chief investigator, Edwin Atherton), on March 16, 1937. The Atherton Report disclosed that each of the city's four police captains controlled and regulated gambling, prostitution, and other illegal activities in his own district. Because of close police supervision, powerful criminal syndicates never developed in the city. This situation contrasted directly with that in Eastern cities. A further difference lay in San Francisco's lack of ward and machine politicians. Because of progressive-era reforms intended to introduce effective government procedures, wards did not exist in San Francisco. Instead, the city-county council was elected on an at-large basis. This method did not prevent corrupt politicians from operating in the city. These men simply did not make use of the ballot box and elective office. The grand jury found that Pete and Thomas McDonough, who abandoned ward politics when the reformers achieved a model government in San Francisco, then entered the bail bond business and played a major role in the city's crime and corruption. Until exposed by the investigations, the McDonoughs served as middlemen between the police and criminals. They handled payoffs, decided who would be raided when such an action seemed necessary for public appearance, and—through contacts in government and the criminal justice system—protected police officers when they got into trouble. Indeed, the Report observed, "the McDonough Brothers [company] was discovered to be a fountainhead of corruption, willing to interest itself in almost any matter designed to defeat or circumvent the law."

In an insightful M.A. thesis entitled "Commercialized Amusements in New Orleans," Elbert S. P'Pool, a long-time New Orleans resident and a former clergyman, in 1930 outlined some of the factors responsible for the city's situation. From personal experience P'Pool attested to the fact that "all reform movements are handicapped by lack of public support." Further undercutting the efforts of reformers was the problem that not only did the " 'good people' not wish to be disturbed," but also they were opposed to "unfavorable publicity" because they did not want "their city to get a bad name in the outside world." In this predominantly Catholic city, support of the Church was essential to effect change. Yet little aid or comfort could be expected from this quarter, P'Pool observed, because of the basically conservative nature of the Church. Protestants, however, were no better, for "very few Protestants of the city have any desire or inclination to jeopardize their interests by crusading for any civil or social reforms." The commonality of interests of the underworld combined with official complicity and widespread graft and corruption completed the sordid picture.[12]

Observers of the situation in San Francisco during the 1920s and 1930s confirmed that the conditions described by P'Pool applied to that city as well. The Atherton Report, for example, found a parallel between these two port cities with their conservative Catholic majority and apathetic Protestant minority. Both were "open towns," where the prevailing attitude was to leave well enough alone so that residents and tourists alike could enjoy themselves and obtain whatever they might want—whether gambling, women, narcotics, or some other illegal commodity.

In contrast to the San Francisco situation, however, New Orleans politicians dominated the city's underworld and used police clout to maintain the status quo. In both cities a number of criminal groups existed but were relatively weak and easily controlled by police and politicians. Significantly, when a national figure entered the New Orleans crime picture, he did so at the request of local politicians.

Prior to World War II, criminal organizations in New Orleans were relatively small and weak. In part this lack of power resulted from the absence of a dynamic, ruthless, far-sighted underworld leader who could consolidate activities under his control and (whether through reason or brute force), convince his fellows of the necessity of cooperation. The city's major Italian criminals included bootlegger and narcotics dealer Sylvestro ("Silver Dollar Sam") Carollo, who at the age of two was brought to the United States in 1898; Carlos Marcello, who, although still in his twenties, was an ambitious narcotics dealer and a gambler with a promising future; Anthony Jules Cigali, born in New Orleans in 1891, who concentrated on gambling activities; and former bodyguard to Huey Long (and close friend of New Orleans mayor Robert S. Maestri) James Brocato, who used the name Moran. The New Orleans-born Moran was also a well-known local gambler and bootlegger. These and other Italians competed in the bootlegging, gambling, and narcotics markets with Irish, Jewish, Creole, and Anglo-Saxon criminals.[13]

New Orleans did not lack criminals during the 1920s and 1930s, but produced no equivalent to John Torrio or Lucky Luciano. Furthermore, politicians controlled moneymaking concerns so tightly that outsiders were not sufficiently tempted to move in on the lucrative tourist trade. Even Frank Costello, who in 1935 received an invitation to move his slot machines to the city and share the wealth with both politicians and police, did not pose a threat to local authorities, since his primary interests lay elsewhere.[14]

Public apathy and indifference to widespread open vice, gambling, and other illegal activities proved to be a major factor in shaping the New Orleans response to entrepreneurial crime during the pre-World War II decades. Official venality faced no effective opposition. Observers of the Huey Long era noted that the residents of Louisiana and

31. Syndicate power Frank Costello (*left*) with his attorney during court appearance in New York in 1935, the same year in which Costello moved his slot machine operations from La Guardia's New York to the more congenial climate of New Orleans. (Chicago *Tribune* Photo)

its principal city "had a tolerance of corruption not found anywhere else in America," a condition rooted in history.[15]

The pervasive atmosphere of corruption in New Orleans permitted vice, gambling, and other illicit operations to take place openly and without social stigma. As a result, both Anglo-Saxon and French-American residents participated in such operations long after they might have stopped had a powerful reform current stigmatized them as undesirable or antisocial (as was the case in most other cities in the nation). Consequently, new immigrants interested in a career in entrepreneurial crime had to compete with the very active native operators.

Since the 1950s the combination of an effective criminal leader, Carlos Marcello (born Caloreo Minacore), and a small but active and vocal reform movement has pushed the leaders of competing crime organizations out of operation, to be replaced by the Italian syndicate.

The victorious Italian organization headed by Marcello absorbed members of the defunct syndicates. Marcello was born on February 6, 1910 in Tunis, North Africa, of Sicilian parents. Also called "The Little Man," Marcello was brought to New Orleans at the age of eight months to join his laborer father. In the late 1930s "The Little Man" served as Frank Costello's local agent and later his partner in gambling ventures, prominent among which was the Beverly Club, opened late in 1945. His relationship with Costello opened doors—which Marcello quickly entered—to wealth, power, and important political contacts. The result, as one reformer noted in an interview (April 1974), has been that—although twenty years earlier New Orleans contained four major syndicates staffed by Irish, Jews, Anglo-Saxons, and Italians with no one group's being dominant—there now exists one syndicate, and it is controlled by Italians. Furthermore, this organization is far more powerful than anything the city has known before.[16]

The emergence in recent decades of a strong, centralized criminal organization in New Orleans contrasts with the earlier parallel development in that city and San Francisco. Bay Area politicians and police have succeeded in keeping local criminal organizations relatively weak. Local police-politician strength is due in part to the absence of dynamic and efficient gang leaders able to weld the criminal elements into an effective organization. (Similarly, politicians of the pre-World War II decades held a tight rein over the underworld in a number of cities, including Kansas City, where the Democratic Party was supreme, and in the Republican stronghold of Philadelphia.)

Powerful criminal organization such as that which appeared in New Orleans during the 1950s has been for decades a reality in Chicago. The same factors which during the past two decades encouraged the growth of syndicates in New Orleans operated since the 1870s in Chicago: able underworld leadership, strong pressure from reform elements, and compliant city politicians. Chicago had a long, distinguished tradition of political and social reform. Mike McDonald and his associates organized its first gambling syndicate in an effort to counter the reforms of Mayor Joseph Medill, who promised in 1871 to drive the criminal elements from the city. The gamblers responded by winning the next election for a mayoral candidate sympathetic to their needs and interests. The Chicago pattern emerged: a strong criminal organization exerting great influence over politicians, political processes, and the police. Prior to prohibition, however, the forces of the underworld lacked firm coordination and tight organization. Under the guidance of John Torrio the system of politician-police-criminal cooperation was perfected. When Al Capone succeeded to Torrio's position in 1925, he did not disturb this arrangement.[17]

In Chicago's First Ward, Capone continued the tradition established long before by predecessors John Torrio and "Big Jim" Colosimo, of cooperating with the ward's Democratic politicians and supporting machine-backed candidates in exchange for a free hand in operating bootlegging, vice, and gambling activities. Capone apparently made it clear that Kenna and Coughlin would get the gangland vote and remain free of interference so long as they followed orders and kept out of syndicate business. Everyone knew who was really in charge in the First Ward. After an audience with Capone, the story goes, a shaken Coughlin admitted that "we're lucky to get as good a break as we did," and, still in a state of fright from the ordeal, verbalized his relief that "the Big Fellow" had not decided to take over the political organization in the ward. The effects of this traditional arrangement showed clearly in the 1927 mayoral election, which was of crucial importance to the city's bootleggers.

During this campaign, Capone's group contributed between $100,000 and $260,000 to the Republican ticket, headed by former two-time mayor (1915–23) William Hale Thompson. In some wards Capone's men used threats and muggings to encourage support of Republican candidates, but—apparently pursuant to long-term arrangements with Kenna and Coughlin—Capone, himself a Republican, made no attempt to influence the First Ward vote and permitted it to go to the Democratic candidate, William Dever. Dever's margin of 7,145 votes (11,076 to Thompson's 3,931) was the largest he obtained in any ward; all Italian precincts voted for him. Instead of operating in the First Ward (which included the central business district, called "The Loop"), the Capone organization went in force into the West Side and also allied with Vincent "the Schemer" Drucci (then heading the O'Banion gang), in order to control the North Side vote as well.

The election's key issue lay in the enforcement or non-enforcement of the liquor law, in the view of ethnic voters as well as the underworld. Dever, the incumbent mayor, had supported the "wets" in 1923, but steadfastly enforced the anti-liquor laws as mayor, with a rapid decline in popularity as a result. Thompson, in contrast, promised to "open 10,000" new drinking establishments, since (he proclaimed) he was himself "as wet as the Atlantic Ocean." His visions of a "wide open town" held a special attraction for the underworld. Gambler and vice-resort operator Jack Zuta, a Jewish member of the North Side gang, contributed $50,000 to "Big Bill's" campaign, explaining to friends that he would quickly recoup several times that amount when his candidate took office. The campaign itself was corrupt and violent. Drucci died from police bullets under highly suspicious circumstances; both candidates spread lies about each other. On election day Capone sent strong-arm squads against the Democratic bully boys, particularly on the West Side, with "orders to meet and beat the enemy."

Once again in office, Thompson lost no time in fulfilling his "wide open town" pledge. Parasites, swindlers, criminals, conmen, and schemers of every type flooded into Chicago. Capone received ample repayment for his contributions to the Republican cause. The new administration permitted him to move his business operations from the suburbs back to Chicago, and in addition appointed his personal friend and political contact Daniel A. Serritella to the post of City Sealer. In 1928 Serritella became Republican Committeeman in the First Ward, a job which, along with his other political contacts, seemed to indicate a promising career in politics for the young Italian. His indictment for attempting to defraud the people of Chicago during the 1931 mayoral campaign (a decision that was overturned because of insufficient evidence in 1933) cost him his career and damaged Thompson's election hopes.

A relationship between criminals and politicians similar to that in

Chicago evolved in New York City. For at least seventy years prior to prohibition, local politicians made use of underworld elements to win elections and remain in power. In exchange, criminals were permitted to practice their particular occupations with minimal official interference. Politicians, however, comprised the dominant element and made use of the police to keep their underworld allies in line. This arrangement began to disintegrate during the 1920s, at least in part because of Tammany boss Charles F. Murphy's death in 1924. A shrewd, pragmatic politician who used any means available to ensure the continued success of the Party, Murphy was also a man of intelligence, personal honesty, and integrity. In the years between 1902, when he became leader of the Hall, and 1924, he led Tammany to heights of success never before reached. According to historian Nancy Joan Weiss, "None of Murphy's predecessors—not Croker, not Kelly, not Tweed—enjoyed his power on the municipal, state, or national level." His death dealt a disabling blow to the machine, for, as J. Joseph Huthmacher has observed, "None of Murphy's successors in the leadership matched his political acumen." Newspaperman Arthur Krock wrote bluntly, "The brains went out of Tammany Hall when he died." [18]

The ensuing struggle for control of the Tammany machine between various ambitious but not overly able district leaders produced no one powerful victor. The strongest force in Tammany during the late 1920s and early 1930s was probably James J. Hines, leader of the Eleventh Assembly District in Manhattan. Unlike earlier Tammany leaders, Hines became directly involved in providing political protection for Dutch Schultz and other criminals, including Luciano, Costello, Lepke, and Brooklyn rackets kingpin Joe Adonis.

Evidence presented in two trials in 1938–39 revealed Hines's role as political protector of Schultz, as well as his complicity with Schultz in the numbers racket. In February 1939 the jury returned a verdict of guilty against Hines and, after appeals failed, in October 1940 the former political leader began serving a four-year sentence. [19]

Two other factors of great importance in the emergence of powerful and politically influential syndicates in New York during the 1930s

32. New York political leader and protector of gangland figures James J. Hines (*center*) dispensing turkeys to the needy during the depression (New York *Daily News*)

were the good supply of potential syndicate leaders (among them Luciano, Lansky, Costello, and Lepke) who possessed shrewdness, farsightedness, ambition, and organizational ability in abundance; and the guidance these young businessmen of crime (most of them in their thirties) had in John Torrio, one of the most intelligent criminals in the nation's history. Respectfully dubbed "The Fox" by Internal Revenue agents, Torrio provided the priceless assets of knowledge and experience for his younger associates during the early 1930s.

The Democratic Party's national convention in Chicago in 1932 underlined the special position Luciano and Costello occupied with Tammany leaders. At that conclave Costello shared a suite at the elegant Drake Hotel with James Hines; Luciano and Albert Marinelli (leader of New York's Second Assembly District) occupied another. This sharing of quarters was of symbolic as well as practical significance, for it demonstrated that criminal syndicate leaders from New York had attained a position of power and influence equal to that of local political party bosses.[20]

Ironically, the other key element in the rise of syndicate leaders was the presence in the city of strong and dedicated reform elements. Under the leadership of Fiorello La Guardia (who became mayor in 1933) and Thomas E. Dewey (as Special Prosecutor and then as District Attorney), reformers achieved successes in their crusade to jail criminals and to break up the unholy alliance of machine politicians and underworld leaders. During that decade Frank Costello's slot machines were cleared out of the city; Jimmy Hines was convicted of protecting Dutch Schultz's policy racket and sent to prison; and fellow Tammany Hall strongman Albert Marinelli was exposed as the creature—some suggested the creation—of Lucky Luciano and associates, and in November 1937 was forced to resign his position as County

33. New York County Clerk Albert Marinelli (*left*) talking with fellow Tammany District leader Sheriff Dan Finn in July 1937. Four months later District Attorney Thomas E. Dewey accused Marinelli of being Lucky Luciano's man in Tammany Hall. (New York *Daily News*)

Clerk; other major syndicate leaders such as Luciano and Lepke were prosecuted in the courts. In addition, reformers exposed a vast range of business and labor racketeering which, at the expense of the people of New York and of the nation, provided the syndicates with huge financial return.

Although this flurry of reform-directed activity appeared to be destroying the criminal-politician alliance, results fell far short of the objective. Contrary to reformer expectations, these successes probably furthered the growth of underworld influence in local politics. In good times and bad, politicians need guaranteed sources for campaign funding; they also require help on election day. With reformers uncovering wrongdoing and in the process drying up at least some of the legitimate sources of income, machine politicians began to rely heavily on unsavory sources for manpower and money. "Starved by lack of patronage," from Washington as well as from La Guardia's administration, "a money-hungry" Tammany Hall found it necessary, notes sociologist Daniel Bell, to turn to Costello and other criminals for support. Even before his fiefdom crumbled under the onslaught of reformers, Jimmy Hines revealed at least a part of the politicians' rationale justifying their alliance with known criminals. Hines had reportedly asked a favor for some underworld character from Edward P. Mulrooney, the former police commissioner, and Mulrooney refused it. "Jim, why do you bother with that type?" Mulrooney asked. "They are no damn good." According to Hines, he replied, "Ed, you know we need those fellows on election day and we can't forget them between elections." [22]

While local machines in New York and Chicago, cities with strong reform traditions, might have needed financial and electioneering aid from "those fellows" in order to continue functioning smoothly, politicians and police in New Orleans and San Francisco obviously did not, at least in the period before 1941. That these two cities contained no criminals in sufficiently strong positions to dictate to law enforcement officials or to politicians, underlines the fact that no one single pattern of syndicate crime growth existed during the period before World War II. Books and articles that concentrate on New York

City implicitly or explicitly give the impression that events in the nation's first city determined what happened elsewhere. Parallels did exist, but the New York situation was not precisely that of other cities, and in some respects was not remotely analogous. The major difference between New York and other cities lay in its large number of Italian criminals, vastly more than in any other city in the nation. Of course, criminals have always amounted to only a small proportion of the entire group; yet the very size of the Italian population in New York—approximately a million members of the first and second generation in 1920—also meant a substantial number of Italian criminals.

Before the 1920s New York contained several "Mafia" bands. During these years no one group established its hegemony over the others, although the Morello brothers' organization occupied a position of primacy, particularly after 1916—the year that leaders of the Brooklyn-based Navy Street / Coney Island gang murdered East Harlem gang leaders Nicholas Morello and Charles Ubriaco. Even after this event, however, the Morellos faced many rivals. As subsequent events would demonstrate, their most powerful competition came from a Lower Manhattan Sicilian gang led by Giuseppe Masseria. Following the release of their brother-in-law Ignacio Saietta ("Lupo the Wolf") from federal prison in the early spring of 1922, the Morellos (Giuseppe, Vincent, and half-brother Ciro Terranova) and their allies Umberto Valenti and Totò D'Aquila, both powerful "Mafia" leaders, moved to eliminate Masseria. Unfortunately for them, their rival proved to be quicker and more deadly. On May 8, just as Lupo and the Morello clan were readying themselves to move against the pudgy little Sicilian, Masseria carried out a three-pronged attack on his enemies. In the late morning, Vincent Morello was murdered on East 116th Street. A few hours later, gunmen killed Joseph Peppo, an ally and business partner of the Morellos. After a lapse of a few hours, and in the same neighborhood, Masseria and his gunmen caught another rival, Valenti, walking along Grand Street near Mulberry, and opened fire. They managed to wound Valenti's bodyguard, who later died, but Valenti survived unharmed. Both the Peppo and

Valenti incidents took place near police headquarters; after the attempt on Valenti, police officers apprehended Masseria. Although the evidence for a conviction seemed overwhelming, a jury found "Joe the Boss" innocent.

The events of May 8 seemed to convince the Morellos that they should accept Masseria's claim to "Mafia" leadership. Valenti then carried on alone. In August he finally had what appeared to be a golden opportunity to eliminate his rival. On August 9, 1922, apparently after bribing Masseria's bodyguard, Valenti's men caught "Joe the Boss" in a trap. At about two o'clock in the afternoon Masseria emerged from his Lower East Side home at 80 Second Avenue near Fifth Street. As he crossed in front of Heiney Brothers Women's Wear shop at 82 Second Avenue, two men approached him with guns drawn. When they came within five feet they began to fire. The 35-year-old gang chieftain deftly dodged, ducked, and jumped around in his efforts to elude the bullets. The shots shattered the plate glass window of Heiney's shop and reduced Masseria's hat to "unsalvageable rubble," but "Joe the Boss" escaped unharmed. The "torpedoes" ran to a waiting car, leaving the "Mafia" leader exhausted but alive.

The dramatic nature of the thwarted assassination embellished Masseria's reputation and standing in "Mafia" circles and greatly increased the awe in which the Italian community held him. His position seemed secure, especially after he staged the brutal public murder of Valenti immediately following a peace conference. Masseria arranged to have two gunmen waiting outside the meeting place, a spaghetti house on East 12th Street, and walked outside the restaurant with his intended victim. His men did not miss. In the aftermath, Lupo, the Morellos, and other potential rivals quickly made peace and at least outwardly accepted Joe as "The Boss." Ciro Terranova remained the "Artichoke King" until the 1930s; he, his Morello relations, and his brother-in-law Lupo offered no further challenges to Masseria or to Masseria's successor, Salvatore Maranzano.[23]

Prohibition added a vital dimension to the Italian-colony crime situation by making opportunities available to gain power and money undreamed of in previous decades. In the 1920s "Mafia" leaders in New York and other cities organized Italian district residents in the manufacture of booze, which American generation criminals sold in the outside community.

During the decade the American "Mafia" became known also as the *Unione Siciliana*. The new name was apparently first used in Chicago by a legitimate mutual-benefit society organized in 1895 to provide for insurance and fraternal needs of unskilled immigrant laborers. Even before prohibition the local "Mafia" gained control of the society when *Capo* Anthony D'Andrea became its president. During the 1920s members of the fraternal society were forced to operate stills in their homes, and the name of the mutual insurance organization came to denote the criminal society. The fraternal group, as Denis Tilden Lynch noted, "exists in various localities in the East and Middle West as separate entities which have no official relations with one another. Many of the criminal element were recruited from these organizations." [24]

In 1925 honest members of the Chicago fraternal society attempted to end the identification with crime by changing the name to Italo-American National Union, but the damage to its reputation was permanent. Sometime during the mid-twenties the use of name *Unione Siciliana* to identify the "Mafia" organization appeared in New York, although it is impossible to determine the precise date.

American second-generation criminals served as distributors of booze produced in the Italian colony. Thus these "Americanized" criminals operated on two fronts, but by the late 1920s they wanted to reduce their involvement in immigrant district rivalries in order to maximize their contacts and opportunities in the economically lush outside community. Apparently, however, "greaseballs" like Masseria opposed innovation. Because of his control over a vital source of bootleg booze, "Joe the Boss" held a powerful weapon in his dealings with Luciano and associates. Masseria had no intention of permitting signs of independence in the younger generation. Charlie Lucky envied the position of power and relative independence that his old friend, Brooklyn-born Al Capone, enjoyed in Chicago. Finally, in

1930, a long-simmering power struggle between two "greaser" factions for control of New York's "Mafia," one led by Masseria and the other composed largely of recent arrivals from Fascist Italy, led by Salvatore Maranzano, burst into open warfare. Luciano saw the opportunity he had been waiting for, and used it successfully.

Masseria reigned supreme until 1927, when Salvatore Maranzano landed in New York and almost immediately began his strategies to unseat "Joe the Boss." Benito Mussolini's campaign in Southern Italy to eliminate secret societies forced high-level Sicilian *mafiosi* out of Italy during the late 1920s (the alternatives were imprisonment or acceptance of Fascist supremacy). The 43-year-old Maranzano, one of these refugees, arrived in the city with a high opinion of his own talents, connections with the other recently-arrived ex-*mafiosi,* and a great deal of money. Apparently he immediately established working relations with American "Mafiosi" who were dissatisfied with "Joe the Boss" and his autocratic ways. During the following four years, until his death in 1931, Maranzano increased his forces by smuggling Sicilian criminals into the country, usually men who were fleeing Fascist police. Both sides contained recruits from mainland Italy as well as from various towns and provinces of Sicily, but Maranzano's forces appeared to be more unified because most of the lieutenants, as well as some of the followers, came from the leader's home district of Castellammare. The bosses in the Masseria gang, in contrast, were more diverse in origin.[25]

Basically, the struggle occurred between long-time residents and newcomers. The Masseria-led faction consisted of old-time ethnic colony extortionists who had little, if any, contact with *mafia, Camorra,* or similar societies in the homeland. Those who had criminal records in Italy were generally guilty of crimes of passion or of brigandage. The Maranzano element, referred to at the time as "the outsiders," consisted largely of genuine *mafia* members and leaders, forced to leave Italy by Mussolini's campaign against secret societies.

Caught in the middle in this fight were the "Americanizers," many of them born in Italy. Members of this latter group, unlike the former Sicilian *mafiosi* and the American "Mafiosi," arrived in the United States as infants or children and grew to maturity in the New World

34. Jaunty young Detroit syndicate leader Pete Licavoli with two friends in 1930. (United Press International)

environment, absorbing its ideas, habits, and patterns of behavior as they matured. An examination of fifty-eight top and middle-management syndicate leaders operating in ten cities (Newark and Jersey City are included with New York City as Metropolitan New York) in 1931 shows that approximately two-thirds (or 39) were under the age of 40. A few were still in their twenties, including New York's Joe Adonis, Gerardo "Jerry" Catena of Newark, and Mario Balestreri of San Francisco. Detroit's Pete Licavoli was 28; Umberto Anastasio (Albert Anastasia) of Brooklyn and James Licavoli of Cleveland were 27; and Joseph Bonanno at 26 was the boss of one of New York's five major Italian syndicates. Those in their thirties included New York's Luciano, Joseph Profaci, Joseph Biondo, and Vito Genovese, all 34; Mike Miranda, 35; Joe Magliocco, 33; Anthony "Tony Bender" Strollo and Thomas "Three Finger Brown" Lucchese, both 32; and Michael Coppola, who was 31. Chicago's Al Capone was 32. Alfred Polizzi of Cleveland was 31; Kansas City syndicate leader and political power John Lazia was 34, as were Detroit's Joseph Zerilli and James Colletti of Pueblo and Denver. Denver booze baron Joseph Roma and New Orleans leader Sylvestro Carollo were 35.

Although the overwhelming majority of the men had been born in Italy (43 of the 58), they viewed themselves as Americans because they grew up in the American urban environment. Thus Luciano was 9 years old in 1906 when he arrived from Sicily with his parents; Neapolitan Joe Adonis was 6. Sylvestro Carollo of Sicily was 2, Sicilian Lucchese 11, Anastasia, also of Sicily, 13, and Genovese of Naples, 15. New York's Frank Costello, who was born in Calabria in 1891, entered the United States when he was 4, a year older than Chicago's Frank Nitti when he migrated. Sicilian Frank Milano of Cleveland and Joseph Di Giovanni of Kansas City were both 14 when they arrived, and Mike Coppola was brought to the United States from Salerno when he was 5 months old. Even elder statesman John Torrio, the oldest on the list (born in Naples in 1882), was of the American generation, for he was brought to the United States at the age of 2, and grew up in New York City. By contrast, Salvatore Maranzano, although two years younger than Torrio, was 43 when he left Italy after four decades in the Sicilian milieu. "Joe the Boss" Masseria was also a grown man (in his twenties) when he reached New York from Sicily, as was Palermo native Ignacio Saietta, born in 1877. Among the American-born were Al Capone (Brooklyn, 1899), Jerry Catena (Newark, 1902), Willie Moretti (New York, 1894), Pete and James Licavoli (St. Louis, 1903, 1904), Anthony Cigali (New Orleans, 1891), Tony Strollo (New York, 1899), and Tony Parmagini (San Francisco, 1890).[26]

The ''Americanizers'' looked down on the *mafiosi* and the ''Mafia,'' viewing both factions as ''greaseballs.'' ''Actually we never got along,'' Joe Valachi recalled, ''because they have a different way of living.'' [27]

Luciano and his followers joined forces with Masseria, according to Nick Gentile, because of the conviction that ''Joe the Boss'' was the weaker of the two ''greaseball'' leaders and thus would be easier to eliminate. Operating with practical cunning, Luciano apparently decided that it would be easier to effect the murder from a position as trusted lieutenant than as a distrusted rival. On April 15, 1931, Masseria and Luciano went to Scarpato's Italian restaurant in Brooklyn's Coney Island section and sat down to what would be the leader's last meal. After eating and playing cards, Lucky went to the men's room. While he was washing his hands, he later told the police, he heard shots and returned to find ''Joe the Boss'' dead; of course he had no idea who had committed the crime. The exact composition of the murder squad is still unknown, but the killers were certainly dispatched by Lucky and probably included his next-in-command, Neapolitan Vito Genovese.[28]

After hearing of the murder, Gentile, who was in New York at the time, stated that he hurried to Luciano's home, where he witnessed the opening discussion between Lucky and Vincenzo Troia, a representative of Maranzano. Luciano apparently did not operate from a position of weakness, for (in Gentile's words) he directed Don Vincenzo to inform his boss that ''we have killed Masseria not to serve him, but for our own personal ends.'' Luciano then threatened continued war if Maranzano harmed even one of his former enemies and gave Maranzano twenty-four hours in which to decide whether he would accept Luciano's terms or prepare for a war ''to the end.'' The conditions were met, and a few days later a peace conference was held in Chicago under Al Capone's auspices.[29]

35. Crowds estimated at 5,000 waited outside Joe Masseria's apartment building for a glimpse of the murdered "Mafia" chieftain. (New York *Daily News*)

After his return to New York, Maranzano staged a victory celebration which, Joe Valachi recalls, was held "in a big hall around Washington Avenue" in the Bronx. During a speech that evening Maranzano justified the late war and the killing of Masseria by claiming that the latter "had sentenced all the Castellammarese to death without cause."

Valachi, a very low-ranking member of the Castellammare forces, claims that Maranzano also decreed the organizational structure of New York's Italian syndicates (a structure that author Peter Maas notes "still exists") as well as the internal relations of these groups which Valachi called "families" but which in the 1930s were generally referred to as *borgate* (literally, villages, or, in the New York context, sections). It is impossible to verify or disprove Valachi's statements (which most writers have accepted as fact), since Valachi was the only person present in the hall that evening who has shared his recollections of the meeting. However, his description of Maranzano's proclamation concerning the formation of the five New York *borgate*, the restructuring of relations within each *borgata*, and the placing of Italian crime in New York on a sound business basis, suggests that Valachi confused some events from this meeting with conferences, limited to top management, that took place a few months later and after Maranzano's murder.

By August 1, 1931, Maranzano and Luciano had settled their differences as well as questions concerning the official relations between them and between themselves and their followers. A banquet was held to honor the new leader, and a three-day celebration which (as a New York *Sun* reporter with excellent police department contacts pointed out later) was no secret to the authorities. Ostensibly a religious festival to raise money for the Maritime Society of Sciacca, the festivities proclaiming Maranzano's assumption of "Joe the Boss's" leadership took place in the same Coney Island restaurant where Masseria had been murdered. "Several thousand Italians" attended, most from the New York metropolitan area, but many from elsewhere in the East and from other sections of the country. The only question in the minds of police, reflecting the uncertainty of their Italian-colony informants, was whether Maranzano or Luciano "took up the leadership that Joe the Boss surrendered by dying last spring." That question, the *Sun* reporter believed, received a definitive answer with the September 10 murder of Maranzano.[30]

The first days of August were busy ones for the Castellammare native. According to Gentile, Maranzano overthrew the existing "Mafia" democracy, the governing commission of six leaders representing "Mafia" groups in the various cities of the country. He proclaimed himself the reigning "Boss of Bosses of all the Mafias in the United States." Contrary to Valachi's recollections, Maranzano became more dictatorial than Masseria had ever been, and made a quantum jump beyond anything attempted by any of his New York predecessors. He proclaimed as his domain Italian-colony crime in New

York, and through his new lieutenant, Luciano, a piece of the non-colony crime controlled by Italians in Manhattan and other boroughs. Even New York comprised only the center of his kingdom, which—in his view—encompassed all the Italian colonies of all the cities of the nation.[31]

"Joe the Boss" had been tyrannical during his nine-year dominance over Italian-colony crime; the "Boss of Bosses" during his brief tenure proved to be insufferable. He brooked no opposition, nor would he tolerate the presence of any potential rival. During the last month and ten days of his life Maranzano plotted the deaths of sixty gangsters in New York and other cities. His list included Luciano and Genovese (who had eased Maranzano's rise to power by eliminating his predecessor and chief rival) as well as the Chicago peacemaker, Capone. Unfortunately for the "Boss of Bosses," his intended victims had laid their own plans.

At approximately 2:45 P.M. on September 10, 1931, "four men carrying guns strode into the three-room suite which was run under the name of the Eagle Building Corporation." Announcing that they were federal agents, the gunmen (recruited from among Luciano's non-Italian syndicate acquaintances) ordered Maranzano's secretary, Grace Samuels, and nine men waiting in an anteroom to line along the wall. While two men guarded these ten, the other two "policemen" walked into the inner office, where they brought a violent end to the reign of the "Boss of Bosses." Maranzano did not die without a struggle; the coroner found six stab wounds and four gun shots in his body. Ironically, at the time of the murder another non-Italian gunman, Vincent "Mad Dog" Coll, was on his way to Maranzano's office to work out the details of a contract to kill Luciano and Genovese.[32]

As had been the case after Masseria's murder, the syndicate called a meeting in Chicago to work out arrangements for the succession to Maranzano's position. The power and prestige enjoyed by Capone among his peers in New York and around the country were emphasized by the prominent role he played in the events that occurred in New York during 1931. According to Gentile, who served as a delegate at the conference, members reached a decision, apparently at the urging of Luciano, to eliminate the position of "boss of bosses" and establish a commission of six members. Thus the delegates returned to a concept originally proposed at the first Chicago conference in 1931, held following Masseria's murder. (At the earlier meeting, however, Maranzano had pressured delegates to reject the plan and to appoint him Masseria's successor in the reinstated position of "boss of bosses.") There existed a major difference between the new group of commissioners and its predecessor. The old governing body was to have been composed of "Mafia" chiefs, and its power limited largely to Italian-colony crime. Luciano's new creation was, in effect, a board of directors, composed primarily of men in command of illegal organizations operating mainly in the larger American community.

The commission consisted of four New York leaders: Luciano, Vincent Mangano, Joe Profaci, and Joe Bonanno; and two non-New Yorkers: Chicago's Al Capone and Cleveland's Frank Milano. Capone's prominence was short-lived, for on October 24, 1931, he was sentenced to five years in federal prison for income tax evasion. Luciano's position, in contrast to his predecessor's almost imperial rank, was that of first among equals. He stressed his break with the past and with Southern Italian tradition by refusing to accept tribute money from his associates at the Chicago conference. (In contrast, his predecessor Maranzano had collected $100,000 at the banquet held to celebrate his new status as "Boss of Bosses." [33])

Luciano's succession completed the process of merging the large and powerful New York "Mafia" units with the emerging syndicates of the second generation. The conflict between old and new resulted in the triumph of the Americanizers. Although the new organization was not Sicilian (or Southern Italian), neither did it function like an American industrial concern. Working relationships, far more impersonal than in Southern Italy, were also far more personalized than in a legitimate American corporation. At this point in their development, syndicate leaders had not learned to hire corporation lawyers and other professionals skilled in the nuances of operating legitimate big businesses. Luciano, Costello, Torrio, and their associates adapted or adopted business ideas they learned from the lawyers, politicians, bankers, and businessmen they associated with and often lived near. The modified or appropriated ideas had to fit organizations containing sizable numbers of men with little or no formal schooling, a handicap shared by many, if not most, of the leadership. Luciano, Capone, and their peers were largely uneducated and unsophisticated in the intricacies of management theory; hence the organizations they created and the operating processes they adopted were primitive and unsophisticated compared with those of a large American business concern. Considering the low level of education of their subordinates, it is understandable—and, in fact, a sign of their shrewdness—that these young captains of illegal business utilized terms familiar to their followers even though these terms were inaccurate translations of the actual institutions they represented. For example, *borgata* and *famiglia* were used to denote a criminal syndicate, and *Unione Siciliana* to refer to the combination of all the individual Italian crime syndicates in New York. The terms, and the rather primitive institutions they described, functioned adequately, however, for the needs of the men involved, and filled a larger need in that they served as the point of departure for developments in organizational structure and procedure in the decades since. Changes do not appear to have been extensive or significant. The principal difference in the 1970s seems to be that syndicate leaders can and do hire specialists in business techniques just as they have for decades hired specialists with needed physical and legal skills.[34]

The organizations themselves were ideally suited for the enrichment of the leadership. Ordinary members—"soldiers," as Valachi called them—received no salary; the boss, who apparently owned or had "a piece" of virtually everything of moneymaking value, gave nothing for free. The chief owed his men protection: against police raids, harassment, or arrest; against the legal system; for families of men found guilty and sent to prison or killed in the line of duty. The leader did not always fulfill these obligations, except against the possible encroachment of other gangs into his territory or his business operations. The limited aid a gang member could expect was indicated in an exchange between Valachi and U.S. Senator Jacob Javits during testimony before the McClellan Committee:

Senator Javits:	Did they [the Genovese organization] give you any protection in the 35 years?
Mr. Valachi:	No.
Senator Javits:	They did not furnish lawyers?
Mr. Valachi:	Never.
Senator Javits:	Or bondsmen?
Mr. Valachi:	Never. I got my own bondsmen, my own lawyers.
Senator Javits:	What use were they to you during that time?
Mr. Valachi:	As I say, they feel that they protect you in anything you have, whatever business you may have, and somebody wants to step on your toes, then you run to them and they protect you.[35]

Unlike members of the more closely knit and paternalistic "Mafia" organizations of an earlier day, who received a fixed weekly salary, syndicate members from bosses on down were expected to operate like highly motivated entrepreneurs. The potential profits, for underlings as well as for those in top and middle-management positions, could be huge; but so were the risks, especially for ordinary members, who had neither the wealth nor the connections enjoyed by the leadership to depend on when trouble struck.

The lowly "soldier" had to "scrounge," generally on his own, to find opportunities in gambling, narcotics, prostitution, racketeering, or any other ventures that might return a profit. "You get nothing, only what you earn yourself," Valachi stated in testimony before the McClellan Committee. At the same time he had to be sure not to infringe upon the territory or illicit business ventures of a member of his or some other Italian organization. Leaders or their lieutenants sometimes offered help to members seeking opportunities. Whether aided or not, "soldiers" had to share their profits with the leaders. In an insecure and hostile world it made good sense to keep the bosses—who, after all, could provide protection even if they often did not—happy and contented. A boss who did not receive a "cut"—a respectable "cut" at that—was not a happy boss.[36]

The practical-minded Luciano apparently did not concern himself with drawing up organizational plans and flow charts, or with coining new names to distinguish the organization and its component parts from that of his "greaser" predecessor. Nor, when he succeeded Maranzano, did Charlie Lucky disturb the internal structure or relationships of the *borgate*. Unlike Maranzano, he was not obsessed with appearances or with an ambition to remold underworld institutions according to a local and personal model. Even in 1931 Luciano seemed to have his goals set far beyond the Italian community and Italian criminal organizations.

The objectives of maximizing profits and eliminating, or at least minimizing, obstacles in the way of making more money, determined Luciano's actions, whether inside or outside the Italian group. In order to realize his goals, he needed the full backing of his fellow Italians. Except in a few instances, he sought no revenge against Maranzano's associates and allies, although he had the opportunity and the precedents provided by Maranzano. As a result, throughout the 1930s, Luciano's New York organization, with its five *borgate*, was known as the *Unione Siciliana*, the term used to identify only the immigrant colony group—the American "Mafia"—in the previous decade. There is no evidence of the use of *Cosa Nostra* during the 1930s; the term apparently has come into use in the New York area since World War II. Furthermore, during this period the geographic designation *borgata* appears to have been favored to denote the individual organizations. The almost exclusive use of the term "family" in recent years reflects the solidification of control over New York Italian syndicates by groups of relatives, through blood ties or marriage. During the 1930s, however, blood ties and family connections could not in themselves guarantee a position of prominence in a *borgata*. Nick Gentile related in his autobiography an incident that occurred in 1935, when Joe Parlapiano, who ran gambling activities in Lower Manhattan for the Mangano syndicate, wanted to bring his son into the gambling operation as a partner, and proposed his plan at a meeting of his associates in the venture. This suggestion met with strong opposition, according to Luigi Marciano, who told the story to Gentile. " 'I too claimed the same right for my son,' Marciano stated, 'and so did the others present. Since it was not possible to admit them all, none were admitted.' " [37]

In each *borgata* a boss and one or more sub-bosses occupied the positions of leadership. They were aided by their immediate subordinates, the "head of ten" (*capodecina*), or section leaders, who served in the syndicate's middle-management positions. Each *borgata* was composed of one or more "groups of ten." Group members, known as "brothers" or "soldiers," were small entrepreneurs who staffed the lowest rank in the syndicate. They, in turn, employed non-*borgata* members in their various illegal business ventures. The only innovation that far-sighted businessman Luciano introduced was a grievance procedure designed to head off potential discontent among lower echelon *Unione* members. Upon succeeding Maranzano, he decreed the creation of a new position within each New York *borgata,* that of *consigliere,* or counselor, to serve as an arbiter of disputes between the leaders and ordinary members. (Later the function of advisor to the syndicate leader was added to his duties.) The office of *consigliere* recognized both the tremendously increased power of the bosses and the distance between them and ordinary gang members— mere hired help who, if they lacked legitimate means of airing grievances, might well turn to other means, most likely the violent ones with which they had greatest familiarity. It also recognized that by the early 1930s syndicate crime had become a big business operation and that management action on the part of syndicate leadership provided the best way to prevent organized protest against that leadership and provide alternate channels for venting frustrations. In subsequent years syndicate leaders elsewhere gradually recognized the value of the idea and eventually adopted it for their own use. As in the legitimate business world, criminal syndicate bosses exchanged ideas and techniques, and sometimes personnel, with leaders in other cities.

During the 1930s Luciano, his associates in New York, and their contemporaries in Chicago, Detroit, and other cities developed a system in which the integrity and independence of the individual syndicates were of primary importance and the power of the syndicate boss within his organization virtually unlimited. Illicit enterprises were developed through the activity of the individual *borgata*, in that each organization staked out territory and business activities and wielded supreme power within its own boundaries. Although a system for airing and dealing with grievances among organizations also evolved during the late 1920s and early 1930s, no central authority limited or infringed upon the autonomy of the boss in his organization.

A number of conferences took place during and after the prohibition era, but apparently none of them created a national crime organization. So far as can be determined, no single national leader or centralized bureaucratic body was formed to coordinate activities among syndicates across the nation, or to function as permanent organization between meetings. The conferences about which knowledge exists seem to have been held for specific purposes, and were local or regional in character and representation.

Meetings were held for a number of reasons—to settle disputes, choose successors for slain or deposed leaders, divide local or regional markets, or discuss production, supply, and distribution problems. Some gatherings consisted of Italian criminals and limited their discussions to problems of interest to them. Others involved only Jews or Irish or some other ethnic group; still others were formed of members of a variety of ethnic syndicates.

Of course, Americans who had no connections with syndicates also utilized conferences. In 1926 two visiting British industrialists, F. Vernon Willey and Guy Locock, President and Assistant Director respectively of the Federation of British Industries, observed the activities of legitimate businessmen. "The American 'convention' habit," they noted "may appear to consume a great deal of time, but there is no doubt that the habit of meeting together frequently and exchanging experiences has proved to be of the greatest value to American industry." That habit proved also to be of value to American crime.[38]

Unlike their industrialist and business counterparts, crime syndicate bosses or their representatives found it expedient to hold their confer-

36. Chicago Police Department photo of local syndicate figures Paul Ricca (1) and Rocco Fiaschetti (5) and three visitors arrested outside a Chicago hotel on April 20, 1932: Sylvester Agoglia (2), a Brooklyn and Miami gunman; New York gangland powers Lucky Luciano (3) and Meyer Lansky (4); and Harry Brown, a "race track man" with no police record. (In author's possession)

ences away from the glare of publicity and news media coverage. As a result, authorities learned about some of the meetings after they had taken place, and doubtless never learned about others. Nevertheless, police managed to interrupt two meetings in progress. One was a 1928 conference of Italians in Cleveland; the other was an all-Jewish meeting in New York in 1933.

On December 5, 1928, Cleveland police arrested twenty-seven suspicious-looking out-of-towners at the Hotel Statler. Nearly all the visitors came from two metropolitan areas, New York and Chicago, although one arrived from Buffalo, one from St. Louis, and one from Tampa. All registered at the Statler and occupied luxurious suites. Arresting officers reported in awe that "virtually all wore new silk underwear and fine linen" and transported their belongings "in new and expensive leather bags." Possibly this finery contrasted with the appearance and standard of living of local criminals, since Detective Captain Emmet J. Potts observed that the men "looked more like prosperous sales representatives of some large business concern than thugs." Captain Potts might have been more accurate than he knew, because one of the purposes of the meeting appears to have been to assure the steady supply and uninterrupted distribution of corn sugar, a product vital to whiskey production. In the hours before their arrest, four of the visitors held "a long conference with one or two men known as bootleg overlords of Cleveland by virtue of a monopoly over the city's corn sugar supply." [39]

The Cleveland police suggested at the time—and their theory has been echoed by many writers on crime since—that another objective was to select a successor to recently slain Chicago "Mafia" leader Tony Lombardo, or to win the support of New Yorkers for a choice already made. A companion theory, and one that is East-Coast oriented, is that delegates met to choose a successor to Frank Yale of Brooklyn, said by some to be national president of *Unione Siciliana,* and, like Lombardo, a recent murder victim.

Early in 1933 New York police learned through underworld informants about a meeting of local Jewish syndicate leaders being held at the Hotel Franconia on West 72nd Street in Manhattan. Police descended upon the Franconia and arrested nine men: Benjamin ("Bugsy") Siegel, business associate of Meyer Lansky; Louis ("Lepke") Buchalter and his partner Jacob ("Gurrah") Shapiro; Joseph ("Doc") Stacher; Harry Teitelbaum; Harry ("Big Greenie") Greenberg; Louis ("Shadows") Kravitz; Phillip ("Little Farvel") Kovolick; and Hyman ("Curly") Holtz. Although it is impossible to be certain, the conference was probably devoted to a discussion of how to diversify illegal operations and overcome problems created by repeal of the Eighteenth Amendment. [40]

In addition to these and other conclaves limited to a single ethnic group and its particular personal or business problems, syndicate members met also in multi-ethnic conferences. One of the most important multi-ethnic conferences took place at the President Hotel in Atlantic City May 13–16, 1929. Local gambling and political kingpin

Enoch J. ("Nucky") Johnson hosted the event. Many major East Coast bootleggers attended, led by a New York delegation that included Luciano, Costello, Lansky, Schultz, and Torrio (who apparently served as chairman). Al Capone headed a contingent from Chicago. At the working session delegates apparently discussed means to decrease what was viewed by participants as an excessive individualism and cut-throat competition in the bootlegging business along the East Coast and in the Middle West. The conference did not bring an immediate end to the divisiveness and bloodshed growing out of the traffic in illegal booze, but it seems to have been an early effort to coordinate activities between syndicates composed of a number of ethnic groups and to divide the market among them. In this respect it helped prepare the way for the establishment in 1932 of the "Big Seven," a cooperative venture of leading East Coast bootleggers which for several months prior to Repeal controlled the importation and distribution of liquor from Canada.[41]

The Atlantic City conferees seem also to have dealt with Capone's excessive use of violence in establishing dominance over Chicago-area entrepreneurial crime. Just three months before, on St. Valentine's Day, Capone gunmen had massacred seven members of the rival North Side organization. This event was followed by the murder on May 7 (just five days before the Atlantic City meeting) of long-time Capone gang members John Scalise, Albert Anselmi, and Joseph "Hop Toad" Giunta. The three Sicilians had schemed to dispose of Capone and take over his empire. "Scarface Al" learned of their plans and at a banquet ostensibly held to honor them for their loyal service, he and associates literally beat them to death. The corpses, with hardly a bone unbroken in any of the three bodies, were dumped in the Indiana countryside near Hammond. On the way back from Atlantic City Capone and his bodyguard were arrested in Philadelphia. Whether he was ordered by his peers at Atlantic City to give himself up for a jail term as punishment for his excessive behavior in eliminating competition, as some writers have claimed, whether—as others maintain—he arranged for his own arrest in order to have a safe rest far from the problems infesting his Chicago domain, or whether his ar-

37. Capone gunmen John Scalisi (*center*) and Albert Anselmi (*right*) at a 1927 court appearance in Chicago. Two years later their battered corpses were found in the Indiana countryside. (Courtesy Chicago Historical Society)

rest resulted from the diligence and honesty of Philadelphia's police (as no one has yet claimed), Capone nevertheless was found guilty of carrying a concealed deadly weapon and sentenced to a year in prison. Safely behind bars, Capone allegedly said, "I do feel secure for the first time in a long while."

The conferences apparently most significant and far-reaching in their future impact took place in 1934 in New York and Kansas City. In the course of investigations in Brooklyn in 1940, which resulted in breaking up a syndicate "hit" squad created at the 1934 meetings, authorities obtained information about the conclaves held six years before. According to members who turned informers, John Torrio was the guiding genius behind the meeting in New York. According to Brooklyn Assistant District Attorney Burton B. Turkus, who related the information received from the informers, "Each boss remained czar in his own territory, his rackets unmolested, his local authority uncontested." Participants at this meeting created a central board composed of all the individual syndicate bosses. Its purpose was to determine common policies and procedures and to arbitrate jurisdictional and other inter-syndicate disputes. An "extermination department" headed by Abe Reles, ("Pittsburgh Phil") Strauss, and "Happy" Maione was made available to any of the member organizations to carry out strong-arm assignments. Syndicate bosses could call on this group or use their own specialists. Concluding that the plan offered an effective balance between autonomy and mutual cooperation, the Eastern syndicate bosses quickly put it into operation. According to the Brooklyn informers, at a second conference later in the year in Kansas City, syndicates in other parts of the country adopted Torrio's plan.[42]

From the beginning, the misdirected insights of New York *World-Telegram* reporter Harry Feeney—in Turkus's words, "a round little Irishman who could smell a story a mile away"—distorted the entire thrust of the investigation. Apparently Feeney helped to shape the story as he wrote it, a contribution that contemporary law enforcement agents did not recognize. On the "very first day of the investigation," Turkus recalled in 1951, Feeney "pointed up the nation-wide connections," and the following day, he "came up with the inspiration for the name"—"Murder, Inc." Feeney erred both in the geographic extent of the meeting and in his choice of name for the organization.[43]

The organization in question, which contemporary criminals called the "Combination," did not possess nation-wide influence. Criminal syndicates, some of them powerful and others merely pretending to power, existed at the same time in other areas of the country, but the largest markets for the services provided by entrepreneurs of crime lay in the East and (to a somewhat lesser extent) in the Middle West. Thus, the foci of syndicate activities, and the strength of the "Combination," lay in these two highly urbanized and industrialized sections of the country. Essentially the "Combination" was an expansion of the idea developed by the Big Seven under Torrio's direction during prohibition. Leading East Coast criminal entrepreneurs, most of whom had participated in the Big Seven experiment, attended the conferences. These men had practical experience of the advantages of cooperative activities. In addition, they respected Torrio's intelligence and innovativeness. Members at both meetings focused on the continued functioning of independent syndicates, each pursuing its separate business interests. Like the Big Seven group before it, the "Combination" had as its guiding principle the prevention of uncontrolled competition. Thus, murder did not provide the "Combination's" reason for existence nor its major activity. The "Combination" utilized murder for purposes of expedience in the operation of illegal business, since the primary and all-consuming objective of participants was to make money. For this end, any means was justified.[44]

Criminal entrepreneurs portrayed themselves as harassed and misunderstood businessmen, misrepresented by the press and victimized by the unfounded accusations of venal politicians. Like Al Capone, who claimed, "All I do is to supply a public demand," syndicate leaders argued that the numbers business, slot machines, bet-taking on horse and dog races, prostitution, "muscling in" on labor unions or small concerns, were all business operations like banking or selling hardware. During the Depression decade, Americans probably believed that little difference existed between the morals and scruples of the so-called big-time criminals and ordinary merchants and businessmen.[45]

8

The 'Thirties: No Depression for the Syndicates

During the 1930s, when the nation as a whole suffered the effects of the worst depression in its history, the syndicates operated on a business-as-usual basis. Even with the end of prohibition in 1933 America's crime organizations continued to grow and prosper. Although the millions of dollars formerly gained from the illicit liquor trade no longer flowed in, numerous other areas of activity more than made up for repeal. During the 1930s gambling returned to its position as the principal source of underworld income. Additional millions poured in from loan-sharking, from syndicate-controlled whorehouses, and from expanding traffic in narcotics. During this decade, Lucky Luciano, for example, was arrested on a charge of organizing prostitution in New York; and although he maintained at the time and later that he never had any connection with or interest in prostitution, a jury found the evidence sufficiently convincing to judge him guilty. The expanding syndicates were also testing the potential for profit in the comparatively new labor and business rackets.

While these areas of enterprise—some of them venerable standbys and some relatively new and untested—absorbed most of the attention of the ex-bootleggers who directed America's crime syndicates, entrepreneurs did not abandon the now-legal liquor trade. With the end of prohibition in 1933, the highly sophisticated industry developed by bootleggers went into decline, although it did not entirely disappear, and criminal syndicates have continued to produce and sell illicit liquor right down to the present day. The two largest stills known to authorities were discovered after enactment of the Twenty-first Amendment. One that apparently had operated for years was found in Zanesville (in the Cleveland area) in January 1935. The estimated value of the plant reached at least $250,000. Machines produced both beer and liquor; the daily production of beer reportedly amounted to over 36,000 gallons, and "5,000 gallons of 190-proof alcohol of the highest grade were produced every twenty-four hours." During the following month, federal, state and local authorities discovered another still in Elizabeth, New Jersey, "second in size only to the one at Zanesville" and valued at $200,000.[1]

Clever, far-sighted entrepreneurs did not have to abandon the liquor business and did not have to continue to operate as bootleggers in the years after repeal of the Eighteenth Amendment. When the demise of the noble experiment occurred, syndicate bosses who had anticipated it already had signed agreements with distilleries to serve as importers and distributors for their products. These companies, it should be pointed out, also employed men who had had no connection with the illicit alcohol trade during prohibition. The former bootleggers did, however, have the advantage of knowing the business, of having contacts with potential buyers, and, when necessary, of being ready and able to employ violent means of persuasion when other sales techniques failed. To illustrate, in 1934 the Midwest Distributing Company, a wholesale liquor firm, received the exclusive distributorship for Seagram products in Jackson County, which included Kansas City. The Schenley line went to Superior Wines and Liquor Company. Joseph ("Scarface") Di Giovanni, who had arrived in the United States with his parents in 1903 when he was 15 and was prominent in Kansas City underworld activities during the 1920s, was president of Midwest, and his brother Vincent headed Superior. Thus, in effect, the Di Giovannis monopolized the liquor trade in the entire Kansas City area.[2]

Frank Costello was another of those who continued to profit from the distribution of alcoholic beverages long after the end of prohibition. Costello and "Dandy Phil" Kastel, his close associate in this and other illegal ventures beginning in the late 1920s, became agents for

38. Pete and Joe Di Giovanni at the time of their appearance before the Kefauver Committee, which investigated their involvement, along with their brother Vincent's, in Kansas City liquor business. (Kansas City *Star*)

Alliance Distributors, Inc., a New York corporation formed at the time of repeal in December 1933 for the purpose of importing and distributing liquor from Canada and overseas. Alliance handled, among others, Scotch whiskey produced by Whiteley Distilleries of London, whose brands included King's Ransom, Auld George, and House of Lords. In 1938 Costello provided financial backing for Kastel and Irving Haim (another prohibition-era bootlegger) to purchase all the stock of J. G. Turney and Sons, Ltd., of London, the holding company for Whiteley Distilleries. Once in control of the company, the new owners appointed Costello the "personal agent" for Turney and Sons in the United States. His contract provided, according to the minutes of the company's Board of Directors, that "Mr. Costello shall use his best efforts to promote the interests of the company in the United States by personal contact with the wholesale and retail merchants, and the consuming public, by frequenting first-class hotels and restaurants, and asking to be supplied with the company's brands marketed in the United States." These services as roving ambassador of good will for the Turney Distilleries were considered to be so valuable that Costello received a salary of £5,000 (approximately $25,000) per year and a commission "equal to 5 shillings on every case in excess of 50,000 cases per annum, shipped by the company to the United States of America." [3]

In the forefront among legal liquor promoters stood John Torrio, who through frontmen serving as officers, directors, and stockholders, owned and operated the importing firm of Prendergast and Davies. In early December 1933, just one month after founding the firm, the three original owners had a falling out and in consequence decided to sell their interest to Torrio for $62,000. The purchase turned out to be one of great bargains of the decade, for, according to a confidential Internal Revenue Service report prepared in 1939, "Prendergast & Davies Co., Ltd., importers and wholesalers of liquors, was the biggest corporation of its kind in New York City from the day of Repeal, December 5, 1933[,] until well into the middle of 1935," when IRS started to investigate Torrio's connection with the company. The firm then began to disintegrate, but until that time "its business ran into the millions of dollars every single month." It had exclusive rights to the products of several of the nationally known distillers and importers. "Its delivery trucks were as familiar a sight at the door of big and little retail stores, restaurants, night clubs and hotels," the report noted, "as the mailman is at your own door." [4]

Although the beverage business continued throughout the 1930s to be a very profitable form of activity, gambling (including horse racing and dog racing, slot machines, casinos, and the numbers racket) became the largest source of income, followed by business and labor racketeering. In 1931 illegal gambling brought in an estimated $500 million per year, as compared with an estimated $2 to

39. A relaxed and confident John Torrio posed for photographers during his 1939 trial in New York on charges of income tax evasion. (New York *Daily News*)

$3 billion from bootlegging. By 1935, numbers alone accounted for at least $100 million a year in a single city, New York.[5]

The growth in the syndicates' "take" from gambling showed in the huge increase in Frank Costello's profits from slot machines in the 1930s. During the 1920s Costello had concentrated primarily on bootlegging, although he did not entirely abandon the gambling activities he had developed in the preceding decade; but in the late 1920s and early 1930s, still in partnership with Phil Kastel, he began a large-scale move into gambling and other areas, along with his stake in the legal liquor business. Thus, in 1931 Costello and Kastel obtained the New York territory from the Mills Novelty Company of Chicago, the largest makers of slot machines in the country. During its first year in existence, Tru-Mint Company, the company Costello and Kastel set up to handle their slot-machine business, placed 5,186 machines at various locations in the city, in speakeasies, cigar stores, candy stores, and grocery stores. The yearly "take" from the slot machines has been estimated at from $18 to $36 million, but not all of it (as Leonard Katz has noted) was clear profit. "There were very, very heavy expenses. Half the police department and all of Tammany Hall was on the payroll." This exaggeration was close to the truth.[6]

40. New York Mayor Fiorello La Guardia destroying slot machines in October 1934. The machines were eventually dumped into Long Island Sound. (United Press International)

Although illegal in New York, the slot machine business was carried on openly with the approval of police and politicians until the election of reform mayor Fiorello La Guardia. In 1934, one year after entering office for his first term, La Guardia began a campaign against the slots and other open manifestations of syndicate crime in the city. In the face of this official pressure, Costello relocated his machines in New Orleans. According to a statement by Costello before a New York grand jury in 1939, he "was invited to come to New Orleans in the early part of 1935 by a man named Senator Huey P. Long." Costello went on, "He asked me to put slot machines in Louisiana; he was going to pass some kind of ordinance for the poor, the blind—a kind of relief, to get a certain percentage—and we would have to pay so much per machine. . . . I got Phil Kastel, which is my associate, to go down there and work the thing out." According to the Internal

Revenue Service, there was strong circumstantial evidence that after Long's assassination in September 1935 Costello arranged with New Orleans's newly-inaugurated mayor, Robert L. Maestri, to place the machines "in almost every business establishment," where they "were unmolested by the police." The 8,100 slot machines, valued at $942,000, grossed an estimated $32,840,000 during the following ten years.

In the 1930s, Italians also moved into the numbers business in New York's Harlem section, a field of economic activity whose potential for profit was earlier recognized by Dutch Schultz. "Numbers" was a variant form of "policy," which appears to have originated in the London lottery shops in the first half of the eighteenth century and was soon transplanted to America. By the early nineteenth century, policy was firmly established as the favorite gambling game of masses of people in the United States, since even the poor could bet their pennies and nickels in hope of hitting a winning number on the designated lottery. An 1890 Michigan court proceedings described how the game was played. For a "sum of money, usually from five to 50 cents," a bettor could select any number or combinations of numbers from 1 to 78. If the player was successful, he had a "hit." If he selected two numbers, he had a "saddle"; three made a "gig," four a "horse." Winnings were based on how many of the numbers selected came out in the drawing. In the case of a "gig," the player received ten dollars for a five-cent bet. Thus the winner of a "gig" received 200 times the amount bet, which to a slumdweller equaled a bonanza; but the odds against scoring a "hit" were overwhelming. If the drawing consisted of twelve winning numbers, the odds against a player's selecting a "gig" were 76,076 to 1; for a "horse" the odds leapt to 1,426,425 to 1. Policy players faced not only the tremendous odds against a winning combination; because of the manner in which the winning numbers were selected—by drawing numbered slips from a bowl or numbered balls from a barrel or wheel—operators could manipulate the odds, and hence "fix" the game in their favor. (As St. Clair Drake and Horace Cayton have shown in their study of black Chicago, the game has not changed essentially in the succeeding years.) [7]

Early in twentieth-century New York, a simplified form of the game was introduced based on choosing the probable last three numbers of the Federal Reserve Clearing House report. Since it was impossible to tamper with the Clearing House figures and since they were published daily in the newspapers, the "numbers game" quickly became very popular along the East Coast, although Chicago and most of the rest of the country have remained loyal to policy down to the present. In an attempt in the late 1920s to destroy the numbers game, newspapers were asked to (and agreed to) print the reports in round numbers. Operators simply turned to other sources of published numbers, the most popular being pari-mutuel totals from various race tracks across the country. At Schultz-controlled numbers banks a favored track was Cincinnati's Coney Island, which "The Dutchman" owned.

The winning number was determined in this way: the total odds paid on the first three races run were added together and the final digit before the decimal point was the first of the three in the lucky number. The other numbers were obtained in the same way: the second digit was determined by adding the odds in the fourth and fifth races, and the final digit from the total odds on the sixth and seventh races. The odds against choosing the winning number were enormous. "The bettor takes a 1,000-to-1 chance that he can pick a set of three digits anywhere between 000 and 999 which will appear in an agreed-upon tabulation at a race track, clearing house, or elsewhere," reporter Tom Poston wrote in a series on the numbers racket for the New York *Post* in 1960. "If he wins, the most he can get is 600-to-1 (really 599-to-1 since the original wager is included in the payoff). Some banks pay as little as 300-to-1 in the case of certain numbers that the policy operators consider 'hot' at a given time." During the 1930s Schultz used another technique to reduce the betting public's chances of winning. Since he owned the race track at which the payoff number for his Harlem "banks" was determined, he would, on occasion, have the odds manipulated so that the winning number was one on which fewest bets had been made.[8]

In the pre-Schultz days in Harlem, numerous independent bankers conducted the game, each for himself, each providing the required capital, and each taking the resulting profits. These profits were enormous. Puerto Rican-born José Enrique ("Henry") Miro began 1927 as a fireman and boiler scaler on steamships. Before the end of the year he began policy operations in Harlem. Internal Revenue Service agents found that between 1928 and 1930 Miro made so much money that, after operating expenses and payoffs to authorities, he deposited $1,083,154.73 in ten different bank accounts. He also purchased an apartment house for $47,000 and a two-family residence on Long Island for $22,500, and maintained two automobiles during the three years—and "they were different each year." [9]

In 1931 Miro and West Indian native Wilfred Brunder (another successful Harlem numbers banker), who had prospered for years because of their ability to buy police-politician protection, became victims of a reform wave in the city. When Samuel Seabury's investigation of official corruption in New York City publicized the activities and wealth of the two numbers leaders, they left the city and turned their operations over to Brunder's lieutenant, Joseph Matthias Ison. Schultz now moved in to take over the Harlem numbers business. Whether this action was spurred by Seabury Commission accounts of how lucrative the numbers game was, or whether Schultz had long coveted the business, is not clear; but once the decision was made, Schultz moved quickly. He had Ison picked up by two of his gunmen, and "persuaded" to accept a new partner, Schultz. "There were threats made," Ison later recalled, and an ultimatum: "We will give you a week to decide on this matter." After consulting with his attorney, Dixie Davis (who later became Schultz's lawyer), Ison accepted Schultz's offer. When a few months later Miro and Brunder ended their brief self-exile and returned to Harlem, Schultz arranged a partnership before they could open their business operations again. In short order Alexander Pompey, Marcial Flores, Edwin and Elmer Maloney, and most, but not all, of the Harlem bankers fell under his control. If Schultz's words did not sway them, the threats of his gunmen generally did. The result, one Harlem numbers runner recalled in the late 1960s, was that "you worked for Schultz or you didn't work at all."

41. Michael ("Trigger Mike") Coppola (*left*) and Joseph ("Pip the Blind")
Gagliano during a trip to Colorado in the early 1930s. Coppola took over
Dutch Schultz's Harlem numbers empire after The Dutchman's murder in
Newark, N.J., on October 23, 1935. (From the collection of Ralph Salerno)

The numbers racket proved to be an extremely lucrative part of the
Schultz corporate structure: the Harlem "banks" contributed approximately $20,000,000 to his annual income, and rival syndicate tycoons
plotted to divest him of this and other moneymaking operations. In an
era of organization and cooperation, Schultz was an anachronism—a
stubbornly independent and uncompromising individualist who, in the
name of progress, had to be eliminated. Following his fatal shooting at

the Palace Chop House in Newark on October 23, 1935, members of "the Combination" split his empire among themselves. Michael ("Trigger Mike") Coppola, a Luciano lieutenant, received the Harlem numbers business.

At the same time that the numbers racket was being organized and centralized, syndicate chiefs moved into horse racing. "Horse race tracks, owned through front men but controlled by underworld partners, became rich sources of revenue as the numbers racket developed." Prior to the 1930s, race tracks had been poor investments. Gangsters discovered that just as the numbers payoff could be "fixed" by manipulating results from the race tracks on which the winning numbers were based, so could betting in horse and dog racing be controlled. Both became popular with the mobsters. The races themselves could, of course, be fixed; hence, they made even more profit, at the same time reducing risks for syndicate-controlled bookie operations. Horse tracks and dog tracks in Miami and Los Angeles and most places between came under the influence or the control of criminal syndicates.

In the decades after the Civil War, horse racing emerged as a popular sport, but a reaction against it started in about 1890 because of widespread scandals involving dishonest bookmakers and rigged races. As Fred S. Buck has observed, "Under the dominance of bookmakers, many of whom were either unscrupulous or downright dishonest, racing had reached such a low estate that its eventual death seemed to be in sight." Under pressure for reform, after the turn of the century one state legislature after another outlawed both racing and wagering on the outcome. Although Kentucky and Maryland never deviated in their support of horse racing, by 1911–12 it was banned throughout the heavily populated urban-industrial states of the East and Middle West and in the vacation centers of Louisiana and California.[10]

Racing began to revive during the 1920s in Illinois, New York, Louisiana, and certain other states, in part because of growing appreciation of track betting as a source of tax revenue, and in part because of the growing popularity of pari-mutuel wagering. Under the pari-mutuel system bettors wager among themselves, and the track receives a small percentage for handling the bets. The advantages for the bettor include the opportunity to bet on any horse—a privilege often denied by bookies if they feel sure a horse will win—and there is no "balancing of the books" by limiting the amount that can be bet on any one horse. Through the 1920s racing "thrived in New York, Maryland, Kentucky, Illinois, Louisiana, and Florida, but," as John McDonald has noted, "still had no real national following." [11]

This situation changed radically after 1930. By the end of that decade, eighteen states had regulated tracks attracting an estimated 8,500,000 customers who bet a total of approximately $400 million. The reason stated most frequently for the about-face by state legislatures was a need for new sources of revenue during a period of depression. In many states, lavish outlays of money from underworld sources were said to be of at least equal importance in securing passage of the required laws. Thus Toney Betts, long-time racing editor of the New York *Post*, recalled in the 1950s that during the Depression, New York and other states, in their effort to balance their budgets used "mutuel machines, with little political hacks behind the windows." Despite diligent state efforts to encourage on-track betting, "handbooks, horse-rooms, telephone offices, tipster bureaus and the racing wire-service began doing bigger business than ever before as millions dreamed of getting out of hock with the horses." [12]

A widespread bookmaking activity operated in conjunction with the syndicate-run or mob-controlled horse tracks and dog tracks. The key to bookie operations, the race wire services, provided track odds, scratches, and race results to bookie joints from tracks located across the country. King of the wire services, as well as of the *Daily Racing Form* and the *American Racing Record,* was former Hearst circulation manager Moses L. ("Moe") Annenberg. According to the Internal Revenue Service, which collected evidence of his income tax evasion, Annenberg "from his offices in Chicago operated one of the largest rackets ever developed in this country which consisted of a monopoly of the telegraph service from practically all race tracks in the United States, Canada, Mexico, and Cuba." Annenberg was brought to trial, and the prosecution established the huge size of the wire service when records were introduced to show that it was the American Telephone and Telegraph Company's fifth largest customer. Annenberg was convicted on one count of income tax evasion, and on July 1, 1940, was sentenced to a three-year prison term.[13]

During the late 1920s and early 1930s the public, as John Kobler has observed, went "mad about dog racing." Grandstands and parimutuel booths could not be built fast enough to keep up with the crowds that flocked to the races. From 1909, when the mechanical rabbit that made the sport possible was invented by Oliver P. Smith, until 1931, dog racing was illegal across the nation. Despite this obstacle, dog tracks operated throughout the 1920s in Chicago and other cities with the backing of criminal syndicates and the bought acquiescence of local enforcement authorities. In the late 1920s Italian and other criminal entrepreneurs like John Torrio, Jake Guzik, and Al Capone recognized the opportunities the already popular resort city of Miami offered for development of horse and dog racing and casino gambling under their control or that of their friends and associates. In 1931 Florida became the first state to legalize dog racing, but other states soon followed. The greed and stupidity of so many syndicate leaders manifested itself in the manner in which they exploited the sport. "The Chicago, Detroit, Cleveland, and Buffalo criminal organizations moved into their new field with great vigor," Wallace Turner observed in 1965, "exploiting it just as they did the crap tables and blackjack games in their illegal gambling houses. They almost finished dog racing, even before it caught on. The sport was almost wiped out by public awareness of its crookedness." Support was quickly restored, however, by the passage of legislation to establish more effective public control over the tracks and to effect the removal of "undesirables" from connection with the tracks. That these actions were successful in severing dog racing's ties with syndicate crime is questionable.[14]

Gambling houses, large and small, fancy and plain, located in or near most of the nation's large and not-so-large cities as well as in resort areas, provided another lucrative source of syndicate income.

"Willie" Moretti was one of the forward-looking entrepreneurs of American syndicate crime, and in 1928, at the age of 34, he left a profitable bootlegging business in his native New York City to establish an even more profitable one across the Hudson River in Bergen County, New Jersey. During the 1930s Willie and his brother Salvatore headed an organization that served a wide range of gambling interests and collaborated with the "Longie" Zwillman syndicate in Essex County and the Mack and Ben Golden gang in Passaic County, as well as Luciano, Costello, Kastel, and other New York City underworld leaders. As New York *Times* crime reporter Meyer Berger observed years later, "the Morettis had their bookmaking agents among workers in the major factories in Bergen, they shared the bookmaking profits pouring into the New York mob's astonishingly widespread New Jersey wire system, and they were partners in plush casinos and so-called 'sawdust,' or dice barns deep into Pennsylvania." The premier casino in Bergen was the Marine Room in the Riviera night club, located on the Palisades just north of the George Washington Bridge. The Riviera operated openly as a night club with big-name entertainers, and anyone with the money could get in to see the floorshow. Entry to the gaming room, protected by guards, was considerably more difficult. "All players had to be known," Berger recalled. "Outsiders saw only the dining rooms."

Other Bergen County gambling places were operated more quietly and discreetly. Abandoned or run-down estates located far from a main road were generally chosen so as not to invite public attention and possible complaints that might force authorities to take action. Unlike the Riviera, these places were run strictly as gambling halls. Entertainment of any type was barred as being irrelevant to the casino's purpose, which was to enable customers to bet as much money as possible in the time they were at the club, and without distractions. In contrast to the casinos catering to a more affluent clientele, Berger observed that the lower class "sawdust" joints were generally located in "old garages, old barns, old factories, with no nearby residential district."

During the 1930s criminal entrepreneurs operated or backed such thriving operations as the Beverly Hills near Newport, Kentucky, across the Ohio River from Cincinnati; the Thomas Club, in the Cleveland suburb of Maple Heights; the Southern Club in Hot Springs, Arkansas; and casinos in the Miami and New Orleans areas. As sumptuous as these and other gambling clubs seemed to contemporaries, they paled in comparison with the post-World War II luxury hotel-casinos of Las Vegas.[15]

Loan-sharking comprised another very lucrative Italian syndicate activity that often had connections with numbers or other types of gambling. A study conducted by the Russell Sage Foundation in the mid-1930s found that the gross annual income from loan-sharking in New York City was in excess of $10 million. Simply stated, loan-sharking involved lending money at a higher rate of interest than that charged by legal lending institutions. The advantage to a gambler who was down on his luck—in fact, to anyone in deep financial difficulty—was that the money was generally advanced with no questions asked. The disadvantage was an interest rate of 20 per cent or more, compounded weekly. As Nick Gentile recalled, the loan sharks with whom he was familiar during the mid-1930s "lent five dollars to receive six dollars back at the end of the week." This loan, if not repaid quickly, piled up until the interest exceeded the amount of the original loan.[16]

By the mid-thirties Italians were reaping a sizable share of the proceeds from policy, racetrack, casino, and other forms of gambling, often in partnership with criminals of other ethnic backgrounds. Thus, when dog racing came to Massachusetts in 1935 it was under the control of Mario Ingraffia, Hyman Abrams, Louis D. Fox, and Arthur C. Barron. These four men, who had been notorious liquor smugglers in the late twenties and early thirties, owned the controlling stock of the Bay State Greyhound Association, Inc., which opened a dog track outside Boston on November 30, 1935.

Profits from gambling and other operations were often used to finance the purchase and distribution of narcotics (or "dope," as it was then called), which in itself formed a profitable activity. Although in the 1930s it was not the moneymaker for the syndicates that it became thirty years later, narcotics did bring in at least $500 million per year during the pre-World War II decade. Organizations operating during the twenties continued to flourish during the depression years. Thus the far-flung operations of the San Francisco-based Mario Balestreri gang, which as early as 1929 was said to have "agents throughout the west coast" with "especially strong connections in Los Angeles," continued to conduct a multimillion dollar business in illegal drugs until 1938. In that year the San Francisco-born mob boss, who dealt also in gambling and counterfeiting activities, was found guilty on a narcotics law violation and sentenced to a five-year prison term.[17]

The Gulf city of New Orleans functioned as a major port of entry for narcotics brought into the country for distribution throughout the South and as far west as Kansas City, and in itself comprised an important market for dope. The arrest on September 18, 1931, of Arthur Sunseri, a banana inspector for a local fruit company, for selling morphine illustrated the use that drug importers made of New Orleans's position as a major shipping point. The famous French Quarter was the center of the local drug traffic, although suburban entrepreneurs also took a prominent cut. In the late 1930s future syndicate leader Carlos Marcello apparently used his bar in Algiers (located across the river from New Orleans) as headquarters for his narcotics operations. The 26-year-old Marcello was, according to the *Times-Picayune,* one of the city's busiest wholesalers.[18]

One of the largest drug rings in the United States developed from a local Kansas City operation in the 1920s, and supplied much of the United States from Chicago west to the Rocky Mountains. Prior to October 1931, dope traffic in Kansas City had been under the control of Lonnie Affrenti, who apparently had limited objectives, contacts, and financial resources. As a result, the drug traffic in Kansas City was a small-time operation until Affrenti left the city in order to—as a Bureau of Narcotics report put it—"evade criminal prosecution for violation of the Narcotics Laws." With his departure a vacuum was created, and two of the city's most prominent bootleggers, Joseph De Luca and Nicolo Impostato, immediately moved to fill it. De Luca had been arrested in 1931 and convicted early the following year for violation of the National Prohibition Act; and in general, with repeal impending, the liquor business was not so attractive a field as it had formerly been. Apparently eager to switch to the narcotics business, the two men organized the highly efficient and financially successful Kansas City Narcotics Syndicate, which was unique among contemporary Italian and Jewish gangs dealing in drugs in that it concentrated exclusively on this commodity. Other gangs, such as those of Balestreri, Gentile, Buchalter, and Luciano, combined narcotics with other illegal activities.[19]

The Bureau of Narcotics was apparently aware of the existence of the Kansas City organization during most of the 1930s; but even though, with Nick Gentile's arrest in New Orleans in 1937, the federal agency obtained an address book containing the names of several of the Kansas City dealers, it was unable to crack the Narcotics Syndicate case until 1941–42. A confidential Bureau report prepared in connection with the prosecution of the gang in 1942 admitted that "the inner workings of the 'Kansas City Narcotics Syndicate' were so well concealed that it was not until the past year [1941] that the higher-ups of the organization were definitely ascertained by officers of the Bureau of Narcotics." The beginning of the end for the gang came with "a number of purchases of narcotic evidence made in Kansas City, Missouri[,] during the latter part of 1941 and early part of 1942." This action resulted in the arrest of Carl Carramusa, Charles Taibi, Felippo Pernice, and Samuel Pernice and the seizure of a shipment of opium and heroin.

Further investigation revealed the structure of the organization. Joseph De Luca was the "major financier and chief of the supervisory board," and Nicolo Impostato, who arrived in Kansas City in 1929 from Chicago to serve as "strong-arm man" for the John Lazia forces, acted as "general manager" of the syndicate. Other prominent members included: Joseph Patito, legal advisor; James De Simone, traveling representative and liaison man between the organization and its sources of supply; Carl Carramusa, wholesale jobber; Charles W. Bengimina, wholesaler; Charles Taiba, Louis Ventola, and Patsy Ventola, "runners"; and Felippo and Samuel Pernice, "who furnished the place of concealment at Kansas City, Missouri, for the contraband narcotics."

During the course of the investigation, in March 1942, Carl Carramusa agreed to provide authorities with full information concerning his "past narcotic activities," and implicated all members of the Kansas City Narcotics Syndicate. Carramusa stated that during the period of his employment as a jobber, from February 1, 1939, to February 15, 1942, the syndicate carried on a million-dollar-a-year operation. Carramusa's confession also provided authorities with the previously unknown fact that the Kansas City organization maintained a branch office at St. Louis and kept it supplied with heroin from its own stock. Thomas Buffa supervised the St. Louis operation, and Tony Lopiparo worked as general manager. Although some of the heroin and opium they sold came through New York City, "the major source of contraband narcotic supplies for this organization during the past ten years had been the notorious Antinori family of Tampa, Florida." The Bureau of Narcotics report stated further that Ignazio Antinori and his two sons, Paul and Joseph, had "long been identified with the smuggling of narcotics, aliens and liquor, and formerly owned their own boat in which they carried on extensive smuggling activities between Havana, Cuba, and the Florida mainland."

The members of the Kansas City Narcotics Syndicate and their associates and suppliers came to trial in 1943 and, in large part through the testimony provided by Carramusa, Impostato, Taiba, Felippo and Samuel Pernice, Carramusa, De Luca, De Simone, and Paul and Joseph Antinori, were found guilty and sent to prison for terms ranging up to six years. For his help in cracking the case Carramusa received a pardon in 1943. Two years later, while he was living under an assumed name in Chicago, the underworld repaid him for what his fellow criminals considered an act of treachery. In June 1945 he died from the effects of a gunshot volley fired by "persons unknown."

New York City contained numerous gangs that carried on large-scale operations in narcotics, but, unlike the Kansas City syndicate, they took part in other illegal activities as well. During the 1930s, all the major Italian syndicates in New York were involved in the narcotics traffic, as were many of the Jewish organizations. Louis ("Lepke") Buchalter headed a huge narcotics operation, as well as dominating business and labor racketeering in the city of New York. A Bureau of Narcotics report described him as "drug peddler, extortionist, labor racketeer, and murderer." His was a multi-faceted and active career in the world of crime, and in all of his endeavors it could be said that Lepke did things spectacularly, even to the point of being the only top underworld figure of his generation—or since—to be tried, convicted, and executed (on March 4, 1944, at Sing Sing) for murder. Lepke's involvement in various rackets, including the fur and garment industries, and his connection with "Murder, Inc." were better known to the public, but his downfall came about as a result of his activity in the dope trade.[20]

At least as early as 1932, Lepke was known to have been importing and distributing illegal drugs. In November 1937 he and twenty-nine other persons were indicted for involvement in a scheme to smuggle narcotics into the port of New York "in the baggage of ostensible round-the-world tourists" between October 1935 and February 1937. According to Bureau of Narcotics reports, the Lepke ring smuggled more than $10 million (retail value) worth of heroin and other drugs into the United States. Most of the drugs came from the Japanese Concession of Tientsin, China, and were smuggled "through the Customs lines of New York City from the swankiest liners that sailed the seas," including the *Queen Mary,* the *Berengaria,* the *Majestic,* and the *Aquitania.* Convicted of narcotics law violations and after unsuccessful appeals, Lepke began to serve a twelve-year sentence on the drug charges and an unrelated two-year sentence for anti-trust violations. He did not serve the full time, being found guilty of murder in 1941 and executed three years later.

Lucky Luciano, New York's most important Italian syndicate leader, had a piece of nearly every lucrative illegal action in the city. Arrested on drug charges in 1916 and 1923, Luciano maintained that after the second arrest he never again involved himself in narcotics, al-

42. New York City Police Department mug shots of Vito Genovese, taken
December 4, 1934. (In author's possession)

though he did admit to pursuing the more socially acceptable lines like
gambling and bootlegging. It is doubtful that Luciano did remain aloof
from narcotics, since it appears that in the spring of 1933 he sent his
lieutenant, Vito (Don Vitone) Genovese, to Fascist Italy to lay the
foundation of a narcotics smuggling ring. The Fascist government's
cooperation made it possible for Genovese to report to Luciano and
other syndicate leaders, on his return to the United States in the fall of
1933, that the network was ready to function. The result was a multi-
million-dollar business and a steady supply of narcotics practically
guaranteed by the Italian government. When he was forced to flee the
United States in 1937 in order to avoid prosecution for murder and
racketeering, Genovese returned to Italy. There he directed the narcotics smuggling program he had created on his earlier visit, and the
immense wealth this brought him made it possible to entertain (most
lavishly) Mussolini, as well as Count Ciano and other Fascist
leaders.[21]

Nicola Gentile, at the time a high-level traveling representative of
the Italian syndicates, also found it necessary to flee the United States
and return to Italy in 1937. Gentile, as it developed, was involved in

the distribution of narcotics in a number of American cities. On October 6, 1937, federal agents arrested Gentile and five others in New Orleans for violation of narcotics laws. Zio Cola was among seventy-four persons involved in "a dope syndicate described as a $5,000,000 to $25,000,000 business with nationwide operations." Gentile returned to his homeland, and there continued in the narcotics business, allegedly with an old associate, Lucky Luciano, who himself had been released from prison in New York and deported to Italy at the end of World War II.[22]

Luciano, who had enjoyed virtual immunity from the law during the years after he eliminated "Joe the Boss" Masseria and Salvatore "Boss of Bosses" Maranzano and thereby won control of New York's Italian underworld, was the prime target in Special Prosecutor Thomas E. Dewey's war on racketeering in the city. In 1936 Luciano was charged with ninety counts of compulsory prostitution (later reduced to sixty-one). In later years he claimed that he was not worried when the trial began on May 13, 1936, since he felt that no one would believe that he would involve himself in so low a trade as prostitution. The prosecution contended that "Little Davie" Betillo had under Lu-

43. Lucky Luciano (*center*) following conviction in June 1936 on charge of compulsory prostitution. (Reprinted from New York *Post*)

ciano's orders organized the whorehouses of New York, two hundred of them with three thousand girls, into a $12 million-a-year business. On June 7, 1936, the jury returned a verdict of guilty on all sixty-one counts, and Luciano was sentenced to 30 to 50 years in prison. Luciano did not serve the full term. In 1946 Dewey, by now Governor of New York, freed him on condition that he leave the United States and return to Italy.[23]

During 1936, while New York's special prosecutor was developing his case against Luciano, the man Dewey branded "the whoremaster of Gotham," a San Francisco grand jury was examining vice operations in the West Coast metropolis. The Atherton Report, released in March 1937, reported the existence of widespread and organized prostitution in the city. In one section of the North Beach area, houses of prostitution were so plentiful that "tenants in some buildings have been forced to put signs on their front doors announcing the fact that they are private residences." Unlike the situation in New York with its "Little Davey" Betillo, San Francisco's prostitution was not directed or controlled by any one person. The grand jury learned that although a wide range of ethnic operatives as well as Americans of Anglo-Saxon background were involved, "the French group or 'syndicate,' as it is sometimes referred to by the sporting fraternity, had become the most highly organized unit in the entire graft set-up." Behind the French, Jewish, and Anglo-Saxon pimps regularly collecting their share of the prostitution profits for permitting the uninterrupted conduct of business was a sizable portion of the city's police officers led by all the departments' captains and their middlemen, the McDonough brothers.[24]

In the heart of Mid-America (Chicago) prostitution was carried on as usual under the direction of Capone's successors and without interference from law enforcement officers in Chicago and suburbs. In contrast to New York, where the discovery that prostitution had been set up on a factory system elicited howls of public outrage and revulsion, in Chicago the business-like operation of whorehouses was an accepted fact of life. To Chicagoans Dewey's revelations of how New York's prostitutes were organized and exploited to increase criminal syndicate profits had a familiar ring. The Capone houses had been run that way for years.[25]

For the remainder of his life Luciano, who died in Italy in 1962 of a heart attack, maintained that he was the victim of a frame, and he may well have been correct. On the basis of his coverage of the prostitution trial, crime reporter Michael Stern, who interviewed Luciano in Italy in 1949, agreed with him that it was "questionable whether the evidence produced at the trial was sufficient to prove beyond a reasonable doubt that he was guilty on this count." Stern noted the irony that "Lucky, who had broken just about every law on the books, was finally brought to a well-merited justice for a crime of which he was least guilty. It is ironic, also, that his name shall go down in infamy as synonymous with Vice Czar when it was a racket he practiced least, if at all." Journalist Hickman Powell, in his comprehensive study of the trial, argued that Luciano had received exactly what he deserved, even if it might have been more than the evidence warranted. In his view the objective of jailing syndicate bosses justified any means used to realize that end. "True, the sentence he got was proportionate more to the manner of his operations than to the specific crime of which he was convicted. Up to now the income tax laws had been the only effective weapon against the racketeer. This conviction was something new. Luciano became the first top-rank American racketeer ever to go to prison for a crime involving moral turpitude." [26]

Both Stern and Powell used the term "racketeer" in the broad sense of any activity that serves as a source of income. In the midst of the bootlegging era in the 1920s, when alcohol was far and away the biggest moneymaker, America's emerging crime syndicates found a form of illegal enterprise which by the following decade would take its place as a major source of income as well as a means to enter legitimate business and organized labor. New York crime reporters Craig Thompson and Allen Raymond described racketeering as it developed in the 1920s and 1930s as "a system whereby, through the creation of a so-called trade association, by the connivance, cooperation or control of a labor union, and the use of a strongarm squad, a process of shaking down merchants or other industrialists was smoothed out to machine efficiency." Put concisely, by criminologist John Landesco, it was "the exploitation for personal profit, by means of violence, of a business association or employees' organization." [27]

Strictly speaking, this form of illegal activity was not new, but before the 1920s the extent was limited and the methods employed were primitive. Long before prohibition, Ciro Terranova (Morello) and other members of his family operated a very profitable racket in controlling the artichoke trade in New York. Terranova's method of operation, as Thompson and Raymond stressed, was "rather more direct and effective than that of the elaborate rackets fixed, leech-like, on the bigger industries of later years." Terranova created a monopoly. At about $6 a crate, he bought all the artichokes shipped into the city from California, and then sold them at a 30-to-40 per cent profit, through a produce company specifically set up for the purpose, to retailers in the city. The dealers could have bought the artichokes directly from the California market but, journalist Fred Pasley pointed out in 1931, "stories were current of the strange things that had happened to dealers who had done that." [28]

Gordon L. Hostetter of the Employers' Association in Chicago claimed that the word "racket" was applied for the first time "to those unholy alliances between business men, labor leaders, politicians, and underworld characters" in the early 1920s and that by 1927 some fifty rackets were openly flourishing "like jungle plants" in Chicago. Among the lines of business racketeers then controlled or were attempting to control were "window cleaning, machinery moving, paper stock, cleaning and dyeing, laundries, candy jobbers, dental laboratories, ash and rubbish hauling, grocery and delicatessen stores, garage owners, physicians, drug stores, milk dealers, glazers, photographers, florists, bootblacks, restaurants, shoe repairers, fish and poultry, butchers, bakers, and window-shade men." [29]

By the spring of 1928 the State's Attorney's office had uncovered and identified 107 separate rackets flourishing in Chicago. The following year the Chicago Crime Commission estimated that racketeering in its myriad forms contributed $136 million per year to the city's criminal syndicates. By 1931 the figure amounted to $200 million. As was true of other forms of entrepreneurial crime in the city, the Capone forces came to control the majority of Chicago's rackets. According to Capone biographer John Kobler, the figure may have been as high as 70 per cent of the racketeering practiced in the city. In April 1931 the New York State Crime Commission reported its findings that racketeers extracted from $200 million to $600 million a year in New York City alone. "The toll in Philadelphia was estimated at $100,000,000; in Detroit at $75,000,000; in Los Angeles at $50,000,000 and in Cleveland and Pittsburgh at $25,000,000 each." [30]

Racketeering did not exist across the entire spectrum of the American business world, but was concentrated in specific industries and businesses that required modest amounts of capital or skill to enter and contained an oversupply of labor. The tendency of racketeering to appear in small, unstable, and disorganized industries led Walter Lippmann to observe in 1931 that it was essentially "a perverse effort to overcome the insecurity of highly competitive capitalism." Thus, rather than criminals forcing themselves on their victims, it was often the harried businessman faced with the constant threat of cut-throat competition, who turned to underworld elements and invited their help in dealing with excessive competition or with troublesome labor problems. Labor leaders also employed gangster aid in their organizational efforts. Criminals excelled in the techniques of violence and terror that labor unions in these industries utilized to win and enforce the closed shop. Whether hired by capital or labor, once they gained a foothold, racketeers had every intention of staying on, not as hired specialists but as partners. [31]

Beginning in the late 1920s New York's Lepke Buchalter, Lower East Side born and bred of Russian Jewish parents, involved himself in the garment racket, first as Hyman ("Curley") Holtz's lieutenant and, after 1931, as boss. Authorities charged that Lepke, with the assistance of his long-time friend and associate Jacob ("Gurrah") Shapiro, "maintained complete domination over the city's garment industry" and extorted at least $15,000,000 from garment manufacturers and from businesses allied with the garment industry. Those who "failed to bow to the gang's orders" suffered "destruction, acid throwing, mayhem or murder.'' By similar methods Lepke, Shapiro, and their army of sluggers and gunmen established their control over the fur industry, the shoe trade, the baking industry, the poultry market, and the taxicab business, among others. Lepke's power rested in part on personal qualities (including shrewdness, organizational ability, and ruthlessness) and in part on his close connections and good working relations with other underworld leaders, including Meyer Lansky, Bugsy Siegel, and Lucky Luciano. Thus, Lepke shared the cabaret racket with Lansky and Siegel and the cleaning-and-dyeing racket with Luciano. By 1932 the mild-mannered, soft-spoken, sad-eyed Lepke ''ruled absolutely and autocratically as any czar over a feudal state.'' He continued as ''the acknowledged leader of this branch of underworld activity'' in New York until 1939, when he surrendered to authorities and was brought to trial on charges of violating Federal narcotics laws.[32]

Racketeers in New York and other urban centers attempted to emulate Lepke's success in squeezing money from local businessmen. Business racketeers often made effective use of labor union pressure to force compliance with their wishes from recalcitrant independent businessmen. An example of union pressure was provided in the late 1920s in the building industry in the Bronx, by the Plasterers' Information Bureau, Incorporated, organized in New York on April 3, 1928, by Antonio Monforte and Tomasso Gagliano. Plastering contractors in the Bronx were forced to join the Bureau and to pay fees to it. Incendiary fires at building sites were used to ''encourage'' reluctant contractors to join. Monforte and Gagliano set up another corporation, United Lathing Company, which furnished lathes to building contractors. To help them gain control of the lathing industry, Monforte and Gagliano hired Michael McCloskey, who was known as the ''czar'' of the Lathers Union. McCloskey was a ''walking delegate,'' which meant that he had the power to appear at any construction site and issue a strike order that would immediately be obeyed. When he did this and the contractors came to him to find out the reason, they would be sent to talk with Monforte, who would demand payment of 5 per cent of the contract fee. If this condition was met, the strike would be called off; if not, it would continue, and the building under construction would usually undergo a destructive fire. Through these techniques, Monforte and Gagliano extorted huge sums of money from intimidated contractors. An investigation by the Intelligence Unit of Internal Revenue Service determined that just one of four known companies created by Monforte and Gagliano extorted $457,886.34 in a single year, 1929. IRS amassed sufficient evidence on the Bronx building racketeers' activities to result in convictions for income tax violations. Monforte received a sentence of two years in federal prison and a $1,000 fine, and Gagliano one year and three months in federal prison. Ten of their associates received prison sentences ranging from four months to one year.[33]

Although the profits enjoyed by Monforte and Gagliano were not insignificant, they were of minor proportions compared to the income of Fulton Fish Market "Czar" Joseph ("Socks") Lanza. In 1923 Lanza, who at the age of 14 had started working as a fish handler at the market five years before, organized his fellow workers into a union, the United Seafood Workers' Union. By the late 1920s the American Federation of Labor-affiliated union was a thousand-man force in local politics as well as in the economy. Because of the tribute exacted from "every dealer, big and small, retailer or wholesaler" at the Fulton Market, Lanza influenced the price of fish not only in New York but throughout much of the nation. The union served as the principal basis of Lanza's $20-million-a-year racket. He operated unimpeded until 1933, when indictments were returned against him by a federal grand jury in New York. Although he was prosecuted in the Federal Courts and served a two-year sentence for violation of the Sherman Anti-Trust Act, Lanza maintained control of the Fulton Market until he died on October 11, 1968.[34]

Like Lanza, who ran his union and the Fulton Market as a fiefdom, Albert Anastasia maintained an iron hold over the International Longshoremen's Association (ILA) and the New York waterfront. The ILA had been gangster-infested and corrupt long before prohibition. Former boxer and Five Points Gang chieftain Paolo Vaccarelli, better known as Paul Kelly, "contributed to the early influx of criminals on to the waterfront," but it was during the 25-year-reign of an Irishman, Joseph P. Ryan, that corruption of the ILA and the waterfront was completed. Ryan, who became president of the ILA in 1927, was, in the words of labor historian John Hutchinson, "tolerant of poor morals and the evils of the industry, light in his claims on the employers, casual in his concern for the longshoremen." Italian and other criminals quickly took advantage of the opportunities offered by this type of leadership. As Irish lawbreakers solidified their control over the North (or Hudson) River piers—and the numerous rackets practiced there—serving the European passenger lines, their Italian counterparts moved in on the Brooklyn waterfront, where they seized control of ILA locals 327, 327–1, 338, 338–1, 1199 and 1199–1. These were the Camarda locals, named after the ILA vice president and official head of the six Brooklyn locals, Emil Camarda, and his two brothers, Anthony and Joseph.[35]

In 1929 a political organization called the City Democratic Club was formed in South Brooklyn. Although the Board of Directors of this club included many of the most respected professionals and businessmen in the Italian community, they were "in effect" (the New York State Crime Commission maintained) "a front for a group of notorious criminals" who used the club as a headquarters for conducting racketeering, gambling, and other illegal operations in Brooklyn. The club membership was also utilized to increase the influence of Italian syndicate leaders among borough politicians. Prominent among these underworld powers were Vincent Mangano, head of one of New York's five *borgate,* whose domain included large-scale gambling interests in Brooklyn and Lower Manhattan as well as the waterfront rackets; Joe Adonis, who served as the syndicate's intermediary with Brooklyn police officials and politicians, and whose business interests after 1933 included the rackets empire formed by Frank Yale and, after Yale's murder in 1928, continued by Anthony Carfano; and Albert Anastasia, later identified as director of the Abe Reles-led group of Brooklyn-based syndicate exterminators employed by "Murder, Inc." According to the New York State Crime Commission, the crimi-

44. Albert Anastasia (*left*), reputed boss of Brooklyn waterfront, with his attorney during 1955 court appearance on charge of income tax evasion. (United Press International)

nal leaders of the City Democratic Club also controlled the destinies and oversaw the activities of the Camarda locals.

Under Anastasia's direction, organized theft of goods on the piers and hijacking between the piers and the inland terminals, kickbacks from employers in return for guarantees that work would be done, and loan-sharking (approximately $200,000 worth a year) were among the variety of rackets practiced on the waterfront. It was said that on some piers it was almost impossible for a longshoreman to obtain work unless he promised the hiring boss to borrow money from the resident syndicate usurer. The time-honored system of hiring dock workers known as "the shape-up" was continued and exploited. "Its most simplified form" is as follows:

> When word goes out that dock workers are needed at a particular pier, they form in a large semicircle around the hiring foreman. The hiring foreman then selects the men he wishes to hire and "blows the whistle." The men who are hired then file into the pier; those not hired drift away.[36]

The syndicate takeover of the waterfront did not go unnoticed by authorities, although it did go virtually unpunished. In April 1940 newly elected District Attorney of Kings County (and later Mayor of New York) William O'Dwyer ordered an investigation of the Brooklyn locals. In May he received documentary evidence of grand larceny and embezzlement of union funds and the forgery and destruction of union books. At a meeting the following month O'Dwyer informed ILA President Ryan and Vice-President Emil Camarda of the facts uncovered by the investigation. Ryan promised thoroughgoing reforms and later announced that the charters of three of the Camarda locals would be revoked. The changes occurred only in appearance and not in substance. The revoked charters were replaced immediately by new ones, with no change in the men who exercised control over the old locals. "Even today," observed the New York State Crime Commission in 1953, "these locals continue under the domination of the same officers who had controlled them for many years." [37]

Among the most notorious union takeovers was that of the International Alliance of Theatrical, Stage Employees and Motion Picture Operators. In 1932 George Browne, business agent for the Stagehands Local 2 of the IATSE in Chicago, ran unsuccessfully for president of the union. The following year Browne met William ("Willie") Bioff, a minor figure in Chicago crime but originator of a racketeering scheme of major proportions. Bioff teamed with Browne in a shakedown of local theater owners, who soon found that only by submitting to extortion could they keep their establishments open and operating. The two men became so successful that they attracted Frank Nitti's attention. In 1934 Nitti, who was Capone's successor as the chief of Chicago's criminal syndicates, advised Browne to run for president of the IATSE and promised underworld support as well as pressure on delegates at the upcoming election (in June) in Louisville. In exchange, Browne was to turn over 50 per cent of all money extorted from union members and from management. This amount was later raised to 75 per cent. Browne and Bioff found themselves permitted to keep the remaining 25 per cent and divide it between themselves. Marshaling support for Browne at Louisville and sharing in the profits after Browne's successful campaign for president of the IATSE were Luciano, Lepke, Zwillman, and other Eastern and Midwestern syndicate powers, in addition to Nitti and his Chicago associates.[38]

The relationship among syndicate leaders of different ethnic groups was illustrated by an exchange between Frank Nitti and Lepke which came to light during trials of the Chicago-based extortionists in the early 1940s. In early June of 1934 Lepke traveled to Chicago to discuss strategy for the up-coming convention in Louisville. Nitti gave Lepke a message for Luciano: "Local 306 [the New York projectionists] was to vote for Browne for president." "I won't have to see Lucky on that, Frank," Lepke replied. "I can handle it myself. I'll also see Kaufman of New Jersey [Louis Kaufman, business agent of the big Newark local] and see that Longie [Zwillman] delivers that outfit."

With Browne in office, the union and its underworld backers moved to extort hundreds of thousands of dollars from theater owners on threat of ruinous strikes and shutdowns. The lucrative ventures had Hollywood for the major prize. From the early 1920s to 1933 the IATSE had enjoyed some influence, but in the latter year had engaged in a jurisdictional dispute with the Painters, Carpenters and Electrical Workers over studio sound technicians which all but destroyed the IATSE in Hollywood, reducing membership from 9,000 to less than 200. Just three years later, however, the gangster-controlled union revived and won the right to represent 12,000 of Hollywood's movie

45. Frank Nitti (*center*), Chicago syndicate boss, flanked by his attorneys Rocco de Stefano (*left*) and Ben Short in 1933 photo. (Chicago *Tribune* Photo)

employees. In addition to the use of strong-arm methods, union organizers gained worker support by negotiating a union shop and a wage increase for members. After consolidating their power, Bioff and Browne demanded a $2 million payoff from the movie studios or, as Bioff later admitted in court, "we would close every theater in the country." Industry leaders balked at this extortion, but between 1936 and 1940 they paid more than $1,100,000 to the union leaders. The racketeers' appetite for money proved to be insatiable. Not only did Bioff and Browne force management to pay, but they also exacted tribute from union members as well—a 2 per cent levy on earnings. When the gang's demands became intolerable, the victims began to talk before a federal grand jury in New York City.

The first indictments were returned in 1941, against Browne, Bioff, and Nick Circella, a Capone gambling-house proprietor. Circella and Browne received eight-year sentences in federal prison, Bioff a ten-year sentence. On March 18, 1943, further indictments were returned against Frank Nitti, Louis Campagna, Paul Ricca, Phil D'Andrea, Frank Maritote, Charles Gioe, John Rosselli, Louis Kaufman, and Ralph Pierce. When he received word of the indictment, Nitti, who had been in ill health for a number of years (suffering from stomach ulcers), committed suicide. The others stood trial on charges of violating federal anti-racketeering statutes.

Browne and Bioff gave damaging testimony concerning the conspiracy. On December 31, 1943, Campagna, Ricca, D'Andrea, Maritote, Gioe, and Rosselli were found guilty; each received a ten-year prison sentence and a $10,000 fine. Louis Kaufman received a seven-year sentence and a $10,000 fine; the case against Pierce was dismissed for lack of sufficient evidence.[39]

The stranglehold on Hollywood and the legitimate theater had been broken, but efforts to infiltrate and dominate labor unions continued in other fields, and in succeeding years pressure intensified from syndicate criminals attempting to take over or to use legitimate businesses either as fronts for illegal enterprises or as legal sources of income. All

46. Willie Bioff (*center*) prior to court appearance in 1943 in connection with Chicago syndicate takeover of motion picture unions. (The Chicago *Sun-Times*)

47. Joe Adonis leaving court surrounded by reporters during a 1940 probe of Brooklyn rackets. (New York *Daily News*)

this activity, however, lay in the future, a bright one indeed for the leaders of American syndicate crime. The years following repeal appeared to herald a decline in the opportunities and fortunes of syndicate crime leaders, and many contemporary observers, mistaking this surface appearance for reality, believed that the forces of law and order were finally about to win over evil and wrongdoing. In their view, at long last law enforcement agencies had the underworld "on the run." Thus Harold Seidman wrote in 1938 that "for the time being, at least, the heyday of New York and Chicago gangsters appears to be at an end." The following year *Collier's* magazine described Lepke Buchalter as the "Last of the Mob," a "key man of the combination which *once* ruled the New York underworld." As the decade of the 1930s drew to a close, no less an authority than J. Edgar Hoover confidently proclaimed that "not one" criminal syndicate was still in operation.[40]

A new era in the war on crime appeared to be dawning with the imprisonment of major syndicate leaders such as John Torrio, Lucky Luciano, and Lepke Buchalter, and of political allies such as Tammany Hall leader Jimmy Hines. In 1940 Joe Adonis, whose political influence had for years spared him from prosecution by local authorities in spite of his racketeering and gambling activities, faced action by an official who could not be bought or influenced. John Harlan Amen, a special racket's prosecutor appointed by Gov. Herbert Lehman, brought charges of kidnaping, assault, and extortion against Adonis. The prosecution had what appeared to be a strong, although not impregnable, case. Astute moves by his attorney, however, enabled Adonis to gain an acquittal on February 24, 1941, without even standing trial. Nevertheless, on the eve of Japan's attack on Pearl Harbor, observers of America's underworld found extensive evidence to support their thesis that the vast and hugely lucrative business of syndicate crime to which prohibition had given so great an impetus was—in fewer than ten years after repeal—in the process of breaking apart (or at least was heading into a difficult period). Actually, far from heralding the death throes of entrepreneurial crime, World War II, with its diversion of public attention from the activities of crime syndicates, its shortages, its needs for cooperation at any price between capital and labor, and its frenzied emphasis on pleasure to compensate for the pains of sacrifice, ushered in a new and even more profitable era for America's criminal entrepreneurs.[41]

9

The Summing Up—
And a Glimpse Beyond

In Southern Italy, secret criminal societies like the *mafia* formed part of the fabric of life. Like other newcomers to the United States, immigrant criminals attempted to re-create in their new homeland the institutions and the traditions with which they were familiar. Efforts to transport the *mafia* to the Italian districts of American cities met with only limited success, for in the process of transferring across the ocean, familiar institutions underwent change. Honest, hard-working peasants as well as criminal parasites found it impossible to re-create the Old World way of life in America's "Little Italies," no matter how earnestly they tried. Extortion activities that had thrived in Sicily altered in style and frequency because core areas of all American cities (except New York) did not contain sufficiently high concentrations of Italian immigrant populations to provide lucrative opportunities. The constant, heavy turnover of residents as newcomers from overseas arrived to replace those who had moved out of the ethnic colony prevented the formation of a stable or unchanging colony life. The Sicilian *mafia* and similar criminal societies thrived in static surroundings like that of western Sicily, whereas change and mobility characterized American cities. Furthermore, the successful *mafia* leaders generally did not move to the United States, except for short visits, until the 1920s, when Mussolini's Fascist regime forced many to relocate. In this decade and the following one, a number of *mafia* chieftains migrated to the United States.

Most of the men who joined immigrant district ("Mafia") gangs had not belonged to *mafia* groups in the homeland. Their turning to crime was not a denial of the American way of life, but rather comprised an effort by common laborers who lacked skills to find "success." They used the most readily available means at their disposal. In doing so, they adjusted to the materialistic nature of American society, which preached honesty, virtue, and hard work, but placed major value on possession of money and power, with little concern evinced as to how that money and power were acquired. These Italian newcomers, however, found it necessary to concentrate their activities on that huge body of Italian immigrants which was honest, hard-working and long-suffering. If immigrant colony bands grew so bold as to murder a non-Italian—like Chief Hennessy of New Orleans or the Pennsylvania game warden Seeley Houk—native responses were quick and violent.

Homeland *mafia* and *Camorra* members who arrived in this country were attracted by the type of society to which they came, one that seemed to offer few rigid barriers to success. Many, of course, decided to emigrate rather than face police action against them in Italy. They could have emigrated to a number of countries, but chose the United States instead of France, England, Brazil, or Argentina simply because they expected to get rich faster in America.

The factors that attracted Italian criminals to the United States, and encouraged formerly honest and hard-working immigrants as well as members of the second generation to turn to crime, were present as early as the 1880s and 1890s. Also present was the response that immigrant criminal activity elicited from the native community: contempt, fear, loathing, and, when the occasion arose, violence.

From the early years of immigration to the United States, Italians found themselves plagued by the fact that the American public identified them with *mafia* activities and therefore with criminality. Discussing the Italian experience in Baltimore during the 1920s and in the years since, Sara Jean Reilly noted the dilemma of the "ninety-nine per cent of the Italians" in Baltimore during the 1920s who were "obedient, laborious and the best of citizens," but who were "trapped

by the distorted image of the Italian, for national publicity sensa-
tionalized the exploits of Al Capone and the Mafia mobster, and often
ignored the law-abiding Italian.'' This assessment is accurate; furthermore, some group members have complicated their problems (and
often made themselves appear ridiculous) by denying the existence of
Italian-American crime and criminals. Ethnic defensiveness has played
into the hands of criminals, who have convinced many honest compatriots that the Italian good name has been tarnished by reports of the
activities of criminals with Italian names. The notoriety, of course,
stems from the actions of the criminals themselves rather than from the
publicity these elicit.[1]

On close examination, the Italian colony (''Mafia'') organizations
that developed in American cities during the decades prior to prohibition do not appear to have been so powerful or effective as contemporary journalists and law enforcement officials made them out to be.
The secrecy, rituals, and exotic behavior encouraged American observers to indulge their imaginations and ascribe to these societies all
kinds of wondrous evil powers. This belief in the omnipotence of
Italian-colony criminal gangs led to the orgy of hysteria and violence
that New Orleans experienced following Hennessy's murder in 1890.

The one urban center where ''Mafia'' organizations possessed
strength was New York City, and there competing groups devoted as
much time and effort to fighting each other as they did to their various
moneymaking projects. Other cities suffered less internecine warfare,
but also lacked the lush opportunities that made New York's Italian
colonies so attractive a market for criminal gangs. An essential charac-
teristic of the American ''Mafia'' was its locus of operations—that is,
entirely within Italian immigrant districts. Black Hand gangs also
played on the longsuffering residents of these neighborhoods. Some
''Mafiosi'' engaged in Black Hand extortion, but most of these crimes
were the work of individuals or small, independent gangs.

More important in the long run than the more highly publicized
Black Handers or the ''Mafiosi'' were the American-generation crimi-
nals whose growth to maturity coincided with the onset of prohibition.
These men, whether born in Italy or the New World, grew up as prod-

ucts of the American urban environment. They viewed themselves as Americans and chose to use crime as the vehicle to material success. They despised immigrant-colony criminals and had little desire to associate with or emulate the "greaseballs." Indeed, they did not hesitate to eliminate the oldtimers whenever expedient.

In the pre-Volstead years, American observers typically concentrated on tales of Black Hand bomb throwers and "Mafia" blood oaths, and failed to recognize the significance of the youthful entrepreneurs. While attention was directed elsewhere, these young men made their debuts into crime in the larger American environment involving gambling, prostitution, narcotics, and the labor wars. The experience gained from such activities and the contacts formed with members of other ethnic groups as well as politicians and the police in the years before 1920 served them well during the 1920s and 1930s. The vital ingredient came with the enactment of prohibition. The "noble experiment" gave these young men the opportunity, which they exploited to the utmost, to eliminate the hated Italian-colony "Mafia" rivals and to establish powerful criminal syndicates, often in combination with Jewish associates.

Entrepreneurial crime provided an important means of upward economic mobility for members of the American generation, most of whom were born in Italy and raised in the United States. Although group unity and cooperative effort figured prominently in Italian successes within the highly competitive world of American entrepreneurial crime during the 1920s and 1930s, the individual played a role of key importance. Individual men had a profound impact on the high level of achievement Italians enjoyed during that era. The situation in entrepreneurial crime from the enactment of the Eighteenth Amendment until American entry into World War II exhibited considerable fluidity; during this period syndicate leaders were highly receptive to ideas that promised to maximize profits and reduce risks and uncertainty. Able businessmen of crime like Costello, Luciano, Lazia, Capone, Adonis, and, above all, Torrio, were innovators and experimenters. The institutions and procedures they and their associates in New York and other cities across the country created during the late twenties and the thirties provided the framework within which criminal syndicates have functioned ever since.

By 1941 the age of the innovator and of the individual had ended. In the decades since then, syndicate leadership has devoted primary attention to preserving and expanding upon the gains made during the 1920s and 1930s. The syndicates have had an economic stake in preserving the status quo. As family men, leaders have felt obliged to look out for the interests and welfare of relatives and friends. Proud and devoted fathers like Carlo Gambino, Joe Bonanno, and Joe Profaci wanted their children to marry well and attain success. Like the fictional "Godfather," Vito Corleone, they and other syndicate leaders willingly paid for the means whereby their offspring might gain acceptance in the legitimate world—in medicine, law, or some other prestigious career—and at the same time they indicated a strong desire to keep control of the syndicate within the biological family; if this was not possible, then they made an effort to keep it within the extended family (consisting of nephews, cousins, and other relatives)—if necessary, bringing in outsiders through marriage or godparentage. Carlo Gambino was one of those who, the New York *World Journal Tribune* noted in 1966, "likes to keep things 'in the family.' " Thus, Don Carlo's son married "the daughter of Thomas Lucchese, listed by the FBI as the head of another Cosa Nostra family. . . . And Gambino's daughter is married to a doctor who is head of the Manhattan clinic of the International Longshoremen's Association," a union Gambino inherited from his predecessor as syndicate boss—Albert Anastasia.[2]

There is significance of symbolic as well as practical nature in the change of designation for New York Italian-American syndicates from *borgate* (the preferred term in the 1930s) to "families." "Italian-American criminal syndicates are rightly called 'families,' " one observer noted in 1972, "because the relationships established within them produce kinship-like ties among members, ties which become stronger when they are legitimated through marriage or godparenthood." [3]

Illicit enterprise flourished during World War II and in the three decades since the end of that conflict. Like other successful businessmen, syndicate leaders and members have catered to public demands for illegal services and commodities in short supply. During the war the U.S. Government rationed scarce and essential items such as gasoline, rubber, meat, and tin. "Unfortunately," historian A. Russell Buchanan has observed, "the patriotic honesty of millions of citizens in living up to the rationing requirements was marred by the willingness and even eagerness of other persons to turn the war into sources of personal profit or convenience." According to Marshall Clinard's sociological study of World War II black marketeering, extensive violation occurred "in a large number of commodities at the producing, wholesaling, and retailing levels," which indicated "the pervasiveness of the black market." Americans who had done without necessities during the Depression indicated extreme willingness to spend their unprecedentedly high incomes from defense jobs on choice steaks, liquor, tickets for stage shows, extra gasoline, new cars, and other items in short supply. Thus, according to evidence collected by the Kefauver Committee in 1951, the Joe Adonis-controlled Kings County Buick Company of Brooklyn "ran up an unsavory record of black market deals during World War II." In an allied black-market activity, Joe Valachi, who admitted that he "wasn't so big" an operator, made about $200,000 from the illegal sale of gas ration stamps between mid-1942 and 1945. The former syndicate "soldier" and other black marketeers operated "without any interference from the law." In fact, their business was often carried out with the connivance of authorities, including employees of the Office of Price Administration, which administered wartime rationing. Valachi recalled that "certain OPA people themselves started sneaking them [rationing stamps] out and selling them." Black-market operations were widespread and highly lucrative. According to records kept by the OPA, at least 2,500,000 gallons of gasoline daily were diverted to illegal usage throughout the war—and gasoline was only one of hundreds of items that could be obtained through the black market. Shortages did not disappear immediately with the war's end, and neither did black market operations.[4]

The war proved to be a boon to syndicate gambling operations such as horse racing, dog racing, bookmaking, the numbers racket, and casino gambling. One commentator has maintained, in fact, that "the modern racing boom actually began early in World War II," when the federal government took the position that "racetracks were good for the war effort because they siphoned off money that otherwise would have been chasing scarce goods." [5]

By 1951, gambling—still syndicate crime's greatest source of revenue—brought an estimated $20 million a year, with annual net profits of approximately $7 million. Although nearly all the money came from illicit activities like bookmaking, policy, and slot machines, the underworld also discovered the possibilities of legal gambling in Nevada. The state had legalized gambling in 1931, but not until the 1940s did Benjamin ("Bugsy") Siegel recognize the tremendous opportunities for profit from legalized casino gambling in Nevada. [6]

At the time it opened, in December 1946, the "fabulous Flamingo Hotel" appeared to be a six-million-dollar miscalculation. Siegel built the Flamingo and believed that, along with Las Vegas and Nevada, it would have an important place in the criminal syndicate scheme of things. As Meyer Lansky's partner, and one who had played an important role in New York City's underworld activities during the 1920s and 1930s, Siegel proved accurate in his assessment of the potential of Las Vegas. He did not live long enough to enjoy the fruits of his labor, since he was murdered on June 20, 1947, in Los Angeles, apparently on orders from East Coast and Middle West syndicate leaders who had backed his Flamingo enterprise and believed that he had let them down. [7]

The doubting underworld establishment soon changed in its attitude, and through the construction of multimillion dollar gambling casino-hotel complexes contributed heavily to making Las Vegas a postwar boom town. Thus, when former California gambler Wilbur Clark encountered financial difficulty in his efforts to build the Desert Inn Hotel in 1948, former Cleveland leaders Moe Dalitz, Morris Kleinman, Thomas J. McGinty, and Sam Tucker provided the funds to complete the project in exchange for a controlling share of stock in the corporation. Lansky and his brother Jake, along with Frank Costello,

Miami's Edward Levinson, Hyman Abrams of Boston, New Jersey's Joseph ("Doc") Stacher, Isadore ("Kid Cann") Blumenfeld of Minneapolis, Pete Licavoli of Detroit, Chicago's Tony Accardo, and numerous other syndicate bosses, invested (either openly or through fronts) in the casino-hotels that sprang up in Las Vegas during the early 1950s.

Many casino backers were Italians, but investors represented a variety of ethnic backgrounds, a reflection of the fact that the nation's crime syndicates contained numerous non-Italian elements. Nevertheless, two developments during the 1950s underscored Italian involvement. First, the Kefauver Crime Committee in 1951 emphasized the role of Italians and publicized the alleged existence of a "nation-wide crime syndicate known as the Mafia." Second, in the central New York town of Apalachin, in November 1957, police broke up a meeting on the private estate of Joseph M. Barbara, who operated a soft-drink bottling plant in the area. At least fifty-seven men—and perhaps as many as a hundred—had gathered at Barbara's home for the purpose, the host maintained, of enjoying social activities and a barbecued steak dinner. Authorities suspected that other reasons existed. They were unable to prove wrongdoing, but publicized information about Barbara's guests fanned public fears about Italian criminal activities since all the men identified by authorities were of Italian birth or extraction. Most of the guests came from New York, New Jersey and Pennsylvania; some had arrived from Florida, Texas, Colorado, California and Cuba.[8]

The testimony of former syndicate "soldier" Joseph Valachi (at the time serving a twenty-year term at the Atlanta federal penitentiary on a narcotics conviction) before the McClellan Committee in 1963 reinforced the prevailing public impression that syndicate crime involved Italians almost to the exclusion of other groups. The President's Commission on Law Enforcement and the Administration of Justice reinforced this view in 1967 by stating that "the core" of American syndicate crime consisted of twenty-four groups or "families," whose membership was "exclusively Italian." Although the power of Italian organizations was exaggerated, the *Report*—and other descriptions of syndicate crime published during the late 1960s and early 1970s—accurately pointed out that during the post-World War II decades Italians had made effective use of ethnic group cohesiveness and the family in order to reach a position of primacy in the American underworld.[9]

Since 1941 Italian syndicates have continued to tap traditional illicit enterprises such as gambling, loan-sharking, narcotics, bootlegging (of cigarets, electrical appliances, furs, aspirin, and other products in addition to the prohibition-era staple, alcohol), and racketeering. Organized prostitution has declined in importance, in part because of a more permissive public attitude toward premarital and extramarital sex. During the late 1960s, Italian criminals like Boston's Vincent Teresa tapped a new source of revenue: stolen securities. These securities were generally obtained in one of two ways: either through inside operators in banks or stockbrokerage houses, or by theft of registered mail at airports. In 1971 a congressional committee investigating the involvement of syndicate crime in the stolen securities business found that the securities were disposed of "through confidence men, stockbrokers and attorneys of shady reputation, fences, and other persons who have the ability, technical knowledge, skill, and contacts to sell the securities or to place them advantageously as collateral in financial transactions." The National Crime Information Center estimated the value of government and private securities stolen in 1970 to be at least $227 million. Significant though it is, this figure is less impressive than the 1967 estimates of the President's Commission of some other illicit activities: $350 million annual gross from narcotics, of which syndicate importers and distributors netted approximately $21 million; illegal wagering on horse races, lotteries, and sporting events, $20 billion annually, of which criminal syndicates received perhaps $7 billion. The Commission declined to specify the total profits obtained from loan-sharking, except to "classify the business in the multi-billion-dollar range." [10]

In recent decades criminal entrepreneurs have devoted increasingly more attention to legitimate business. There is some disagreement among authorities as to whether this focus represents an effort to use profits obtained from illegal activities as a means to infiltrate and cor-

48. Carlos Marcello and his daughter Jackie, after leaving Federal Court in New Orleans, January 30, 1975, after he and two associates were acquitted on charges stemming from an alleged night club takeover. (United Press International)

rupt legitimate enterprises, or an attempt on the part of upwardly mobile entrepreneurs to leave a sordid life and gain respectability. The Kefauver Committee, which subscribed to the former theory, noted the presence of syndicate figures in "approximately 50 areas of business enterprise." These included advertising, appliances, the automobile industry, banking, coal, construction, drug stores and drug companies, electrical equipment, florists, food (meat, sea food, dairy products, groceries, cheese, olive oil, fruits), the garment industry, import-export business, insurance, the liquor industry, news services, newspapers, the oil industry, paper products, radio stations, ranching, real estate, restaurants, the scrap business, shipping, steel, television, theaters, and transportation. The desire to "go legitimate" has continued to the present.[11]

Despite prodigious efforts to maintain the status quo, by the 1960s

changes were taking place, not in the structure of entrepreneurial organizations (which have remained much as they were in the 1930s), but
in the area of personnel. The generation of criminal leaders who grew
to maturity during the prohibition era and who, following the lead of
John Torrio and Lucky Luciano, helped create the "Combination,"
clung tenaciously to power into the post-World War II decades. Three
factors contributed to the decimation of the ranks of the "Giants":
death from natural causes; coordinated federal, state, and local law enforcement activities (particularly during the Kennedy Administration);
and internal power struggles, most notably that of the mid-1950s,
which brought Vito Genovese to a position of dominance in the New
York underworld following the murder of Albert Anastasia and the attempted murder of Frank Costello.[12]

Increasingly, criminal syndicates were unable to attract able, intelligent, ambitious Italian-Americans of the younger generation. Careers in crime offered little to these status- and security-conscious
youngsters who had grown to maturity during a period of almost continuous prosperity. They preferred careers as lawyers, doctors, army
officers, or corporation executives.[13]

Official pressures, advancing age of syndicate leaders, and this in-
ability to attract new local talent combined with increasing competition from blacks and Latins to mark the beginning of the decline of
Italian-American syndicates, particularly in the highly competitive New
York City area. Carlo Gambino was among the last of the "old time"
New York bosses still around in 1976, and the 76-year-old Brooklyn
resident was suffering from heart trouble and other physical ills. Efforts by younger leaders to inject new ideas and techniques into syndicate operations suffered a setback on June 28, 1971, when Joe Co-
lumbo, who took the offensive and led Italian-American protestors
against the FBI and others who—he claimed—slurred the Italian-
American name, was shot three times and crippled by a black gunman
at an Italian-American Unity Day parade. In efforts to replenish their
depleted ranks, syndicate bosses in New York and elsewhere reportedly imported ambitious young toughs from Sicily during the early
1970s to do battle with Cubans and blacks in the scramble for nar-

49. Carlo Gambino appeared at Sheepshead Bay police station, Brooklyn, on February 2, 1973, with his chauffeur, who was arrested for driving with a revoked license. (New York *Daily News*)

cotics dollars. "Greasers are taking over the whole operation," one federal informant was quoted as saying in 1973. "Carlos Marcello has spread them through the South and the Southwest. They are in upstate New York. Gambino and Marcello and Magaddino [Buffalo's Steffano Magaddino] are bringing them over. Right here, in downtown New York, the numbers are all theirs." [14]

Before his murder on April 7, 1972, Joey Gallo was said to have advocated another approach to stem the waning power of Italian syndicates: recruitment of blacks rather than warfare with this potentially important pool of manpower. Despite attempted remedies, by 1976 the "golden age" of Italian-American entrepreneurial crime appeared to be at an end. [15]

NOTES TO CHAPTER 1

1. Antonio Cutrera, *La Mafia e i Mafiosi* (Palermo, 1900), pp. 25–27; Albert Falcionelli, *Les Sociétés secrètes italiennes* (Paris, 1936), pp. 184–86; Luigi Barzini, "The Real Mafia," *Harper's* 208 (June 1954):42.

2. "The Mafia in Sicily," *Living Age* 189 (June 1891):633; William A. Paton, *Picturesque Sicily* (New York, 1898), p. 363; Jeremy Boissevain, "Poverty and Politics in a Sicilian Agro-Town," *International Archives of Ethnography*, 50, pt. 2 (1966):222.

3. Bolton King and Thomas Okey, *Italy To-day*, new, enl. ed. (London, 1909), p. 112.

4. Eric Hobsbawm, *Bandits* (New York, 1969), pp. 58, 87, 111; Gino Arias, *La Questione meridionale* (Bologna, 1921), 1:288.

5. Elizabeth Wormeley Latimer, *Italy in the Nineteenth Century and the Making of Austria-Hungary and Germany*, 2d ed. (Chicago, 1897), p. 365; Giustino Fortunato, *Il Mezzogiorno e lo stato italiano*, reprinted in Bruno Caizzi, ed., *Antologia della questione meridionale* (Milan, 1950), p. 167.

6. Leopoldo Franchetti and Sidney Sonnino, *La Sicilia nel 1876* (specifically vol. 2, *Contadini Siciliani*, by Baron Sidney Sonnino) [Florence, 1925]; Napoleone Colajanni, *La Sicilia dai Borboni ai Sabaudi, 1860–1900*, new ed. (Milan, 1951); Caizzi, ed., *Antologia della questione meridionale*.

7. This and the preceding paragraphs are based on Boissevain, "Pov-

erty and Politics in a Sicilian Agro-Town," p. 202; Leonard Moss, "The Peasantry," paper prepared for Symposium on Modern Italy, Columbia University, 1971.

8. King and Okey, *Italy To-Day*, pp. 111–12; Boissevain, "Poverty and Politics in a Sicilian Agro-Town," p. 204.

9. "The Mafia in Sicily," 633; Boissevain, "Poverty and Politics in a Sicilian Agro-Town," 222.

10. Donald Pitkin, "Land Tenure and Family Organization in an Italian Village," Ph.D. dissertation, Harvard University, 1954; Constance Cronin, *The Sting of Change: Sicilians in Sicily and Australia* (Chicago, 1970), pp. 26, 50–63.

11. "The Spirit of the Mafia," *Fortnightly Review* 77 (Jan. 1901):107–8.

12. The discussion of the *mafia* is based on the following studies: Giuseppe Montalbano, "La Mafia," *Nuovi Argomenti* 5 (Nov.-Dec. 1953):165–204; Cutrera, *La Mafia e i Mafiosi;* Eric J. Hobsbawm, *Primitive Rebels, Studies in Archaic Forms of Social Movements in the 19th and 20th Centuries,* 2nd ed. (New York, 1963); esp. chap. 3; Michele Pantaleone, *The Mafia and Politics* (London, 1966), esp. chap. 2; Henner Hess, *Mafia and Mafiosi: The Structure of Power* (Lexington, Mass., 1973); Anton Blok, *The Mafia of a Sicilian Village, 1860–1960; A Study of Violent Peasant Entrepreneurs* (Oxford, 1974); Falcionelli, *Les Sociétés secrètes italiennes,* esp. pp. 184–230; Denis Mack Smith, *A History of Sicily. Modern Sicily: After 1713* (London, 1968); Giuseppe Alongi, *La Maffia nei suoi fattori e nelle sue manifestazioni. Studio sulle classi pericolose della Sicilia* (Turin, 1887); Franchetti and Sonnino, *La Sicilia nel 1876;* Nando Russo, ed., *Antologia della Mafia* (Palermo, 1964); King and Okey, *Italy To-Day,* esp. chap. 5; Salvatore F. Romano, *Storia della Mafia* (Milan, 1963); Domenico Novacco, *Inchiesta sulla Mafia* (Milan, 1963). Only direct quotations are footnoted.

13. Gino C. Speranza, "Petrosino and the Black Hand," *Survey* 23 (Apr. 3, 1909):11; Montalbano, "La Mafia," p. 189.

14. Franchetti and Sonnino, *La Sicilia,* 1:66.

15. Blok, *The Mafia of a Sicilian Village,* p. 173.

16. King and Okey, *Italy To-Day,* pp. 121–22.

17. Cutrera, *La Mafia e i Mafiosi,* p. 27.

18. Montalbano, "La Mafia," p. 170.

19. Quoted in *ibid.,* p. 191.

20. Pantaleone, *Mafia and Politics,* p. 134; Hess, *Mafia and Mafiosi,* pp. 88, 75.

21. Hess, *Mafia and Mafiosi,* pp. 12, 60, 75.

22. Alongi, *La Maffia,* p. 135; Boissevain, "Poverty and Politics in a Sicilian Agro-Town," 224–25.

23. Hobsbawm, *Primitive Rebels,* pp. 49–52 and sources cited there.

24. The discussion of the *Camorra* is based on Giuseppe Alongi, *La Camorra: Studio di sociologia criminali* (Turin, 1890); Marco Monnier, *La Camorra: Notizie storiche raccolte e documentate* (Naples, 1965); Ernesto Serao, "The Truth about the *Camorra,"* *Outlook* 98 (July 29, 1911):717–26, (Aug. 5, 1911):778–87; Arthur Train, *Courts, Criminals and the Camorra* (New York, 1912); Falcionelli, *Les Sociétés secrètes italiennes.*

25. Train, *Courts, Criminals and the Camorra,* pp. 149–50; Alongi, *La Camorra,* p. 134.

26. Serao, "The Truth about the *Camorra,"* 724; Alongi, *La Camorra,* pp. 31–35.

27. King and Okey, *Italy To-Day,* pp. 118–19; Train, *Courts, Criminals and the Camorra,* pp. 160–61.

28. A Veteran Diplomat, "Protection of the Slayers of Petrosino," *New York Times Magazine,* March 28, 1909, p. 4.

29. Italy, Commissariato Generale de'l'Emigrazione, *Annuario statistico della emigrazione italiana dal 1876 al 1925* (Rome, 1926), 149–51; U.S. Congress, Senate, *Reports of the Immigration Commission,* 1(1911):104; Robert F. Foerster, *The Italian Emigration of Our Times* (Cambridge, Mass., 1919), chaps. 5, 6, 7; "The Immigrant in South America," *Blackwood's Edinburgh Magazine* 190 (Nov. 1911):608–18. Despite the title, this article limits itself to an examination of the problems faced by Italian immigrants in Argentina and Brazil and the reasons for the decline of Italian immigration to those countries.

NOTES TO CHAPTER 2

1. Charles Gayarre, *The World From Jackson Square: A New Orleans Reader*, ed. Etolia S. Basso (New York, 1948), pp. 16, 17; Herbert Asbury, *The French Quarter: An Informal History of the New Orleans Underworld* (New York, 1936), p. 19; Gerald M. Capers, *Occupied City: New Orleans under the Federals, 1862–1865* (Lexington, Ky., 1965), pp. 12–13; Joy J. Jackson, *New Orleans in the Gilded Age: Politics and Urban Progress, 1880–1896* (Baton Rouge, 1969), p. 232.

2. U.S. Bureau of the Census, *Seventh Census of the United States: 1850*, xxxvi; *Ninth Census of the United States, 1870. Population,* 1:390; *Tenth Census . . . 1880. Population,* 1:540–41; *Eleventh Census . . . 1890. Population,* 1:672, 676. The assertion that New Orleans contained between 20,000 and 25,000 Italians in 1890 was made by the New Orleans *Picayune,* Oct. 18, 1890. John E. Coxe, "The New Orleans Mafia Incident," *Louisiana Historical Quarterly* 20 (Oct. 1937):1106, claimed that the number at that time was between 25,000 and 30,000.

3. New Orleans *Picayune,* Nov. 12, 1890.

4. Denis Mack Smith, *Italy* (Ann Arbor, 1959), p. 3. U.S. Bureau of the Census, *Report of Vital and Social Statistics in the United States at the Eleventh Census: 1890. Part II. Vital Statistics, Cities of 100,000 Population and Upward* (1896), pp. 198, 284. U.S. Bureau of the Census, *Compendium of the Eleventh Census: 1890: Part III* (1897), pp. 111, 113.

5. Eleanor McMain, "Behind the Yellow Fever in Little Palermo," *Charities and the Commons* 15 (Nov. 4, 1905):156.

6. Writer Jesse White Mario elaborated on the stability of New Orleans Sicilians in an article, "Maffia, Camorra, Brigandage—Alias Crime," in *The Nation:*

> The Sicilians have always had a preference for New Orleans, and their colony there is regarded with pride and hope at home. They have there ten patriotic and benevolent societies, with $20,000 reserve. Only last

January they sent home to their families in Sicily 300,000 lire ($60,000), depositing another $20,000 with the Consul. (52 [April 16, 1891]:315)

7. *Soards' New Orleans City Directory for 1890* (New Orleans, 1890); City of New Orleans, Tax Ledgers for 1890, City Archives; New Orleans *Picayune,* Aug. 6, 1913. Among other successful Italians, E. F. Del Bondio, a commercial merchant residing at 326 Josephine, had an estate of $35,800 in real and personal property; Antonio Augusti, of 33 North Claiborne, a realtor, was worth $37,550; auctioneer and real estate agent Benedetto Onorato, St. Charles Avenue at the corner of Octavia, $26,760; fruit merchant Antonio Campagne of 128½ Felicity, $10,700; liquor dealer Antonio Patorno, 31 Dumaine, $13,000; boss drayman Blanche Otero, 72 Washington Street, $10,600; grocer John B. Canepa of 261 Dauphine, $21,450; fruit dealer Angelo Cusimano, 146 Decatur, $16,000; saloon and restaurant owner Louis Cignoni, 379 St. Ann, $12,950; Peter Lipari, fruit dealer (later, sea captain), 271 Royal, $13,000; Anthony A. Desposito, 108 South Derbigny, $13,325; lumber dealer Lazaro Roca, 203 Esplanade Avenue, $19,550; B. Campiglio, 80 Melpomene Avenue, commercial merchant, $22,500; Giuseppe Passalacqua, 227 Orleans, shoe factory owner, $17,950; fish and oyster dealer Salvador D'Amico, 268 Girod, $11,300.

8. New Orleans *Picayune,* Nov. 12, 1890. According to Charles B. Barnes, *The Longshoremen* (New York, 1915), pp. 263–64, a stevedore is "a man who takes contracts for loading and discharging ships. The term is sometimes applied to a head foreman. It is loosely used for longshoremen." A longshoreman is "a workman employed in discharging or loading the cargoes of vessels or in trucking them back and forth on the pier."

9. This and the following material are from the New Orleans *Picayune,* New Orleans *Times,* New York *Herald,* and New York *Sun* for the period from July 1 to Dec. 31, 1881.

10. Eric Hobsbawm, *Primitive Rebels: Studies in Archaic Forms of Social Movement in the 19th and 20th Centuries,* 2d ed. (New York, 1963), pp. 16–17.

11. John S. Kendall, "Who Killa de Chief?" *Louisiana Historical Quarterly* 22 (Apr., 1939):507; Hodding Carter, *Lower Mississippi* (New York, 1942), p. 318; James D. Horan, *The Pinkertons: The Detective Dynasty That Made History* (New York, 1967), p. 419.

12. U.S. Department of State, *Correspondence in Relation to the Killing of Prisoners in New Orleans on March 14, 1891* (Washington, 1891), pp. 75–83; New Orleans *Picayune*, May 6, 1891; John C. Wickliffe, "The Mafia in New Orleans," *Truth* 10 (Mar. 26, 1891):9; Coxe, "The New Orleans Mafia Incident," p. 1071.

13. Italian criminals showed neither subtlety nor discretion when they murdered to carry out blood feuds or vendettas. In the 1880s as well as in the 1930s, they killed rivals in public view, generally eliminating their victims brutally and making little effort to dispose of the bodies. In this way the killers made clear to the community how effective they were in removing opposition, and struck fear into potential rivals as well as the general public. Some writers have claimed that while Italian-colony violence in the decades before 1880 was not organized, that taking place after Esposito's arrival in the city was organized. Thus, Kendall maintains that Italian murders in the 1860s and 1870s were, "without exception, traced to vendetta or to casual personal difficulty." Since neither bibliography nor footnotes are provided in his articles, it is difficult to be positive as to the source of Kendall's statement, but it probably is based on the official and seemingly comprehensive list prepared by Police Chief Gaster in 1891. Kendall, "Who Killa de Chief?" p. 505.

14. Official coroner reports for New Orleans are located in the City Archives.

15. Kendall, "Who Killa de Chief?" pp. 509–10.

16. Nicholas Gage, *The Mafia Is Not an Equal Opportunity Employer* (New York, 1972), p. 35.

17. New Orleans *Picayune*, July 27, 1890.

18. Kendall, "Who Killa de Chief?" p. 510.

19. This material and following paragraphs are based on records of the Criminal District Court for the Parish of Orleans, in the case of *State of Louisiana vs. Joseph Provenzano, et al.* Section A, No.

13731, Section B, No. 13732 (this includes indictment records, lists of witnesses, affidavits, and a limited number of transcripts of trial proceedings located at Criminal Court Building in New Orleans); New Orleans *Times-Democrat,* New Orleans *Picayune,* New Orleans *Item,* New Orleans *States,* and New Orleans *Mascot* for period from May 6, 1890, to Jan. 24, 1891; Harris Myron Dulitz, "The Myth of the Mafia in New Orleans," B.S. Honors Thesis, Tulane University, 1956; Kendall, "Who Killa de Chief?"

20. For example, Asbury, *French Quarter,* p. 410.

21. New Orleans *Times-Democrat,* July 17, 1890.

22. See lists of witnesses and affidavits, Criminal Court Buildings.

23. The *Stoppagliere* society was a *mafia* organization that appeared in Monreale during the 1870s and quickly gained widespread notoriety throughout Sicily. It would have been more likely, however, for the Provenzanos, who were natives of Monreale, to have been intimately familiar with the inner workings of the *Stoppaglieri* than for the Matrangas, who originated in Piana degli Albanesi.

24. New Orleans *States,* May 16, 1891.

25. Ed Reid, *Mafia,* new rev. ed. (New York, 1964), p. 110; Hobsbawm, *Primitive Rebels,* pp. 46–47.

26. "Romance of the Day. No. III. Organized Assassination," *Illustrated American* 5 (Nov. 8, 1890):351; New Orleans *Times-Democrat,* July 17–19, 1890; New Orleans *Picayune,* July 17–19, 1890; Notes from the Italian Legation in the United States to the Department of State, File Microcopies of Records in the National Archives: No. 202, Roll No. 10, Oct. 1, 1889–Dec. 26, 1892; U.S. Department of State, *Correspondence in Relation to the Killing of Prisoners in New Orleans.* It is impossible to determine the place of birth (in Italy) of the eleventh man.

NOTES TO CHAPTER 3

1. Discussion of the Hennessy murder trial is based on the following: New Orleans *Picayune,* New Orleans *Times-Democrat,* New Orleans

States, New Orleans *Item,* New Orleans *Mascot; Il Progresso Italo-Americano, L'Eco d'Italia, L'Araldo Italiano,* (all of New York), *L'Italia* (Chicago), all for the period from Oct. 16, 1890, to May 31, 1891; John E. Coxe, "The New Orleans Mafia Incident," *Louisiana Historical Quarterly* 20 (Oct. 1937):1067–1110; John S. Kendall, "Who Killa de Chief?," *Louisiana Historical Quarterly* 22 (Apr., 1939):492–530; Harris Myron Dulitz, "The Myth of the Mafia in New Orleans," B.S. honors thesis; Tulane University, 1956; Richard L. Carroll, "David C. Hennessy," B.A. thesis, Notre Dame Seminary, New Orleans, 1957; U.S. Department of State, *Correspondence in Relation to the Killing of Prisoners in New Orleans on March 14, 1891* (Washington, 1891), pp. 48–109; Frank P. Dimaio, a Pinkerton Agency operative who was sent to New Orleans to help find and convict the Hennessy killers, prepared an eight-page memo on the case, in File Drawer #18, dossier labeled "Murder of David Hennessy, Chief of Police, New Orleans, Louisiana, October 15, 1890," located in the Agency's library in its New York headquarters. It is undated but was obviously written long after the event, probably in the late 1930s or early 1940s. Indictment and trial records of the Hennessy case no longer exist at the Criminal Court Building in New Orleans. Whether they were lost, stolen, or destroyed is unknown. The daily press, however, contained daily summaries of the trial proceedings, and these have been used in this study.

2. New Orleans *Times-Democrat,* Oct. 19, 1890.

3. Dimaio memo in Pinkerton Agency files.

4. Coxe, "The New Orleans Mafia Incident," p. 1083; Kendall, "Who Killa de Chief?" p. 517; New Orleans *Times-Democrat,* Apr. 13, 1891; Dulitz, "The Myth of the Mafia in New Orleans," p. 31.

5. New Orleans *Picayune,* Mar. 14, 1891; New Orleans *Times-Democrat,* Mar. 14, 1891.

6. Herbert Asbury, *The French Quarter: An Informal History of the New Orleans Underworld* (New York, 1936), pp. 415–16; Joy J. Jackson, *New Orleans in the Gilded Age: Politics and Urban Progress, 1880–1896* (Baton Rouge, 1969), p. 248; Coxe, "The New Orleans Mafia Incident," p. 1083; Kendall, "Who Killa de Chief?" p. 530.

7. New York *Herald*, Mar. 18, 1891.

8. New York *Times*, Mar. 14, 1891; New Orleans *Picayune*, Mar. 14, 1891.

9. New Orleans *Times-Democrat*, Mar. 15, 1891.

10. There is a vast literature on the lynching and on the resulting crisis between Italy and the United States. Among the more useful items are these: "The New Orleans Massacre," *Nation* 52 (Mar. 19, 1891):232; "The Italian Trouble," *Nation* 52 (Apr. 9, 1891):294; "The New Orleans Outbreak," *Frank Leslie's Illustrated Newspaper* 72 (Mar. 28, 1891):127; "Eleven Italians Killed in the Parish Prison at New Orleans," *Public Opinion* 10 (Mar. 21, 1891):561–65; "Lessons of the New Orleans Lynching" *Public Opinion* 10 (Mar. 28, 1891):585–88; "New Orleans' War on the Mafia," *Illustrated American* 6 (Apr. 4, 1891):318–23; James Bryce, "Legal and Constitutional Aspects of the Lynching at New Orleans," *New Review* 4 (May 1891):385–97; "The Mafia and What Led to the Lynchings," *Harper's Weekly* 35 (Mar. 28, 1891):226–27; *Correspondence in Relation to the Killing of Prisoners in New Orleans;* J. Alexander Karlin, "The Italo-American Incident of 1891," Ph.D. dissertation, University of Minnesota, 1940; J. Alexander Karlin, "The Italo-American Incident of 1891 and the Road to Reunion," *Journal of Southern History* 8 (May 1942):242–46; Notes from the Italian Legation in the United States to the Department of State, File Microcopies of Records in the National Archives: No. 202, Roll No. 10, Oct. 1, 1889–Dec. 26, 1892.

11. John C. Wickliffe, "A Jury of Twenty Thousand," *Frank Leslie's Illustrated Newspaper*, Apr. 4, 1891, p. 146. This justification was unquestioningly accepted by subsequent writers, who embellished it. Herbert Asbury and Hodding Carter, for example, drew on, and expanded, Wickliffe's story; see Carter, *Lower Mississippi* (New York, 1942), p. 318; Asbury, *French Quarter*, p. 416. On the other hand, Luigi Roversi, "The Blood-Red Fiends of New Orleans," *Truth* 10 (Mar. 26, 1891):11 strongly disagreed with Wickliffe's argument.

12. Wickliffe, "A Jury of Twenty Thousand," p. 146; New Orleans *Times-Picayune*, Oct. 29, 1943; New Orleans *States*, Oct. 29, 1943.

13. "New Orleans' War on the Mafia," p. 322; Wickliffe, "A Jury of Twenty Thousand," p. 146.

14. The papers quoted were reprinted in the March 21, 1891, issue of *Public Opinion;* J. Alexander Karlin, "New Orleans Lynchings of 1891 and the American Press," *Louisiana Historical Quarterly* 24 (Jan., 1941):202–3.

15. The admitted Italian citizens were Loretto Comitz, Pietro Monasterio, and Charles Traina. The Italian government claimed that all but Macheca and Romero were Italian subjects. See letter from the Italian consul in New Orleans to the Italian Ambassador in Washington, dated March 19, 1891, in the Notes from the Italian Legation.

16. Karlin, "The Italo-American Incident of 1891."

17. New Orleans *Picayune,* Apr. 22, 1892; George M. Reynolds, *Machine Politics in New Orleans, 1896–1926* (New York, 1926), pp. 13–14.

18. New Orleans *Picayune,* May 6, 1892.

19. New Orleans *Times-Democrat,* Dec. 9–11, 1892; John S. Kendall, "Blood on the Banquette," *Louisiana Historical Quarterly* 22 (July 1939):819–56.

NOTES TO CHAPTER 4

1. New York *Tribune,* Mar. 23, 1891; *L'Italia* (Chicago), Oct. 8, 1892.

2. San Francisco *Examiner,* Nov. 28, 1878; Oct. 20, 1890.

3. New Orleans *Picayune,* July 22, 1881; New Orleans *Times,* July 17, 1881.

4. U.S. Department of State, *Correspondence in Relation to the Killing of Prisoners in New Orleans on March 14, 1891* (Washington, 1891), pp. 66–67; New Orleans *Times-Democrat,* Oct. 19, 1890; New Orleans *Picayune,* May 16, 1891.

5. *La Tribuna Italiana Transatlantica* (Chicago), Feb. 1, 1908; Gaetano D'Amato, "The 'Black Hand' Myth," *North American Review* 182 (Apr. 1908):544, 548.

6. Lindsay Denison, "The Black Hand," *Everybody's Magazine* 19 (Sept. 1908):293.

7. New York *Herald,* Sept. 29, 1902.

8. *Ibid.,* Jan. 26, 1902.

9. This and following paragraphs are based on: New York *Herald,* Apr. 16–Sept. 19, 1903, and Mar. 14, 1909; Arthur A. Carey, in collaboration with Howard McClellan, *Memoirs of a Murder Man* (Garden City, N.Y., 1930), chap. 10. Carey was in charge of the New York City Police Department Homicide Squad.

10. New York *Herald,* Sept. 13, 1903.

11. For example, New Orleans *Times-Democrat,* July 14, 1910. For a variety of interpretations concerning the Spanish origins of Black Hand, see D'Amato, "The 'Black Hand' Myth," p. 544, and Denison, "The Black Hand," p. 293. The term was also used in 1894 to describe the activities of bomb throwers in Europe. See "Record of the Black Hand," San Francisco *Examiner,* June 25, 1894.

12. Denison, "The Black Hand," p. 291; "The Black Hand Scourge," *Cosmopolitan Magazine* 47 (June 1909):32–33; Humbert S. Nelli, "Italians and Crime in Chicago: The Formative Years, 1890–1920," *American Journal of Sociology* 74 (Jan. 1969):385–90.

13. New York *Herald,* Nov. 13, 1909.

14. New York *Times,* May 18 and 22, 1915; New York *Herald,* May 18, 1915.

15. On residential mobility see Humbert S. Nelli, *Italians in Chicago, 1880–1930: A Study in Ethnic Mobility* (New York, 1970), chap. 2, and "Italians in Urban America," *The Italian Experience in the United States,* ed. Silvano M. Tomasi and Madeline H. Engel (New York, 1970), pp. 78–81.

16. Quoted in Denison, "The Black Hand," p. 299.

17. St. Louis *Post-Dispatch,* Aug. 12, 1909.

18. From the official trial transcript of the case of *The People against Salvatore Romano, indicted with Antonio Lecchi, Pasquale Lopipero,* Court of General Sessions of the Peace, City and County of New York, September 22, 1911. The trial transcripts for New York County typed from the official stenographic notes are located at the Criminal Court building in New York.

19. Pittsburgh *Dispatch,* Jan. 10, 1908.

20. Philadelphia *Inquirer,* Mar. 10, 1908.

21. Baltimore *Sun,* Nov. 11, 1908.

22. Official trial transcript of the case of *People of the State of New York against Antonio Buono, impleaded with Benedetto Randazzo, Matteo Pallazzolo, Pietro Brusco and Vica Funnera* [*Mrs. Brusco*], Court of General Sessions of the Peace, City and County of New York, Part V. June 30, 1914.

23. This was the usual procedure followed by Black Hand gangs specializing in kidnapping; see the case of *The People of the State of New York against Pasquale Milone, impleaded with Anthony Siragusa, Vincenzo Acena, Katerina Acena, Francesco Masalusa, and Archillo La Rosa,* Court of General Sessions of the Peace, City and County of New York, Part III, August 7, 1914. The prosecutor pointed out, "Each man in this, Gentlemen, played his own particular part, . . . and each man does one thing, and they are very careful not to do two things" (p. 6).

24. This and following paragraphs are based on the Baltimore *American,* Baltimore *Sun,* and *Il Progresso Italo-Americano,* for the period from Dec. 11, 1907, to Apr. 29, 1908. The trial aroused widespread interest in other cities of the East and Middle West. *Il Progresso,* for example, reported the proceedings day by day.

25. "The Black Hand Scourge," pp. 37–38.

26. San Francisco *Examiner,* Jan. 13, May 3 and 7, 1908. The newspapers used were the Baltimore *American,* Baltimore *Sun,* Boston *Globe,* Boston *Post,* Cleveland *Plain Dealer,* Chicago *Tribune,* Kansas City *Star,* New Orleans *Picayune,* New York *Times,* Philadelphia *Inquirer,* Pittsburgh *Post,* Pittsburgh *Dispatch,* San Francisco *Examiner,* *L'Araldo Italiano* (New York), *Il Progresso Italo-Americano* (New York), *L'Italia* (Chicago), and *La Tribuna Italiana Transatlantica* (Chicago). In order to determine whether Black Hand was indeed a problem that existed among Italians in different parts of the country, Southern and Western as well as Eastern and Midwestern cities were selected for examination. In addition to geographic consideration, an effort was made to offer economic diversity—ocean port cities, railway centers, inland ports, commercial cities, and industrial centers. Another objective was to include a wide range of city size and

of size of the Italian element within the population in 1910—from New York City with 4,766,833 people and 340,765 Italians to Kansas City with 248,381 inhabitants and 2,579 first-generation Italians. (See table below.) Newspapers were chosen as source material for information on Black Hand because they were the only source that was still available in all the cities examined and that provided material on the various questions for which information was desired. Police department records, it was found, are either no longer available or are incomplete in some of the cities; occasionally they are simply unavailable for use. New York's police records for 1908, for example, no longer exist, having apparently been discarded or destroyed. In Chicago, officials told the author that records were "unavailable." The sample obtained through use of newspapers is relatively small (141 cases) and probably over-represents sensational and violent crimes as well as those involving non-Italians (41, or 28 per cent of the cases); even so, newspapers represent the only source still extant that provides information on each city for the entire year, the various nationality groups involved, and city-wide coverage. If the shortcomings are kept in mind, newspaper accounts can provide a useful perspective on the study of the Black Hand, even though the conclusions are suggestive rather than exact.

TOTAL POPULATION AND ITALIAN IMMIGRANT POPULATIONS OF SAMPLE CITIES, 1900 AND 1910

| | TOTAL POPULATION | | ITALIAN POPULATION | |
	1900	1910	1900	1910
New York	3,437,202	4,766,883	145,433	340,765
Chicago	1,698,575	2,185,283	16,008	45,169
Baltimore	508,957	558,485	2,042	5,043
New Orleans	287,104	339,075	5,866	8,066
San Francisco	342,782	416,912	7,508	16,918
Pittsburgh	321,616	533,905	5,709	14,120
Boston	560,892	670,585	13,738	31,380
Kansas City	163,752	248,381	1,034	2,579
Philadelphia	1,293,697	1,549,008	17,830	45,308
Cleveland	381,768	560,663	3,065	10,836

Compiled from population census figures, twelfth and thirteenth U.S. censuses.

27. San Francisco *Examiner,* Dec., 1916, esp. the issues of Dec. 1, 2, and 7; Bob Patterson, "The Mafia Revisited," *California Living, Magazine of the San Francisco Examiner and Chronicle,* Jan. 10, 1971, pp. 18–19.

28. "The Black Hand Scourge," p. 34.

29. Humbert S. Nelli, "The Italian Padrone System," *Labor History* 5 (Spring 1964):159.

30. Final disposition of cases could not be determined because some dragged on in the courts for years after 1908, through appeals.

31. New York *Times,* May 8–July 25, 1908.

32. Frank Marshall White, "The Black Hand in Control of Italian New York" 104 (Aug. 16, 1913):858–59.

33. Chicago *Tribune,* Apr. 25, May 29, 1908; New York *Times,* Apr. 9, 1908.

34. "The Seely Houk Case," State of Pennsylvania, *Report of the Game Commissioners for 1908; Commonwealth vs. Rocco Racco, Appellant,* Paperbook of Appellant. In the Supreme Court of Pennsylvania, Western District, No. 82, October Term, 1909. Pinkerton Agency Files, Drawer #45, "Murder of Seely Houk," located at Pinkerton Agency headquarters in New York; Cleveland *Plain Dealer Magazine,* Mar. 28, 1909. James D. Horan, *The Pinkertons: The Detective Dynasty That Made History* (New York, 1967), chap. 35, drew upon Agency files but misinterpreted agents' reports and other material, and distorted the situation existing in the mining towns.

35. This and the following paragraph are based on Confidential Agent Reports, located in the Pinkerton Files. Reports from Agents #10, #32, and #89 proved to be especially informative.

36. Denison, "The Black Hand," p. 295.

37. Baltimore *American,* Dec. 12, 1907; Baltimore *Sun,* Dec. 12, 1907; Jan. 19, 1908; Boston *Globe,* Feb. 14, 1908; New York *Times,* Nov. 21, 1908.

38. *L'Italia,* Nov. 16 and 30, 1907; *La Tribuna Italiana Transatlàntica,* Nov. 16 and 23, 1907; *L'Araldo Italiano,* Dec. 11, 1907 and Feb. 22 and 29, 1908; New Orleans *Picayune,* Dec. 6, 1907; *Il Progresso Italo-Americano,* Nov. 24, 1907; Apr. 8, 1908; Baltimore *Sun,* Apr. 7, 1908; Cleveland *Plain Dealer,* Jan. 2, 1908.

39. *La Tribuna Italiana Transatlantica,* Jan. 11, Feb. 15, 1908; Chicago *Tribune,* Feb. 28, Sept. 20 and 22, Oct. 14, 1908.

40. The Italian "White Hand" Society in Chicago, Illinois, *Studies, Action and Results* (Chicago, 1908); *La Tribuna Italiana Transatlantica,* Nov. 9, 1907.

41. This and following material are based on *Il Progresso Italo-Americano, L'Araldo Italiano,* New York *Times,* New York *Herald,* Brooklyn *Eagle,* all for the period from Feb. 1 to July 1, 1909; "Blackmail and Murder," *Outlook* 91 (Mar. 27, 1909):656–57; Carlo G. Speranza, "Petrosino and the Black Hand," *Survey* 22 (Apr. 3, 1909):11–14; Frank Marshall White, "How the United States Fosters the Black Hand," *Outlook* 93 (Oct. 30, 1909):495.

42. Michele Pantaleone, *The Mafia and Politics* (London, 1966), pp. 40–41. See also Arrigo Pettaco, *Joe Petrosino* (New York, 1974), pp. 187–89. The only value of this otherwise disappointing study is the inclusion of contemporary Italian police reports.

43. Michael Fiaschetti, as told to Prosper Buranelli, *You Gotta Be Rough: The Adventures of Detective Fiaschetti of the Italian Squad* (Garden City, N.Y., 1930), pp. 283–89; Ed Reid, *Mafia* (New York, 1964; new, rev. ed.), pp. 143, 148–49; *L'Araldo Italiano,* Mar. 18, 1909.

44. Quoted in "Uncle Sam to Fight the Black Hand," *Literary Digest* 50 (June 19, 1915):454; Frank Marshall White, "The Passing of the Black Hand," *Century* 95 (Jan. 1918):337.

45. Edward Dean Sullivan, *Chicago Surrenders* (New York, 1930), p. 224.

NOTES TO CHAPTER 5

1. This and the preceding material are based on Intelligence Unit, U.S. Internal Revenue Service investigative files, and newspaper clippings.

2. Andrew Rolle, *The Immigrant Upraised: Italian Adventurers and Colonists in an Expanding America* (Norman, Okla., 1968), and *The American Italians: Their History and Culture* (Belmont, Calif., 1972);

Howard Chudacoff, *Mobile Americans: Residential and Social Mobility in Omaha, 1880–1920* (New York, 1972), pp. 66–67, 80–82.

3. This and the following paragraph are based on New York *Herald Tribune,* June 19, 1936, "Luciano Began Lawless Career in School Days"; Alberto Consiglio, *La Vita di Lucky Luciano* (Milan, 1963), pp. 11–15; Sid Feder and Joachim Joesten, *The Luciano Story* (New York, 1954), pp. 14–19.

4. Frederic M. Thrasher, *The Gang: A Study of 1,313 Gangs in Chicago,* rev. ed. (Chicago, 1936); Clifford R. Shaw and Henry McKay, *Juvenile Delinquency and Urban Areas* (Chicago, 1942); David Matza, *Delinquency and Drift* (New York, 1964).

5. This and the following paragraph are based on George Kibbe Turner, "Tammany's Control of New York by Professional Criminals," *McClure's Magazine* 33 (June 1909):117–34; Herbert Asbury, *The Gangs of New York: An Informal History of the Underworld* (New York, 1927), pp. 252–98; Jack McPhaul, *Johnny Torrio: First of the Gang Lords* (New Rochelle, N.Y., 1972), pp. 44–53; John Kobler, *Capone: The Life and World of Al Capone* (New York, 1971), pp. 31–34.

6. This and the next paragraph are based on Charles B. Barnes, *The Longshoremen* (New York, 1915), p. 5; Inter-Racial Council, "Distribution of the Foreign-Born and Those of Foreign Parentage in New York City, Arranged by Races and Location in the Five Boroughs," manuscript dated December 1919, in New York City Archives; confidential sources.

7. Barnes, *The Longshoremen,* p. 181; Charles P. Larrowe, *Shape-Up and Hiring Hall; A Comparison of Hiring Methods and Labor Relations on the New York and Seattle Waterfronts* (Berkeley and Los Angeles, 1955), chaps. 1 and 2; Vernon H. Jensen, *Hiring of Dock Workers and Employment Practices in the Ports of New York, Liverpool, London, Rotterdam, and Marseilles* (Cambridge, Mass., 1964), chap. 2.

8. McBride's opposite number on the *Leader* was another circulation war veteran, James M. Ragen, who after World War II engaged in a bitter struggle with the Capone forces for control of the nationwide

dissemination of racing information, which is essential for the operation of illegal handbooks. That battle ended with Ragen's murder.

9. U.S. Congress, Senate, *Hearings Before the Special Committee to
Investigate Organized Crime in Interstate Commerce,* 82nd Cong., 1st
Sess., pt. 6, pp. 43–47 (hereafter cited as Kefauver Committee);
Virgil W. Peterson, *Barbarians in Our Midst: A History of Chicago
Crime and Politics* (Boston, 1952), pp. 220–22; Hank Messick, *The
Silent Syndicate* (New York, 1967), pp. 10–14, 192–97.

10. This and the following paragraph are based on Ferdinand Lundberg, *Imperial Hearst; A Social Biography* (New York, 1936), pp.
149, 153–70; Internal Revenue Service files.

11. For a fuller presentation of the points made in this and the following paragraph, see Humbert S. Nelli, *Italians in Chicago, 1880–1930:
A Study in Ethnic Mobility* (New York, 1970), chap. 4.

12. Turner, "Tammany's Control of New York by Professional Criminals," pp. 119–20, 124–25.

13. Allen F. Davis, *American Heroine: The Life and Legend of Jane
Addams* (New York, 1973), p. 178.

14. Egal Feldman, "Prostitution, the Alien Woman and the Progressive Imagination, 1910–1915," *American Quarterly* 19 (Summer
1967):192; The Vice Commission of Chicago, *The Social Evil in
Chicago: A Study of Existing Conditions* (Chicago, 1911), pp. 32–33,
305; Howard B. Woolston, *Prostitution in the United States* (New
York, 1921), p. 33; Stanley W. Finch, "The White Slave Traffic,"
Address delivered before World's Purity Congress, Louisville, Ky.,
May 7, 1912, p. 7 (reprinted in U.S. Congress, Senate, 62nd Cong.,
3rd Sess., Document No. 982); Walter C. Reckless, *Vice in Chicago*
(Chicago, 1933), pp. 34–35; R. N. Wilson, *Transactions of the Fif-
teenth International Congress on Hygiene and Demography,* IV, pt. 1,
p. 115, cited in Woolston, p. 39.

15. Roy Lubove, "The Progressives and the Prostitute," *The Historian* 24 (May 1962):308; Finch, "The White Slave Traffic," p. 7;
Clifford G. Roe, *The Prodigal Daughter: The White Slave Evil and
the Remedy* (Chicago, 1911), p. 182; Edwin W. Sims, "The White
Slave Trade of Today," *Fighting the Traffic in Young Girls, or War*

on the White Slave Trade, by Ernest A. Bell et al. (Washington, 1911), pp. 49–50.

Contrary to general opinion, pre-World War I prostitutes were recruited largely from among city girls of native birth. Although there were many immigrants and rural Americans among them, Walter Reckless (*Vice in Chicago,* pp. 43–45) has presented information from 77 white slave cases in Chicago during the years 1910 to 1913, from records compiled by the police, information that he believed "may help to put Chicago's former white slave market in its proper perspective." One claim of reformers was that white slavers were corrupting vulnerable, innocent children, whom they found to be easier to ensnare than young girls or mature women. Of the 77 subjects studied, 63 showed actual evidence of pandering. Of the 63, none was under 15 years of age, 29 were between 15 and 19, 15 were between 20 and 24, and 2 were older than 24. The age was not available for the other 17, but Reckless believed that none was below age 15.

Of the 63, 6 were reported as being immigrants (one Irish, one Danish, two Swedish, one Hungarian, one Serbian), though none was newly arrived: all had resided for several years (up to eleven) in the United States. Of the "white slaves," 27 (43%) were from Chicago. Of the remaining 36, 15 (24%) were from large towns, 17 (27%) from small towns; in the other 4 cases, the place of origin was unreported or unknown. As to claims that white slavers held girls prisoners and abused them, authorities found evidence that 3 of the 63 were being held against their will, and 15 were "brutally treated by their pimps."

16. Chicago Committee of Fifteen, Research Data, vol. 25, the University of Chicago Library Special Collections. The Committee of Fifteen was a private agency founded in 1908 for the purpose of aiding and prodding local officials, the police, and the courts in the investigation, prosecution, and conviction of procurers and panderers in Chicago.

17. Davis, *American Heroine,* pp. 181–82.

18. Ophalia Amigh, "More About the Traffic in Shame," *Fighting the Traffic in Young Girls,* p. 117.

19. George Kibbe Turner, "The Daughters of the Poor," *McClure's*

Magazine 34 (Nov. 1909):46; Roe, *The Prodigal Daughter,* p. 99; Theodore A. Bingham, "Foreign Criminals in New York," *North American Review* 188 (Sept. 1908):390.

20. Chicago *Tribune,* June 20, Oct. 13, 1908; San Francisco *Examiner,* Apr. 1936–Mar. 1937; Curt Gentry, *The Madams of San Francisco: An Irreverent History of the City by the Golden Gate* (New York, 1964), pp. 246–52; Charles Winick and Paul M. Kinsie, *The Lively Commerce: Prostitution in the United States* (Chicago, 1971), pp. 113–14.

21. Turner, "Daughters of the Poor," p. 47, and "Tammany's Control of New York by Professional Criminals," pp. 121–25; John Landesco, *Organized Crime in Chicago* (Chicago, 1968), pp. 30–31. This invaluable study is a reprint of Part 3 of the *Illinois Crime Survey,* originally published in 1929.

22. Chicago Committee of Fifteen, Research Data, vol. 25; Chicago *Tribune,* Oct. 1, 1909–Jan. 6, 1910.

23. San Francisco *Chronicle,* May 7, 1937; Denver *Post,* Mar. 5 and 8, 1912.

24. Philadelphia *Inquirer,* Dec. 17 and 29, 1908; Chicago *Tribune,* Feb. 7, July 28, 1908; Roe, *The Prodigal Daughter,* pp. 237, 250–51; Kobler, *Capone,* p. 40.

25. Sims, "The White Slave Trade of Today," pp. 56–57.

26. New York *Times,* Mar. 1, 1919. David Musto, *The American Disease: Origins of Narcotics Control* (New Haven, 1973) p. 5, and n. 13, pp. 253–54, provides more conservative, and probably more accurate, figures.

27. Based on the official trial transcript of the case of *The People of the State of New York against Alexander De Meo,* New York Supreme Court, Criminal Branch, New York County, December 17, 1913.

28. New York *Times,* Nov. 16, 1909, Mar. 20, 1910, July 16, 1936; New York *Herald,* Nov. 16, 1909–Mar. 20, 1910.

29. Kefauver Committee, pt. 6, pp. 401–2.

30. Nelli, *Italians in Chicago,* pp. 105–11, 123; Boston *Globe,* Jan. 3, 1908.

31. New Orleans Police Department Records; Elizabeth Brown, "En-

forcement of Prohibition in San Francisco," M.A. thesis, University of California, Berkeley, 1940, p. 26.

32. Henry Chafetz, *Play the Devil: A History of Gambling in the United States from 1492 to 1955* (New York, 1960), pp. 194–201, and chap. 3, esp. pp. 290–91; Herbert Asbury, *Sucker's Progress: An Informal History of Gambling in America from the Colonies to Canfield* (New York, 1938), chap. 12, esp. pp. 385–86.

33. Herbert Asbury, *Gem of the Prairie: An Informal History of the Chicago Underworld* (New York, 1940), pp. 142 ff.

34. Peterson, *Barbarians in Our Midst,* pp. 84–91; Landesco, *Organized Crime in Chicago,* chap. 3.

35. Frank Marshall White, "How the United States Fosters the Black Hand," *Outlook* 93 (Oct. 30, 1909):495.

36. Eric J. Hobsbawm, *Primitive Rebels: Studies in Archaic Forms of Social Movement in the 19th and 20th Centuries* (New York, 1963), p. 47; Nicholas Gage, "The Mafia at War, Part I," *New York Magazine* 5 (July 10, 1972):30. The Mafia-Camorra confrontation in New York is discussed in Ed Reid's *Mafia,* new, rev. ed. (New York, 1964), pp. 151–62, first published in 1952, and the source of Hobsbawm's discussion and probably of Gage's, although it is impossible to be certain, since that article is not documented.

37. New York *Herald* and New York *Times,* May 18–25, 1915; New York *Times,* Nov. 15, 1909.

38. This and the following paragraphs are based on official trial transcripts in the following cases: *The People of the State of New York against Pellegrino Morano,* New York State Court of Appeals Cases, vol. 2280; *The People of the State of New York against Alessandrio Vollero,* New York State Court of Appeals Cases, vols. 3841 and 3842; *The People of the State of New York against Angelo Giordano, et al.,* Court of General Sessions of the Peace, County of New York, pt. 5, April 22, 1918.

39. Nick Gentile, *Vita di capomafia* (Rome, 1963), pp. 46, 48–52.

40. For a detailed examination of the Powers-D'Andrea struggle, see Nelli, *Italians in Chicago,* pp. 105–11, 123.

41. This and the next paragraph are based on confidential Agent Reports, in Pinkerton Detective Agency files, New York.

42. Nelli, *Italians in Chicago,* pp. 170–81, discusses the structure and activities of Italian-colony mutual benefit and fraternal insurance societies.

NOTES TO CHAPTER 6

1. Charles Merz, *The Dry Decade* (Garden City, N.Y., 1931); Preston William Slosson, *The Great Crusade and After, 1914–1928* (New York, 1930); Andrew Sinclair, *Prohibition; The Era of Excess* (Boston, 1962), pp. 18, 21; William E. Leuchtenburg, *The Perils of Prosperity, 1914–1932* (Chicago, 1958), pp. 213–14; James H. Timberlake, *Prohibition and the Progressive Movement, 1900–1920* (Cambridge, Mass., 1963); Joseph R. Gusfield, *Symbolic Crusade; Status Politics and the American Temperance Movement* (Urbana, Ill., 1963).

2. Willis J. Abbot, "Prohibition in Practice. IV—The Cities of Our Trans-Mississippi States," *Collier's,* 63 (May 17, 1919):13, 28–30; George L. McNutt, "Why Workingmen Drink," *Outlook* 69 (Sept. 14, 1901):115–18; George E. Waring, Jr., "The Drink Problem in New York City Politics," *Outlook* 69 (Oct. 26, 1901):504–8; Sinclair, *Prohibition,* pt. 1.

3. This and the next two paragraphs are based on Timberlake, *Prohibition and the Progressive Movement,* pp. 150–54, 181–83; voting records from Boston, Chicago, and New York.

4. Justin Steuart, *Wayne Wheeler, Dry Boss* (New York, 1928), pp. 149–52; *U.S. Statutes at Large,* 41, pt. 1, 305–23.

5. Roy A. Haynes, *Prohibition Inside Out* (Garden City, N.Y., 1923), p. 11.

6. Clark Warburton, *Economic Results of Prohibition* (New York, 1932), p. 202; J. C. Burnham, "New Perspectives on the Prohibition 'Experiment' of the 1920s," *Journal of Social History* 2 (Fall 1968):51–68.

7. Denver *Post,* Feb. 5 and 19, 1916; Larry D. Engelmann, "O, Whisky: The History of Prohibition in Michigan," Ph.D. dissertation, University of Michigan, 1971, pp. 485, 491–92.

8. New York *Herald,* Jan. 15, 1920.

9. *New York Times,* July 29, 1931; J. Richard (Dixie) Davis, "Things I Couldn't Tell Till Now," *Collier's* 104 (July 29, 1939):38, 40; Craig Thompson and Allen Raymond, *Gang Rule in New York: The Story of a Lawless Era* (New York, 1940), pp. 314–18.

10. U.S. Department of Commerce, *The Balance of International Payments of the United States in 1924* (1925); Frank J. Wilson (as told to Howard Whitman), "How We Caught Al Capone," Chicago *Tribune Sunday Magazine,* June 14, 1959.

11. Merz, *Dry Decade,* p. 65; New York *Times,* July 4, 1920.

12. Chicago *Tribune,* Jan. 18, 1920.

13. Chicago *Daily News,* Nov. 17, 1924; Chicago *Tribune,* Nov. 18, 1924.

14. John Landesco, "Prohibition and Crime," *Annals of the American Academy of Political and Social Science* 163 (Sept. 1932):120.

15. Engelmann, "O Whisky," p. 526; Merz, *Dry Decade,* pp. 66–67.

16. Elizabeth A. Brown, "The Enforcement of Prohibition in San Francisco," M.A. thesis, University of California, Berkeley, 1952, pp. 44–47; Gilman Ostrander, *The Prohibition Movement in California, 1848–1933* (Berkeley, 1957), pp. 178–81.

17. Ostrander, *Prohibition Movement in California,* p. 178; Sinclair, *Prohibition,* pp. 206–7.

18. U.S. Congress, Senate, *Hearings Before a Subcommittee of the Senate Committee on the Judiciary,* 69th Cong., 1st Sess., p. 182; U.S. Treasury Department, *Industrial Alcohol* (1930), p. 48.

19. National Commission on Law Observance and Enforcement, *Prohibition* (Washington, 1931), 1:132 (hereafter cited as Wickersham Report); U.S. Coast Guard Intelligence Division, "Estimate of the Smuggling Situation Subsequent to Repeal of the 18th Amendment" (1932), National Archives, Record Group 26, Box 20.

20. U.S. Coast Guard Intelligence Division, "Estimate . . ."; Wickersham Report 5:383–87.

21. Investigative file of the Intelligence Unit, U.S. Internal Revenue Service, on Consolidated Distilleries, Ltd.

22. This and following paragraphs are based on material in Prohibition Bureau and Internal Revenue Service files, including two reports, dated June 22, 1928, and Oct. 30, 1928, from Special Agent Eugene R. O'Brien to the Commissioner of Prohibition, in the U.S. Department of Justice files, File No. 23–51–467; and the extensive investigative records on John Torrio in the Internal Revenue Service files.

23. U.S. Coast Guard Intelligence Division, "Estimate . . . ."

24. This and the preceding paragraph are based on Engelmann, "O Whisky," pp. 457, 503.

25. Ibid., pp. 520–22.

26. Intelligence Unit, Internal Revenue Service, Treasury Department, *A Report Outlining the Organization, Functions, and Activities of the Intelligence Unit Covering the Period From the Date of Its Establishment, July 1, 1919[,] to June 30, 1936* (Washington, 1936), pp. 94–95.

27. New York *Times,* Jan. 18, 1930; Sinclair, *Prohibition,* pp. 201–3.

28. Merz, *Dry Decade,* pp. 69–71.

29. Humbert S. Nelli, *Italians in Chicago, 1880–1930: A Study in Ethnic Mobility* (New York, 1970), p. 219.

30. Letter from Tony Franzel to the Attorney General and newspaper clippings are in the National Archives, Record Group 60, File No. 23–51–68.

31. John Kobler, *Capone: The Life and World of Al Capone* (New York, 1971), pp. 89–90.

32. Merz, *Dry Decade,* pp. 69–70.

33. Edward Dean Sullivan, *Chicago Surrenders* (New York, 1930), p. 205.

34. Landesco, "Prohibition and Crime," p. 125; Walter Noble Burns, *The One-Way Ride* (Garden City, N.Y., 1931).

35. Intelligence Unit, Internal Revenue Service, investigative files on John Torrio.

36. John Landesco, *Organized Crime in Chicago: Part III of the Illinois Crime Survey* (Chicago, 1968), pp. 92–94.

37. Chicago *Tribune,* May 20, 1924; Chicago *Daily News,* Nov. 17, 1924; Wickersham Report, 4:372.

38. Files of newspaper articles on criminal activity in Chicago during the 1920s, maintained by the Chicago Crime Commission at its offices in Chicago.

39. Landesco, *Organized Crime in Chicago,* pp. 102–5; files of the Chicago Crime Commission.

40. This and the next paragraph are based on the following: files of the Chicago Crime Commission; Virgil W. Peterson, *Barbarians in Our Midst: A History of Chicago Crime and Politics* (Boston, 1952), p. 135; files of Intelligence Unit, Internal Revenue Service.

41. Investigative files of Intelligence Unit, Internal Revenue Service; Boston Evening *Transcript,* Jan. 24–Feb. 3, 1933; correspondence from Dec. 29, 1922, to May 26, 1924, on Solomon's trial and conviction in 1922 on narcotics charges, National Archives, Record Group 60, file No. 12–1751.

42. This and the following paragraph from Philadelphia Evening *Bulletin,* Aug. 23 and 30, 1928; Mar. 26, 1966; May 12, 1968; Mar. 9, 1969; Arthur H. Lewis, *The Worlds of Chippy Patterson* (New York, 1960), p. 239; Richard E. Cichowski, "Philadelphia During Prohibition," manuscript dated 1971, in possession of the author.

43. Arthur Evans Wood, *Hamtramck: Then and Now. A Sociological Study of a Polish-American Community* (New York, 1955), p. 165; Engelmann, "O Whisky," pp. 446–48.

44. Engelmann, "O Whisky," pp. 491–96; Keith Sward, *The Legend of Henry Ford* (New York, 1948), pp. 300–2; U.S. Congress, Senate, *Hearings Before the Special Committee to Investigate Organized Crime in Interstate Commerce,* 81st Cong., 2nd Sess. pt. 9 (hereafter cited as Kefauver Committee).

45. This and the preceding paragraphs are based on: "Murder in Cleveland," an 11-part series of articles on prohibition-era wars in Cleveland in the Cleveland *Plain Dealer* from Dec. 26, 1933, to Jan.

5, 1934; clippings files, Cleveland Public Library; Kefauver Committee, pt. 6; Hank Messick, *The Silent Syndicate* (New York, 1967).

46. This will be examined in detail in Chapter 8.

47. Thompson and Raymond, *Gang Rule in New York,* p. 100.

48. Leo Katcher, *The Big Bankroll: The Life and Times of Arnold Rothstein* (New York, 1959).

49. Intelligence Unit, Internal Revenue Service, investigative files.

50. This and the preceding paragraph are from Denver *Post,* Mar. 25 to 29 and May 8, 1925; Sept. 12, 1926; Aug. 28 and Sept. 16, 1931; confidential sources.

51. U.S. Internal Revenue Service, *Story of the Work of the Intelligence Unit* (1943), 2:4–5, 7–14, 92–100; Kefauver Committee, pt. 4-A, pp. 485–92; files of the Intelligence Unit, Internal Revenue Service; William M. Redding, *Tom's Town: Kansas City and the Pendergast Legend* (Philadelphia, 1947), pp. 248–64, 316–22.

52. San Francisco *Examiner,* Dec. 16, 1928; San Francisco *Chronicle,* Nov. 23 and 24, 1929; Mar. 3 to 24, 1931; Nov. 24, 1934; May 7 and 9, 1937; confidential sources.

53. Based on a research paper prepared in 1930 by two University of Chicago sociology students, under the direction of Ernest W. Burgess. The students obtained their information on the Tavern from an underworld figure connected with the Capone organization and from personal observation in Stickney. J. L. Munday and K. B. Alwood, "Stickney," dated Mar. 18, 1930, in Ernest W. Burgess Papers, II-A, Box 5, University of Chicago Library. These observations are corroborated by other contemporaries such as Mezz Mezzrow, a jazz musician who worked at a Capone roadhouse, the Arrowhead Inn, in Burnham in the late 1920s. See Mezz Mezzrow and Bernard Wolfe, *Really the Blues* (New York, 1946), pp. 49–56.

54. Intelligence Unit, Internal Revenue Service investigative files on Al Capone; Chief Frank J. Wilson and Beth Day, *Special Agent: A Quarter Century with the Treasury Department and the Secret Service* (New York, 1965), chap. 3.

NOTES TO CHAPTER 7

1. J. Richard (Dixie) Davis, "Things I Couldn't Tell Till Now," *Collier's* 104 (Aug. 5, 1939):44; Craig Thompson and Allen Raymond, *Gang Rule in New York: The Story of a Lawless Era* (New York, 1940), chap. 12.

2. Nearly every study of the Maranzano death places the murder on September 11. The lone exceptions are Davis, "Things I Couldn't Tell Till Now," by Dutch Schultz's former lawyer; U.S. Congress, Senate, *Hearings Before the Permanent Sub-Committee on Investigations of the Committee on Government Operations. Organized Crime & Illicit Traffic in Narcotics,* 88th Cong., 1st Sess., pt. 1, p. 232 (hereafter referred to as McClellan Committee); and Peter Maas, *The Valachi Papers* (New York, 1968), p. 114. The latter two were based on police department records. All the city newspapers also accurately reported the murder as taking place on September 10. Among those who believed the death occurred on the 11th are Thompson and Raymond, *Gang Rule in New York,* p. 374; Burton B. Turkus and Sid Feder, *Murder, Inc.; The Story of "The Syndicate"* (New York, 1951), p. 73; Fred J. Cook, *The Secret Rulers: Criminal Syndicates and How They Control the U.S. Underworld* (New York, 1966), pp. 97–98; Ralph Salerno and John S. Tompkins, *The Crime Confederation: Cosa Nostra and Allied Operations of Organized Crime* (Garden City, N.Y., 1969), p. 87; Donald R. Cressey, *Theft of the Nation: The Structure and Operations of Organized Crime in America* (New York, 1969), p. 43; Gay Talese, *Honor Thy Father* (New York, 1971), p. 192.

3. Davis, "Things I Couldn't Tell Till Now," p. 44.

4. Thompson and Raymond, *Gang Rule in New York,* pp. 374–75.

5. Turkus and Feder, *Murder, Inc.,* pp. 73–74.

6. Maas, *The Valachi Papers,* p. 111.

7. Cressey, *Theft of the Nation,* p. 44.

8. Maas, *The Valachi Papers,* pp. 115–16; New York *Times,* Sept. 11 and 15, 1931; New York *Daily News,* Sept. 11, 1931.

9. This and the following two paragraphs are based on files of the Denver *Post* for 1930–33, at the *Post* library.

10. Confidential sources, and San Francisco *Chronicle* and San Francisco *Examiner* for the period between Dec. 1, 1928, and Dec. 31, 1932. Especially useful was the May 22, 1932, issue of the *Chronicle*.

11. This and the following paragraph are based on the text of the Atherton Report, printed in the San Francisco *News*, Mar. 16, 1937, confidential sources.

12. Elbert S. P'Pool, "Commercialized Amusements in New Orleans," M.A. thesis, Tulane University, 1930, pp. 75–76.

13. Statements on syndicate crime in New Orleans are based on material from files of Intelligence Unit, U.S. Internal Revenue Service, U.S. Bureau of Narcotics, and Metropolitan Crime Commission of New Orleans, and from confidential sources.

14. For contrasting views on whether Sen. Huey Long or New Orleans politicians invited Costello into the city, see T. Harry Williams, *Huey Long* (New York, 1969), pp. 865–66; Edward F. Haas, "New Orleans on the Half-Shell: The Maestri Era, 1936–1946," *Louisiana History* 13 (Summer 1972):297.

15. Williams, *Huey Long*, p. 194.

16. Files of Intelligence Unit, Internal Revenue Service, and Metropolitan Crime Commission of New Orleans; confidential sources.

17. This and the following paragraphs are based on the following: Lloyd Wendt and Herman Kogan, *Lords of the Levee: The Story of Bathhouse John and Hinky Dink* (Indianapolis, 1943), pp. 344–45; William H. Stuart, *The Twenty Incredible Years* (Chicago, 1935), pp. 315–17; City of Chicago, Board of Election Commissioners, *Official Precinct Voter Registration Lists* and MS of Official Election Returns, Apr. 5, 1927; Chicago *Daily News,* Apr. 4, 1927; Aug. 27, 1930; Apr. 1, 1931; Chicago *Tribune,* Apr. 2, 1931; *People v. Serritella,* 272 Ill. Appellate Ct. (1933), 616.

18. Charles Garrett, *The La Guardia Years; Machine and Reform Politics in New York City* (New Brunswick, N.J. 1961), p. 176; Nancy Joan Weiss, *Charles Francis Murphy, 1858–1924: Respectability and*

Responsibility in Tammany Politics (Northampton, Mass., 1968), p. 52; J. Joseph Huthmacher, "Charles Evans Hughes and Charles Francis Murphy: The Metamorphosis of Progressivism," *New York History* 46 (Jan. 1965):35; Isabel Paterson, "Murphy," *American Mercury* 14 (July 1928):347–54.

19. New York *Times,* Aug. 1938—Oct. 1940; Thomas E. Dewey, *Twenty Against the Underworld* (Garden City, N.Y., 1974), chap. 9; Rupert Hughes, *Attorney for the People: The Story of Thomas E. Dewey* (Boston, 1940), pp. 212–17, 237–52, 298–314.

20. Intelligence Unit, Internal Revenue Service files; George Wolf with Joseph Di Mona, *Frank Costello: Prime Minister of the Underworld* (New York, 1974), p. 181.

21. On Marinelli see documentation supporting Thomas Dewey's accusations included in Hughes, *Attorney for the People,* pp. 169–73, 183–85. Some of the major rackets operating in New York will be discussed in Chapter 8.

22. Daniel Bell, "Crime as an American Way of Life: A Queer Ladder of Social Mobility," *The End of Ideology: On the Exhaustion of Political Ideas in the Fifties,* rev. ed. (New York, 1962), pp. 144–45; Davis, "Things I Couldn't Tell Till Now," (Aug. 26, 1939), 38.

23. New York *Times,* New York *Herald,* New York *Sun,* New York *Tribune,* May–Aug., 1922; Nick Gentile, *Vita di capomafia* (Rome, 1963), pp. 60–80.

24. Denis Tilden Lynch, *Criminals and Politicians* (New York, 1932), pp. 11–12.

25. Confidential sources; Cesare Mori, *Con La Mafia ai Ferri Corti* (Milan, 1932); New York *Sun,* Sept. 11, 1931. Alberto Consiglio, *La Vita di Lucky Luciano* (Milan, 1963), p. 70, placed Maranzano's arrival in New York in 1929, while Valachi (Maas, *The Valachi Papers,* p. 104) stated that Joe Profaci informed him that Maranzano "had come over here right after the First World War." This, however, was clearly an effort to make the leader appear to be something other than he was—that is, a recently arrived immigrant who had entered the country illegally.

26. The sample group of middle and upper levels of Italian criminal leaders was selected after careful examination of city newspapers, police department records, and interviews with law enforcement officials and others knowledgeable in the underworld situation in 1931 in the New York metropolitan area, Boston, Cleveland, Detroit, Chicago, New Orleans, Kansas City, Denver, and San Francisco.

27. McClellan Committee, pt. 1, p. 96.

28. Gentile, *Vita di capomafia,* p. 112; New York Police Department records, cited in Maas, *Valachi Papers,* p. 103. According to Valachi (p. 104), the killers included Genovese, Frank Livorsi, and Joseph Stracci.

29. This and the following two paragraphs are based on Gentile, *Vita di capomafia,* pp. 112–14, 118–19; Maas, *Valachi Papers,* pp. 104–6.

30. New York *Sun,* Sept. 11, 1931; Maas, *Valachi Papers,* pp. 112–15.

31. Gentile, *Vita di capomafia,* p. 115.

32. New York *Sun,* Sept. 11, 1931; Maas, *Valachi Papers,* pp. 112–15.

33. This and the preceding paragraph are based on Gentile, *Vita di capomafia,* pp. 115, 118–19; confidential sources.

34. Confidential sources.

35. McClellan Report, pt. 1, p. 115.

36. Ibid., p. 109; Maas, *Valachi Papers,* pp. 125–41, presents an excellent picture of the insecurities and problems of life as a lower-echelon syndicate member.

37. Gentile, *Vita di Capomafia,* p. 128.

38. F. Vernon Willey and Guy Locock, "America's Economic Supremacy," *Current History* 23 (Jan. 1926):504.

39. This and the next paragraph are based on Cleveland *Plain Dealer,* Dec. 6–9, 1928; Guy Nichols, "The Prohibition Situation with Special Reference to Chicago," typescript of a 1930 Treasury Department report (the copy examined was located in the Bureau of Narcotics Library); John Kobler, *Capone; The Life and World of Al Capone* (New York, 1971), p. 263.

40. A police department photograph of the nine men is published in Ed Reid and Ovid Demaris, *The Green Felt Jungle* (New York, 1963), between pp. 116 and 117.

41. This and the following paragraph are based on files of the Chicago Crime Commission; Kobler, *Capone*, pp. 265–70.

42. Turkus and Feder, *Murder, Inc.*, pp. 83–84; confidential sources. Writing on the subject in 1971, Hank Messick (who, like Turkus, based his description on an underworld source) maintained that only one conclave was held in 1934 and that in New York; he did agree that a national body was created. Messick, *Lansky* (New York, 1971), pp. 72–76.

43. Turkus and Feder, *Murder, Inc.*, p. 16.

44. Meyer Berger, "Murder, Inc.: Justice Overtakes the Largest and Most Cruel Gang of Killers in U.S. History," *Life* 9 (Sept. 30, 1940):86–88.

45. Edward Dean Sullivan, *Chicago Surrenders* (New York, 1930), p. 205.

NOTES TO CHAPTER 8

1. Hank Messick, *The Silent Syndicate* (New York, 1967), pp. 111–25.

2. Craig Thompson and Allen Raymond, *Gang Rule in New York: The Story of a Lawless Era* (New York, 1940), p. 394; U.S. Congress, Senate, *Hearings Before the Special Committee to Investigate Organized Crime in Interstate Commerce*, 81st Cong., 2nd Sess., pt. 4, pp. 323–24, 370–73 (hereafter referred to as Kefauver Committee).

3. Kefauver Committee, pt. 7, pp. 986–1002.

4. Investigative files, Intelligence Unit, U.S. Internal Revenue Service.

5. Rufus King, *Gambling and Organized Crime* (Washington, 1969), pp. 24–25, citing research from the Wickersham Report; Ted Poston, "The Numbers Racket," New York *Post*, Feb. 29—Mar. 10, 1960,

reprinted in Gus Tyler, ed., *Organized Crime in America: A Book of Readings* (Ann Arbor, 1962), p. 263.

6. This and following paragraphs are based on Intelligence Unit, Internal Revenue Service confidential files and reports; Thompson and Raymond, *Gang Rule in New York,* pp. 378–80; Leonard Katz, *Uncle Frank; the Biography of Frank Costello* (New York, 1973), pp. 85–86.

7. Herbert Asbury, *Sucker's Progress; An Informal History of Gambling in America from the Colonies to Canfield* (New York, 1938), pp. 88–93; Harold F. Gosnell, *Negro Politicians; The Rise of Negro Politics in Chicago* (Chicago, 1935), pp. 122–25; St. Clair Drake and Horace Cayton, *Black Metropolis: A Study of Negro Life in a Northern City,* rev., enl. ed. (Chicago, 1970), 2:470–72.

8. Ted Poston, "The Numbers Racket," *Organized Crime in America,* pp. 262–63.

9. This and the following paragraphs are from Intelligence Unit, Internal Revenue Service files; Paul Sann, *Kill the Dutchman! The Story of Dutch Schultz* (New Rochelle, N.Y., 1971), chaps. 13 and 14; Herbert Mitgang, *The Man Who Rode The Tiger* (New York, 1970), chaps. 9–16; J. Richard (Dixie) Davis, "Things I Couldn't Tell Till Now," *Collier's* 104 (July 29, 1939):37–38, (Aug. 19, 1939), p. 36; Francis A. J. Ianni, *Black Mafia: Ethnic Succession in Organized Crime* (New York, 1974), p. 118.

10. Fred S. Buck, *Horse Race Betting; A Comprehensive Account of Pari-Mutuel and Bookmaking Operations,* New ed. (New York, 1962), p. 10; The *American Racing Manual* for the years from 1904 to 1942 (Chicago, 1904–42); Henry Chafetz, *Beat the Devil: A History of Gambling in the United States from 1492 to 1955* (New York, 1960), p. 386; William H. P. Robertson, *The History of Thoroughbred Racing in America* (Englewood Cliffs, N.J., 1964), pp. 96–97, 196–97; Anthony Comstock, *Race Track Infamy! or Do Common Gamblers Own New York State?* (New York, 1904).

11. Chafetz, *Beat the Devil,* pp. 384, 387; John McDonald, "Sport of Kings, Bums, and Businessmen," *Fortune* 42 (Aug. 1960):114; Buck, *Horse Race Betting.*

12. Toney Betts, *Across the Board* (New York, 1956), p. 28; Joe Mahar, "New York Goes Mutuel," *Turf and Sport Digest* 17 (Jan. 1940):12–13, 46–50.

13. Records and reports of Intelligence Unit, Internal Revenue Service.

14. John Kobler, *Capone: The Life and World of Al Capone* (New York, 1971), pp. 236–38; Wallace Turner, *Gamblers' Money; The New Force in American Life* (Boston, 1965), p. 66.

15. This and the preceding paragraphs are based on confidential sources and New York *Times,* Dec. 4, 1951. This was the second in a series of articles by Meyer Berger entitled "Gambling a World Wide Problem, but Most Corrupting in U.S."

16. New York *Times,* Dec. 4, 1935; Nick Gentile, *Vita di capomafia* (Rome, 1963), p. 142.

17. San Francisco *Chronicle,* Apr. 3, 4, 6, 1929; May 22, 1929; Mar. 13, 1938; Oct. 19, 1938; Jan. 10, 1939; Feb. 16, 1939.

18. New Orleans *Times-Picayune,* Sept. 19, 1931; Mar. 29, 1939; Records of Metropolitan Crime Commission of New Orleans.

19. This and the following paragraphs are from a confidential report of U.S. Bureau of Narcotics "in re: Carl Carramusa, et al," prepared in 1945 and located in the Bureau's Library in Washington, D.C.; Kefauver Committee, pt. 4, pp. 81–100.

20. This and the following paragraph are from U.S. Bureau of Narcotics Report on the "Louis Buchalter Case"; Hughes, *Attorney for the People,* pp. 116–24, 338–40.

21. Confidential sources.

22. Gentile, *Vita di capomafia,* pp. 147–53; New Orleans *Times-Picayune,* Oct. 7, 1937; Michele Pantaleone, *The Mafia and Politics* (London, 1966), pp. 181–83.

23. Hickman Powell, *Ninety Times Guilty* (New York, 1939).

24. Text of Atherton Report, reprinted in San Francisco *News,* Mar. 16, 1937; confidential sources.

25. Confidential sources.

26. Michael Stern, "Lucky Luciano, Vice King in Exile," *Eye* (Sept.

1949), p. 10, copy in Narcotics Bureau Library file; Powell, *Ninety Times Guilty*, chap. 11.

27. Thompson and Raymond, *Gang Rule in New York*, p. 219; John Landesco, *Organized Crime in Chicago: Part III of the Illinois Crime Survey of 1929* (Chicago, 1968), p. 149.

28. Thompson and Raymond, *Gang Rule in New York*, pp. 292–93; Fred D. Pasley, *Muscling In* (New York, 1931), p. 142.

29. Gordon L. Hostetter and Thomas Quinn Beesley, *It's a Racket* (Chicago, 1929), pp. 9–13; Landesco, *Organized Crime in Chicago*, pp. 149–50.

30. Hostetter and Beesley, *It's a Racket*, pp. 13–14; Kobler, *Capone*, p. 233; Pasley, *Muscling In*, pp. 16–17.

31. Walter Lippmann, "The Underworld, Our Secret Servant," *Forum* 85 (Jan. 1931):3; David J. Saposs, "Labor Racketeering: Evolution and Solutions," *Social Research* 25 (Autumn 1958):255–57.

32. U.S. Bureau of Narcotics reports; Burton B. Turkus and Sid Feder, *Murder, Inc.; The Story of "The Syndicate"* (New York, 1951), pp. 288–312.

33. Investigative files, Intelligence Unit, Internal Revenue Service.

34. Confidential sources; Pasley, *Muscling In*, pp. 169–72.

35. This and the following paragraph are based on confidential sources; manuscript records and published reports of New York State Crime Commission, 1952–53, located in Columbia University Library; Kefauver Committee, pt. 7, pp. 280–316, 563–83.

36. New York State Crime Commission, *Fourth Report* (Albany, 1953), pp. 37–39; John Hutchinson, *The Imperfect Union: A History of Corruption in American Trade Unions* (New York, 1970), p. 96.

37. New York State Crime Commission, *Fourth Report*, p. 33.

38. This and following paragraphs are based on Intelligence Unit, Internal Revenue Service, records; confidential sources; Virgil W. Peterson, "The Career of a Syndicate Boss," *Crime and Delinquency* 8 (Oct. 1962):343–44; Malcolm Johnson, *Crime on the Labor Front* (New York, 1950), pp. 18–23.

39. Chicago *Tribune* and New York *Times*, Mar. 19, 1943, to Jan. 2,

1944; U.S. Department of Justice Records; and confidential sources.
40. Harold Seidman, *Labor Czars: A History of Labor Racketeering* (New York, 1938), p. 124; Davis, "Things I Couldn't Tell Till Now" (Aug. 19, 1939), p. 12, emphasis added; Jay Robert Nash, *Citizen Hoover: A Critical Study of the Life and Times of J. Edgar Hoover & His FBI* (Chicago, 1972), p. 82.
41. New York *Times* for period from Apr. 22, 1940, to Feb. 24, 1941; Kefauver Committee, pt. 7, pp. 306–8.

NOTES TO CHAPTER 9

1. Sara Jean Reilly, "The Italian Immigrants, 1920–1930. A Case Study in Baltimore," M.A. thesis, The Johns Hopkins University, 1962, p. 272.
2. Mario Puzo, *The Godfather* (New York, 1969), p. 291; New York *World Journal Tribune*, Dec. 30, 1966; Gay Talese, *Honor Thy Father* (New York, 1971).
3. Francis A. J. Ianni with Elizabeth Reuss-Ianni, *A Family Business: Kinship and Social Control in Organized Crime* (New York, 1972), p. 169.
4. U.S. Congress, Senate, *Third Interim Report of the Special Committee to Investigate Organized Crime in Interstate Commerce*, 82nd Cong., 1st Sess., p. 175; A. Russell Buchanan, *The United States and World War II* (New York, 1964), p. 137; Marshall B. Clinard, *The Black Market: A Study of White Collar Crime* (New York, 1952), p. 39; Peter Maas, *The Valachi Papers* (New York, 1968), pp. 185–88.
5. John McDonald, "Sport of Kings, Bums, and Businessmen," *Fortune* 62 (Aug. 1962):114.
6. U.S. Congress, Senate, *Second Interim Report of the Special Committee to Investigate Organized Crime in Interstate Commerce*, 82nd Cong., 1st Sess., pp. 13–14.
7. This and the following paragraph are based on U.S. Congress, Senate, *Hearings Before the Special Committee to Investigate Organized Crime in Interstate Commerce*, 81st Cong., 2nd Sess., pt. 10, pp.

52–103, 910–13, 930; U.S. Congress, Senate, *Third Interim Report,* pp. 90–94; Intelligence Unit, U.S. Internal Revenue Service files.
8. U.S. Congress, Senate, *Third Interim Report,* p. 150; William Howard Moore, *The Kefauver Committee and the Politics of Crime, 1950–1952* (Columbia, Mo., 1974); Dom Frasca, *Vito Genovese: King of Crime* (New York, 1963), pp. 173–90; U.S. Congress, Senate, *Hearings Before the Permanent Subcommittee on Investigations of the Committee on Government Operations. Organized Crime and Illicit Traffic in Narcotics,* 88th Cong., 1st Sess., pt. 1, p. 6 (hereafter the McClellan Committee). Santo Trafficante, who also lived in Tampa, Florida, was the Barbara guest from Cuba, where he was co-owner of Havana's San Souci Hotel. Under the corrupt regime of Fulgencio Batista, American syndicate-run gambling casinos in Cuba were a valuable source of underworld income. A mutually rewarding arrangement ended when, on January 1, 1959, Batista was driven from the island by Fidel Castro, who just a little over two years before had led a small invasion force. Castro confiscated the syndicate's hotels and casinos without compensation. In 1975, testimony before the Senate Intelligence Committee established that in 1960 agents of the Central Intelligence Agency plotted with syndicate figures John Roselli of Los Angeles and Chicago's Sam Giancana to "remove" Castro. The Cuban leader's death would benefit both the CIA, which hoped the event would topple the island's Communist government, and the syndicate, which hoped that a more congenial government would succeed Castro's and permit the syndicate's return to Cuba. See *New York Times,* July 31, 1975.
9. McClellan Committee, pt. 1; *The Challenge of Crime in a Free Society. A Report by the President's Commission on Law Enforcement and Administration of Justice* (Washington, D.C., 1967), pp. 192–93 (hereafter President's Commission).
10. U.S. Congress, Senate, *Hearings Before the Permanent Subcommittee on Investigations of the Committee on Government Operations. Organized Crime—Stolen Securities,* 92nd Cong., 1st Sess., pp. 2–5, 772–838; U.S. Congress, *Hearings Before the Select Committee on Crime. Organized Crime in Sports (Racing),* 92nd Cong., 2nd Sess.,

pt. 1, pp. 1–2; Vincent Teresa, *My Life in the Mafia* (Garden City, N.Y., 1973), chap. 23; President's Commission, pp. 188–89.

11. U.S. Congress, Senate, *Third Interim Report,* pp. 170–71; confidential sources.

12. Maas, *The Valachi Papers,* pp. 238–49. On the Profaci-Gallo struggle see Raymond Martin, *Revolt in the Mafia* (New York, 1964).

13. Ianni, *A Family Business,* p. 132; confidential sources.

14. Nicholas Pileggi, "Anatomy of the Drug War," *New York Magazine* 6 (Jan. 8, 1973):36; Staff and Editors of *Newsday, The Heroin Trail* (New York, 1974), pp. 207–9.

15. Francis A. J. Ianni, *Black Mafia: Ethnic Succession in Organized Crime* (New York, 1974), pp. 12–13, 180–81.

BIBLIOGRAPHIC NOTE

Most of the literature concerning syndicate crime has been produced by journalists or former journalists. Among the most useful of their works are Fred Pasley, *Al Capone, The Biography of a Self-Made Man* (Garden City, N.Y., 1931), John Kobler, *Capone: The Life and World of Al Capone* (New York, 1971), Craig Thompson and Allen Raymond, *Gang Rule in New York: The Story of a Lawless Era* (New York, 1940), Hank Messick, *The Silent Syndicate* (New York, 1967), and *Lansky* (New York, 1971). Until recently, scholars have tended to shy away from entrepreneurial crime and criminals, with a few notable exceptions. Foremost among these exceptions is John Landesco, *Organized Crime in Chicago: Part III of the Illinois Crime Survey, 1929* (Chicago, 1929; reissued 1968). During the past decade sociologists and criminologists have greatly expanded our understanding of crime in recent and contemporary American society; see, e.g., Joseph L. Albini, *The American Mafia: Genesis of a Legend* (New York, 1971), Donald Cressey, *Theft of the Nation; The Structure and Operations of Organized Crime in America* (New York, 1969), Dwight Smith, *The Mafia Mystique* (New York, 1975), and especially Francis A. J. Ianni with Elizabeth Reuss-Ianni, *A Family Business: Kinship and Social Control in Organized Crime* (New York, 1972).

Historians have been among the last to turn their attention to syndicate activities, but in recent years significant contributions have been made by William Howard Moore, *The Kefauver Committee and the*

Politics of Crime, 1950–52 (Columbia, Mo., 1974), and Mark H. Haller, "Urban Crime and Criminal Justice: The Chicago Case," *Journal of American History* (December 1970), and "Organized Crime in Urban Society: Chicago in the Twentieth Century," *Journal of Social History* (Winter 1971–72). One reason for hesitancy on the part of historians is the mistaken belief that primary source material is limited in extent and difficult to locate, when in fact a storehouse of information is available from interviews and in manuscript or printed form from the files of federal, state, and city agencies and archives; local, state, and federal courts; police departments; prosecuting attorneys; grand juries; private police agencies; and labor unions.

In preparation for this study I conducted research in New York City, Boston, Baltimore, Philadelphia, Pittsburgh, New Orleans, Cleveland, Detroit, Chicago, Kansas City, Denver, Los Angeles, San Francisco, and Washington, D.C. Each city contained a wealth and wide variety of material. Files of federal agencies proved to be particularly useful. My understanding of the bootlegging racket during prohibition was greatly enhanced by information located in the National Archives and in the files of the U.S. Department of Justice.

I made extensive use of the Internal Revenue Service's Intelligence Unit reports and records, as well as those of other federal agencies, including the Narcotics Bureau (now part of the Drug Enforcement Administration), and examined the records of local police departments, courts, and prosecuting attorneys. I was especially fortunate to find, in New York, typed trial transcripts of cases involving Italians. In other cities I had to content myself with material contained in indictment and disposition reports. The Pinkerton Detective Agency's files (at the Agency's headquarters in New York City), although not extensive, offer information on the Hennessy murder, and are even more valuable for the agents' reports on immigrant-colony criminal gangs in western Pennsylvania mining towns.

Particularly useful were the files of the Metropolitan Crime Commission of New Orleans, the Chicago Crime Commission, the New York Waterfront Commission, the New York State Crime Commission, the Chicago Committee of Fifteen, and the Burgess Papers.

These last contain research papers by University of Chicago students from the 1920s to the 1940s on gambling, prostitution, and other underworld activities in Chicago and its suburbs, as well as in Los Angeles and other cities.

When used with discretion, newspapers may add greatly to one's understanding of Black Hand crime as well as syndicate activities during the 1920s and 1930s. Effective crime reporters were (and are) among the most knowledgeable syndicate crime experts, for they have contacts on both sides of the law and as clear an understanding of events and procedures in the underworld as any contemporaries. Among the papers I used were: in New York, the *Times, Herald, Tribune, Sun, News, Post, Il Progresso Italo-Americano, L'Eco d'Italia, L'Araldo Italiano, Cristoforo Colombo;* the Brooklyn *Eagle;* the *Globe, Post,* and *Transcript* of Boston; in Baltimore, the *American* and *Sun;* in New Orleans, the *Picayune, Times-Democrat, States, Mascot,* and *Item;* in Philadelphia, the *Inquirer* and *Bulletin;* the Pittsburgh *Post* and *Dispatch;* in Detroit, the *News;* in Cleveland, the *Plain Dealer;* the Washington *Post;* the Miami *Herald;* in Chicago, the *Tribune, Examiner, News, L'Italia, La Tribuna Italiana Transatlantica;* the Denver *Post;* the Los Angeles *Times;* the *Chronicle, Examiner, News,* and *La Voce del Popolo* of San Francisco; the *Star* and *La Stampa* of Kansas City; in St. Louis, the *Post-Dispatch.*

Especially helpful were the librarians of the Denver *Post,* San Francisco *Examiner,* and Los Angeles *Times,* as well as the photography curators of the New York *Daily News,* Chicago *Tribune,* United Press International, and Associated Press. The New Orleans Public Library has a comprehensive card file of articles from all the local newspapers, but it contains inaccuracies and must be used with care. The New Orleans city archives are also located at the Public Library, and provide coroner's reports, tax records, police department records, and mayors' papers.

The Kefauver Committee investigations (U.S. Congress, Senate, *Hearings Before the Special Committee to Investigate Organized Crime in Interstate Commerce,* 81st Cong., 2nd Sess. and 82nd Cong., 1st Sess.) contain valuable information on the careers of numerous prominent criminals of various ethnic backgrounds across the country. This information is available elsewhere, and so whenever possible I examined the records on which the Committee's questions concerning activities during the 1920s and 1930s were based—that is, files of federal agencies, police department records, and other sources. I made use of the *Report* to fill in the gaps.

Joseph Valachi's recollections are useful descriptions of syndicate life in the 1920s and 1930s. These must be used with care, however, since they present the views of a very low-ranking member. They are recorded in U.S. Congress, Senate, *Hearings Before the Permanent Sub-Committee on Investigations of the Committee on Government Operations. Organized Crime. Illicit Traffic in Narcotics* (88th Cong., 1st Sess.), and *The Valachi Papers* (New York, 1968). More valuable is the Nick Gentile autobiography, *Vita di capomafia* (Rome, 1963). Gentile, who at one time or another lived in New York, Boston, Pittsburgh, Cleveland, Chicago, and Kansas City, was prominent in Italian-American crime from 1915 to 1937 and knew most of the major figures in Italian-colony crime as well as syndicate crime. Contrary to myth, retired syndicate members (and many active members as well) are willing to talk about their avocation and associates, past and present, although generally with the understanding that they not be identified in print.

In the preparation of this survey I interviewed nearly a hundred persons who occupied positions on both sides of the law. As many of these people stipulated that they remain anonymous, I have not identified any interviewees. For a subject like syndicate crime, oral sources are invaluable, but it is essential to corroborate information obtained from interviews with material obtained from other sources—including people as well as manuscript and printed records. I have attempted to do so in each case.

INDEX

Prepared by Susan Young